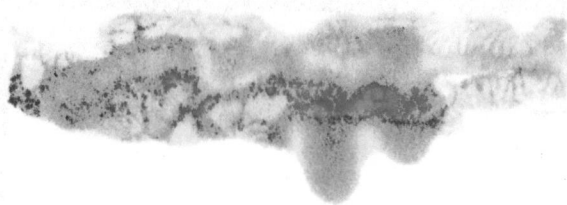

VALUES AND MORAL DEVELOPMENT IN HIGHER EDUCATION

EDITED BY GERALD COLLIER
    PETER TOMLINSON
    JOHN WILSON

A HALSTED PRESS BOOK

JOHN WILEY AND SONS
New York   Toronto

Published in the USA and Canada
by Halsted Press, a Division of
John Wiley and Sons, Inc., New York

ISBN 0-470-16549-9

Library of Congress Catalog Card Number: 74-1599

The Editors acknowledge with thanks permission from the editors and
publishers of the journal of *Moral Education* to reprint the greater part
of Gerald Collier's chapter; permission from the editors and publishers
of the *Bulletin of the British Psychological Society* to reprint the
diagram on page 86 and permission from Holt, Rinehart and Winston
to reprint the extract on page 31 from W.G. Perry, Jr., *Forms of
Intellectual and Ethical Development in the College Years: a Scheme*,
New York 1968

Printed in Great Britain

CONTENTS

CONTENTS cont'd

INTRODUCTION

John Wilson

This book ventures not only into a new field of study, but also into a new methodology: the reader is owed some explanation of its origins, structure and general intention.

In the last few decades there has been more interest and discussion (both at home and abroad) focused on titles like 'moral development' and 'moral education' than ever before. The reasons for this are complex,and would require a book in themselves: though one's mind turns naturally to the breakdown in certain types of authority, to mass education, and to the pluralism of values in most advanced societies. There has been some serious research in moral education, and a good number of hit-or-miss practical or developmental projects. But the subject is still in its infancy; and it is particularly striking that little has been said about moral development in higher education. Nobody, I take it, believe that a person's moral development should grind to a halt at the age of 15 or 16; and it seems important, however difficult, to investigate this particular area as sensibly as possible.

Such an investigation must begin by facing squarely the fact that nobody is yet in a position to conduct anything like a strictly experimental study of the moral effects of what is done in institutions of higher education. Adequate tests and assessment methods are not yet available to take account of the bewildering variety of variables. However, we are now a good deal clearer both about the *aims* of higher education and about the *kinds* of psychological and social factors — admittedly very general — which are relevant to the efficacy of practical methods. Briefly: we cannot say anything like 'This method or practice will have such-and-such effects on such-and-such students', but we can say, 'This *sort* of method or practice looks as if it might fulfil some of our aims, in the light of the general psychological and sociological knowledge that we have: it is at least a good candidate for investigation and discussion.

We find ourselves therefore in what we might call the pre-experimental stage of investigation. This is a very important stage, and we must not be in too much of a hurry to pass through it. Too much educational research has rushed too quickly into statistics and quantification, even in areas which do not lend themselves to such

1

methods. A good deal of hard thinking and discussion is required before we can begin even to formulate sensible and productive experiments. In this process we need to understand and bear in mind both (a) the aims towards which we are working and (b) the relevant evidence from psychology and the social sciences, and to marry these up with (c) descriptions of what goes on in practice. (a), (b) or (c) in isolation is not of much value: it is only putting them together in our minds that is likely to lead to progress in the subject. This, in brief, is what we have to do in this book. The reader will readily perceive that there are gaps, untidinesses, overlaps and perhaps disagreements, but we do not feel inclined to be over-apologetic about them. This condition is the state of the subject, and it would be intellectually dishonest to pretend to a tidiness and coherence which does not exist.

Two other points are, we think, worth making at the outset: first, the practical enterprises described in Parts II and III were not for the most part undertaken *as* attempts at practical moral education in the light of philosophically-derived aims for such education, or for the psychological and sociological study of it. The concerns which moved those responsible for these practical projects (Part III), or which dominate those concerned with teaching particular subjects (Part II), are very varied. What has happened is something like this: a person may have some more or less clear aim in view — say, 'to break down inter-departmental isolation', 'to give the students a sense of identity', 'to show them the importance of language and literature', and so on — and some practical project or style of teaching arises to meet this need. With the increased general interest in moral development, however, we have become increasingly clear that many of these aims and practices overlap, and that our individual aims have wider connotations, which need to be examined. It is less likely today that a lecturer will see himself as *just* a teacher of English or history, for instance: he will want to know about the implications of his subject for the general personality and life-style of the student. In the same way a principal or a tutor will not see himself only as fulfilling a specific, given role in the institution but as, at least to some degree, responsible for the general moral development of the community and its members. Hence the experiences and ideas of the authors in Parts II and III, although perhaps not originally focused on the title 'moral development', are highly relevant to that title. What they have been doing *is*, in fact, 'moral education'; and is now coming to be seen as such.

Secondly, most of these practical projects have taken place within a particular tradition and style of thought of their own. Therefore the language and concepts that naturally used by, say, a lecturer in religious knowledge, a guidance counsellor, an advisor on drama, and a psychologist will all be very different. It would be wrong to deny these different traditions, or to attempt a common language throughout the book, for it will be seen, we believe, that this variety of conceptual frameworks masks a good deal of common ground: in other words, the general aims are much more similar than the different languages imply. Most, if not all, of such aims – however generally expressed – fit within the philosophical framework described in the first chapter of the book. The same point applies to the psychological and sociological considerations in Part I: for the different empirical disciplines too have their traditional concepts and language. The authors have attempted to focus their writing on common aims, without concealing the particular framework in which they have planned and operated. It is precisely the realisation of a common ground, and the understanding that many individual workers have that they are concerned with the same aims, which seems to us very valuable

Reference
(1)   See *Philosophy and Educational Research* (N.F.E.R. publication), John Wilson, 1972.

PART I

THE NATURE OF MORAL DEVELOPMENT: UNDERSTANDING GAINED FROM THE DISCIPLINES

1   THE STUDY OF 'MORAL DEVELOPMENT'

John Wilson

'Moral development' is in inverted commas for two reasons. First, it is the official title for specific studies in post-Piagetian psychology; second, its meaning is unclear, both when it acts as this official title and when (as now) it is used in a wider sense. It is hard to do without some general heading for the subject of our interest, and 'moral development' is perhaps as good as any. But, in the context of this book, its vagueness at once raises two questions; roughly (1) 'What are we talking about under this heading?', and (2) 'In what ways can contributions from various fields (sociology, literature, etc.) be relevant to the study of "moral development"?' In this introductory section I shall try to deal with these questions: sacrificing, since this is not primarily a philosophical treatise, the conceptual complexities inherent in these questions for the sake of brevity.

Meaning and Aims in 'Moral Development'

There is an area of human thought and action, for which 'morality' may stand as a (more or less misleading) title, which is concerned with those principles, rules, ideals and behaviour-patterns that a man takes to be of overriding importance. Not every man may use the word 'moral' in relation to his overriding principles, and not every man may formulate the reasons for his behaviour coherently but every man, in this sense, has a morality. To him some ends, some objectives, some states of affairs, or some class of reasons for action, will seem overridingly important. This is his morality, and — whatever we may want to do with the word 'moral' — the area with which we are concerned.[1]

It would be hard to deny that there are some criteria of success which apply to this area: that is, some general principles or procedures, acceptable or inevitable for any rational person who reflects on the area, in terms of which we may talk of a person 'performing' well or badly in it. Performance in the moral area is surely not wholly *arbitrary*. For instance, it seems clear that principles like 'face facts', or 'get to know yourself and other people' are required by anybody who is going to evolve his own moral beliefs in a serious and sensible way. Similarly qualities we may call 'self-control' or 'being able to act on one's own decisions' seem to be required by any person, whatever his particular moral values. If somebody denied or abandoned such general principles as these, we should say — not that we disagreed with his particular moral values, but that he was not taking morality seriously at all.

Of course people can, and very often do, think and act without reference to these principles: that is, people are very often unreasonable, arbitrary, or even insane. But we know quite well, even without philosophical proofs, that we ought to begin with the principles. Indeed it hardly makes sense to deny them. If a man said that he ought not to face facts, or have enough self-control to act on his own decisions, we should hardly understand him: we could interpret it only as a wilful refusal to think at all. We all very often make such refusals: but we know that we ought not to.

Without the existence of such principles, it would not be possible to talk of 'education' or 'development' in morality at all. Teachers and others would have no publicly justifiable aims. There would be no meaning in saying that pupils were 'better at' or 'more successful in' the area of morality: just as, if there were no rational principles incumbent on any serious person who was trying to do science, we should not be able to talk of educating a pupil in scientific thought and action. Hence the criteria of success — what is to *count as* being 'developed' or 'educated' in morality — are of immense importance to anyone trying to help students and others. For without a clear grasp of these criteria of success, such a person will not be clear even about what he is trying to do, let alone about how he is to do it. So the task of outlining and clarifying these principles, which form the aims of moral education, is an essential first step.

Two mistakes or inadequacies have afflicted, and continue to afflict, much of what is said on this topic. First, people have taken criteria and aims that are *partisan*. This has usually occurred because these people have not seen the problem as one of educating pupils in the moral area (as one might educate them in the areas of science, history, literature, etc.) but rather as a problem of 'how to make pupils moral'[3] — and 'moral', for them, will mean something like 'in accordance with the values I personally favour'. It is one thing to try to produce (by whatever methods) good Christians, good Communists, good middle-class Englishmen, good liberals, good supporters of a technological society, etc. and quite another to try to produce people who are reasonable (educated, sane, sensible, etc.) in this area: people who will raise seriously the important question 'What ought I to do and to feel?', answer them seriously, and act on the answers.[4] Of course it can be said, if we like, that words such as 'reasonable', 'educated', 'sane', etc.

'contain values'; but it is just as obvious that they are not *partisan* values — they are second-order values which are conceptually connected to the notions of being human and being educated. Whether they can intelligibly be questioned at all, and if so how, are interesting philosophical questions: but educators (rightly) take them as given.

At the cost of being repetitive, I should like to stress the importance of appreciating that this is a matter of logic (or, if you like, common sense); it does not rest upon any particular creed, or faith, or axiom. Such principles as 'facing facts', 'not contradicting oneself', 'gaining understanding and so forth do not rely on any intuition or revelation. They are part of what it means to be a thinking human being, as opposed to an animal or a psychopath. Understanding and following such principles is part of what we *mean* (or should mean, if we were clearer) *by* 'being educated' in morality and other areas of life. They are an expansion of the concept of education itself, not a set of particular moral values. I repeat this because it is just as important that students and pupils should grasp this as that educator should. They, and we, would rightly resent any attempt to foist a particular morality or faith on them, but no-one can sensibly object to clarification of what it means to be educated in the moral area. Unless the distinction is firmly grasped, I fear that much moral education will be ineffective (as well as illegitimate).

Secondly, statements of aims and criteria in the moral area have been intolerably vague. There is much talk about 'sensitivity', 'concern', 'awareness', 'a sense of responsibility', 'personal identity', 'commitment', 'an adult attitude', and so on. Such talk is not so much mistaken as inadequate. On the one hand it allows, by its very vagueness, partisan values to creep in under cover of these expressions; on the other, it fails to provide what any clear-headed educator will surely demand — a specific and detailed list of aspects (or elements) in the 'successful performer' in the moral field. Any such list must identify *different* aspects — the items must not overlap with each other — and must also identify *all* aspects required for moral success. The importance of such a list is obvious for the researcher; it ought to be equally obvious for the practising teacher. For without it he cannot know, even in principle, to what aspects his teaching is supposed to relate, what the gaps are, or may be, in the moral development of his pupils, what new methods might help to fill those gaps, and so forth.

This may save us also from a third mistake, which is connected with the second — the belief (better, the fantasy) that moral development rests on some *one* quality or method: 'it's all a matter of X', where X may be 'personal example', 'having concerned teachers', 'the right sort of atmosphere in the institution', 'gaining sensitivity through literature', and so *ad infinitum*. We have to appreciate that moral development involves *many different* types of learning, which can not in principle be done by only one method. We still suffer from the fantasy that 'virtue' is the name of some single essence or property, possessed in large measure by 'virtuous peasants' or 'saints', which we need only transfuse (like blood) into our pupils. We need to stop talking about 'sensitivity', 'goodness', 'virtue', 'concern' and so on, and start getting down to business.

There are, I think, only two serious ways of getting down to business. One, using a tradition which goes back to Plato and Aristotle, involves itemising the virtues for our list. We may reasonably say that there are a number of virtues which (a) can be distinguished clearly from eath other; (b) are 'culture-free', and logically required by any person who is to be successful in the moral area. (For instance, fear will inevitably sometimes stand between any person and that person's goal so that some kind of courage is inevitably a useful tool for any person — not necessarily courage in climbing mountains or facing dragons, but courage to face whatever particular dangers the person meets with. Or again, it is self-evident that 'alertness' and 'determination' or 'self-control' are required since any person will have goals that he cannot immediately attain, and will meet situations which he needs to be able to size up quickly). This is an interesting approach, and some very important work has been done on these lines. There are, however, difficulties, though perhaps not insuperable, which lead one to prefer a different approach. The rationale and central elements of this list have been discussed at length elsewhere,[5] but I need here to produce it in full, since it is relevant to our second question about the relevance of contributions from other fields.

It seems that anyone who wants to be sure of success in the moral area would need at least the following 'components' (abilities, skills, etc.) to which I have given brief home-made titles for the sake of easy reference:

PHIL (HC)	Having the concept of a person (that is, of a conscious and rational language-using creature, with a will, intentions, desires and emotions).
PHIL (CC)	Claiming to use this concept as the criterion for forming and acting on principles of action: that is, accepting that the wants and interests of other people and himself, regarded as equals, are the relevant reasons for moral thought and action.
PHIL (RSF)	Having feelings which support this general principle, at least to some extent: feelings attached to the notion of 'duty' or 'benevolence'.

9

EMP (HC)	Having the concepts of various emotions and moods. moods.
EMP (1) (Cs)	Being able, in practice, to identify emotions and moods in oneself, when these are at a conscious level.
EMP (1) (U cs)	Ditto, when these are at an unconscious level.
EMP (2) (Cs)	Ditto, in other people, when at a conscious level.
EMP (2) (Ucs)	Ditto, when at an unconscious level.
GIG (1) (KF)	Knowing other ('hard') facts relevant to moral decisions.
GIG (1) (KS)	Knowing sources of facts (where to find out).
GIG (2) (VC)	'Knowing how' — a 'skill' element in moral situations, as evinced in verbal communication with others.
GIG (2) (NVC)	Ditto, in non-verbal communication.
KRAT (1) (RA)	Being in practice 'relevantly alert' to (noticing) moral situations, and seeing them as such under the right descriptions (in terms of PHIL, etc. above).
KRAT (1) (TT)	Thinking thoroughly about such situations, bringing to bear whatever PHIL, EMP or GIG he has.
KRAT (1) (OPU)	As a result of the foregoing, making an overriding, prescriptive and universalised decision to act.
KRAT (2)	Being sufficiently whole-hearted, free from unconscious counter-motivation, etc. to carry out (when able) the above decision in practice.

I do not want to claim, either that there are no problems attached to various items on this list, or that it may not need revisions and additions. But I would claim that any serious attempt to taxonomise the logical requirements for success in this area would have to look something like this. There are of course logical requirements, not psychological 'forces' or 'factors' or 'constructs': it is the task of empirical researchers and others to tell us what actual types of training, upbringing, teaching or other empirical phenomena will produce these 'components' in individuals. All I have tried to do here is to produce as clear and complete a list of aims as I can.

Perhaps an example may help to show why some such list as this is essential, and also the ways in which it may be of practical help to the educator. Suppose we come across a phenomenon which seems, *prima facie,* to indicate a lack of 'moral development': for instance, teenagers beating up a Pakistani in London. Now we need to be able to identify, as clearly as possible, just what sort of failure (vice, moral incompetence, etc.) the teenager suffers from – or what sorts, since he may suffer from more than one. Unless we know this, we cannot even begin to think seriously, or do serious research, about what methods of education will help to remedy the failure – and we cannot know what sort of failure it is without consulting a list of this kind.

Thus, going down the list, we might wonder somewhat as follows: 'Is it that he has no proper concept of a person – that he doesn't really count Pakistanis as people – a lack of PHIL(HC)? Is it that he knows Pakistanis are people but thinks that their being people is unimportant compared with their being coloured, or immigrants, or not members of his gang, or whatever – a lack of PHIL(CC)? Is it that he accepts the importance of their being people "on paper", so to speak, but has no feelings which back up this acceptance – lack of PHIL(RSF)? Is his behaviour due to some failure in emotional perception (various kinds of EMP); for instance, does he fail to recognise the strength of his own racial prejudices, whether conscious or unconscious? Might he perhaps think that coloured people don't feel pain in the same way that white people do – is there some straightforward "hard fact" of which he is ignorant (GIG(1))? Is it that he can't communicate with the Pakistani in any other way – would it help if we improved his "know-how" or "social skills" (GIG(2))? Finally, is it that he just doesn't stop to consider things at all, but acts on impulse – that he isn't alert to the situation as required under the heading of KRAT(1) (RA), or doesn't think properly about it as required by KRAT(1) (OPU)? Or that, having done all this, he still doesn't translate his decision into action – a deficiency in the KRAT (2) area?

In this case, as with all such cases, some of these failures are more probable than others. It is likely, for instance, that the teenager lacks PHIL and KRAT more than he lacks GIG. But – particularly since there may be more than one thing lacking – it is both important and difficult to identify them. It is difficult because, in practice, it is not easy to separate out these logically distinct elements. The overlaps between PHIL and KRAT are especially hard to untangle, but not until we can do this can we determine the appropriate methods for a cure. There is not much point in stressing the importance of people to somebody who has no clear grasp of what a person is, or in promoting alertness and determination to someone who uses these qualities to his neighbour's disadvantage. We have, then, to start by *identifying,* both in principle and in practice, what may be or is wrong; then we can go on to explain and to cure.

Before going further, I should like to disarm (as briefly as I may) those who may still find this list of aims alarming or unsatisfactory, rather than merely advising them to pursue the philosophical literature mentioned in the footnotes. Despite the shorthand jargon (PHIL, EMP, etc.), which we have found useful for research purposes, there is nothing very original or exciting about this list. It serves to remind us (as philosophers often do) of what we know quite well already. Few people would deny the importance of having concern for others and regard for their interests; of emotional insight and awareness; of factual knowledge and 'social skills'; of the various aspects of personality sometimes referred to as 'self-control', 'alertness', 'motivation'. The list is no more than an attempt to separate these out in a little more detail, and independently of any particular language-style (whether derived from psychology, religious belief or any other source). We can talk if we like of 'autonomy', 'ego-strength', 'the grace of God', and so on, but it is best, at least to begin with, to keep our feet on the ground.

Some will feel that this list does not provide a 'true basis' for morality; there is a sense of something missing. I can only ask such people to consider whether what they want is, in however uncertain a form, some kind of *authority* to do their morals (and their moral education) for them — if not a personal god, then some 'intuition of human worth', some 'faith in people', or something of that kind. They may be asking at once for a *logical basis* (the ultimate reasons and criteria that make up what we mean by 'successful performance' in the moral area), and also for some *source of moral strength*; certainly this is a common confusion in morality, though less common when we talk about 'the basis' of medicine, or science, or history, or other areas of thought and action which are now publicly refined and accepted. I have attempted only the former. Particular 'sources of moral strength', whether religious or not, are for empirical researchers to discuss: in my list, they would fit into the area I have called KRAT.

In connection with the above, I am not saying here anything against (or for) any particular creed, faith, political affiliation or 'ism'. That is not the educator's, nor the philosopher's, business. Our business is to encourage our students in forms of understanding and criteria of action which are public and demonstrable, not those which are the peculiar property of partisan groups. If we put our allegiance to any partisan group above the principles of reason and understanding, we are not earning our money as educators: we should rather be paid by some propagandist fund.

Finally, for those who wish to pursue the topic in more detail, I do not of course wish to convey the impression that all the (very complex) philosophical problems here have been solved. But they are, I would stress, *philosophical* problems, and to approach them seriously is to do philosophy. I think it is true that most competent philosophers, however many difficulties they might raise, would agree that some such list as I have drawn up is, at least, not hopelessly astray. As I mentioned above, it seems to me not so much questionable as boringly obvious (even though, under pressure from prejudice and fantasy, it is commonly forgotten). So perhaps we can allow it to stand, and get on with the urgent task of translating in into practice.

Let us go back now to the phrase 'moral development'. Two points are commonly made by philosophers about 'development', as the word figures in psychological research. (1) The implication is that 'morality', or something to do with morality, 'develops' in the way that flowers develop from buds, or butterflies from grubs and it is taken analogically with the 'development of the brain'; there is the implied picture of something becoming larger and more complicated or sophisticated in accordance with certain laws of nature (hence the talk of 'stages' in development, rather like stages in evolution). But morality is not (could not be) like the unfolding of a bud or a butterfly: it is, at least in part, something *learned.* Coming to perform successfully in the moral area is more like learning to play chess, or the piano, than it is like simply coming to have bigger biceps or more brain-cells. It is something which we *do* and *learn* for ourselves rather than something which just *happens to* us. (2) The (usually well-concealed) implication or assumption is that the more morally 'developed' a person is, the *better* he is. The later 'stages' of development, it is assumed, are *improvements* on the earlier: it is not just that they come later, or are more sophisticated, or are inevitable for 'normal' children. Many psychologists seem simply to assume this; but, obviously, any 'stage' of development can be sophisticated, characteristic of more age and experience, and (in one sense) 'normal' for human beings, without earning our approval. (No doubt Lucifer, Hitler and de Sade 'developed' as they got older; but they may also have got worse.)

'Moral development' for us — that is, for educators — will not be tied to these ambiguities. The process of development will include anything which contributes to the aims of moral education (as set out in the list of 'components' above). We shall not call it 'development' unless it is an improvement and we shall be willing to look at any factors relevant to it, whether factors of 'natural growth' or 'cognitive learning' (both very obscure phrases). We have to be willing to look at them all, for all may be relevant: but, of course, as educators we may only be able to control some of them — that is, those which fit in with the concept of education.

I do not wish here to restrict unduly the particular factors and methods with which educators can be concerned, but it is as well for them to be clear about certain important distinctions. There are various things we can do with people: we can drug them, sever connections in their brains, inspire them, condition them (and there are various logical types of conditioning), train them for specific tasks, browbeat them, indoctrinate them, make them feel happy, and so on. If we ask 'What is it, specifically, to *educate* them?' we shall probably arrive at some such answer as that given by Richard Peters and others, roughly 'To initiate them into various forms of understanding, "cognitive awareness" and knowledge: basically, to teach them to think and understand, and to care for such understanding'. This marks education off with some (not complete) distinctness from other ways of handling people: and we may try to make further distinctions between training, indoctrinating, conditioning, forcing, browbeating, and so on.

Some of these non-educational processes will be very important for moral education. This is particularly clear when we remember that more sophisticated processes of learning or instruction do not cover all the ground. It is an essential part of the notion of education that the pupil comes to *care for* understanding. In moral education especially, where the 'affective' or 'motivational' side is unusually important, we must not undervalue those non-cognitive processes which are essential for the acquisition of attitudes and dispositions.[7] At the same time, we have to give the cognitive or conceptual side its due weight — a point sometimes missed by empirical workers, particularly in the behaviouristic tradition of psychology.

Contributions to Moral Development

The logical way to go about moral development would be this: first we establish our objectives, in as much detail as possible. Then we see from the examination of these objectives as well as from experimental and other evidence what *sorts* of processes are likely to achieve them. Then we look at these processes in action, and/or try out new ones (having cast them in the form of educational programmes), and see whether they in fact work: that is, whether they do actually increase one or more of the 'moral components' which form our objectives.

When I talk of 'an examination of these objectives' the point is this: *it is not entirely a contingent or empirical question whether certain methods will achieve certain objectives.* To use an old example, if we were asking how to get a pupil to appreciate Shakespeare, there is something logically odd or (ultimately) contradictory in suggesting that this can be done by any methods fairly described as 'conditioning', 'training' or 'indoctrinating'. The statement of the objective,

14

'appreciating Shakespeare', just does not fit these methods. This point applies to many of the 'moral components' as I have described them. For instance, genuine concern for others as people (PHIL) cannot arise solely through conditioning or training processes, or by example, or by an infusion of some magical quality 'love' or 'benevolence', for it implies the quite complicated business of (a) having a clear concept of another person in the required sense (and very few of us actually have such a clear concept); (b) using *that* concept, and not some other, as the criterion of our actions (for instance, being nice to people *qua* people, not *qua* attractive blondes, rich uncles, powerful tyrants, etc.); and (c) actually applying the criterion in such a way that it issues in action. Of these, the conceptual learning could not, even in principle, be achieved by conditioning or training processes. Pupils will have to be *taught*.

The educator, then, will need to look very closely at all the components in order to get a clear view of what methods could, in principle, be relevant. Some seem required, as it were, *a priori':* for instance, it seems clear that many components, or aspects of them, could not be acquired without an adequate use of *language* and conceptual apparatus (pointing to, for instance, the work of Basil Bernstein). So the educator may, in effect, conceptually deduce the importance of certain methods, given these aims. Further, he will want to examine each component in itself. What is *meant,* for instance, by 'being able to identify emotions'? is this a matter of correlating the symptoms of emotion with the person's belief and with his intentional actions? How far is it a matter of induction as against direct perception?[8] In this example, the methods of teaching this ability (EMP) will naturally follow from a proper conceptual (perhaps we should say 'phenomenological') understanding.

As I said earlier, the logical procedure would be to do this first, and then proceed to experiment and the trial of certain methods. But, in fact, we already have a good deal of psychological and sociological research (the names of Piaget, Kohlberg, Durkheim and others are well known in this field), and a good deal of practical methods being used (the names of A.S. Neil, Kurt Hahn, and Thomas Arnold are also not unfamiliar). So we have the very difficult task — much more difficult, I cannot forbear to add, than if we could work straightforwardly from the conceptual points in virgin soil — of trying to determine whether and how various research-findings or approaches are relevant to our aims: that is, to the moral components. Some are not relevant; others are only tangentially or obliquely relevant; most are relevant to aspects of moral development which come under training or conditioning rather than education. A thorough survey of the field would, I am sure, show enormous gaps in our knowledge, gaps due not so much to the lack of time, money or energy on the part of researchers, but (briefly) to the continued though slightly diminishing influence of a naive behavourism which has so far prevented all but the anthropologists and clinical psychologists from being sufficiently concerned with human beings *qua* rational creatures.[9]

This is not to say, of course, that psychological work which may seem at first glance poorly related to the moral components may not, in fact, be highly relevant. Though all men are rational in the minimal sense of being conscious, language-using creatures, few are very rational in the wider sense of being disposed to be reasonable in the moral area. We have, in practice, to face many different types of pervasive irrationality or fantasy – not only in moral thought and action, action, but in the concepts or pictures which people have about the nature of morality itself. Most of these pictures are fantasy-based, and would merit examination and taxonomy by clinical psychologists and others. There is also a more general dislike or opposition to rationality and sanity in this area, often expressed by phrases like 'But people just *aren't* rational!', 'What about the emotions?', 'Reason will only take you so far, you must have faith', and so on. The origins and nature of these fears and fantasies, common to teachers as well as taught, need close study. For people are indeed not always reasonable, and we must be able to identify the opposition.

It is possible to produce a procedure or *modus operandi* for bringing the disciplines, and the experience of practising teachers, to bear on moral development, and I will try now to do this, partly for its own sake, and partly to show the reader how this book is supposed to cohere. We must begin, as I have begun, with a clear statement of aims which must be more or less common ground (in some language or other) to those who contribute otherwise when we talk of 'moral development' we shall not even be talking about the same thing. If it is common ground, those who practise the disciplines can then tell us what research in their disciplines relates to one or more elements listed in these aims (for instance, the relationship of 'living in a folk society' to 'having a proper concept of a person' (PHIL(HC)); or 'forming a close relationship with a teacher' to 'understanding the emotions of older people' (a part of EMP); or, even more obviously, of 'training in social skills' to effectiveness in verbal and non-verbal communication in moral situations (GIG(1) (VC & NVC). Their difficulty here, I think, will be not so much the correct reportage of research, or establishing the *general* relevance of certain activities to the aims of moral development, but to make this relevance at all specific (or even, in some cases, plausible). It is commonly said, for instance, that the study of literature is useful for moral development. But with reference to what components? – does it increase concern (PHIL), awareness of one's own emotions (EMP(1)), awareness of other people's (EMP(2)), or what? And is there any evidence for this? As soon as we try to relate empirical work (or hunches) to the components, we begin to see the complexity of the problems; though this is, at least, no longer to rest content with vague talk about literature 'making for sensitivity' or 'encouraging awareness'.

I do not, of course, suggest that only 'hard' or experimental research findings are worth relating to the components. Much of the value in these disciplines — perhaps particularly in clinical psychology and sociology — is that they give us, if not proofs and predictions, at least a set of concepts which may be an improvement on our old ones. To have learned to talk in such terms as 'social role', 'ambivalence', 'the unconscious', etc. is to have learned something. The approaches of these expertises may teach us more than any 'findings' teach us. What is important, from our viewpoint, is that the disciplines can be shown not to be *autistic;* that their concepts and/or their experiments are not divorced from the real world, but can be deployed to give us genuine information which we would not otherwise possess. This requirement tends to get lost in talk of 'operational definitions', 'empirical co-variances' and so on. We want to know what empirical moves are likely, in practice, to produce people who are genuinely concerned with others, *in the normal sense of that phrase.* Much turns here on whether the assessment-, testing-, or verification-procedures (used by psychologists and others) measure up to this normal meaning: usually they do not.[10]

After those who practise the disciplines have given us as much guidance as they can — telling us, as it were, the *sort* of things which they have reason to believe would be likely to increase the components, the sort of factors we ought to pay attention to — we shall naturally turn to various kinds of practical enterprises designed actually to bring this about. Here the field is even wider, and even more strewn with a large number of current enterprises which have not been clearly thought out, either with reference to the aim of moral development or with reference to the general findings of psychology and other disciplines. However, we can at least consider these enterprises with the aims and the findings in mind; and interchange between these three parts of the business — the philosopher, who will remind us constantly of the aims, the psychologist and his colleagues in other disciplines, who remind us of the general factors of importance, and the practising teachers — is likely to be very fruitful so long, that is, as everyone bears this structure in mind.

It is perhaps worth trying to distinguish, however roughly, between different types of disciplines and enterprises that may be brought to bear in the task. A rough taxonomy might look like this:

A. *Aims.* The analysis of aims is essentially a philosopher's business:

that is (in case this is not universally understood) the business of someone whose expertise lies in the field of the analysis of concepts and meaning. Much of the work here has already been done, and I need say no more about it.

B. *General approaches from the disciplines.* Here we are concerned with bringing to bear the findings of those empirical disciplines whose business it is to study human beings, both in isolation and collectively, in those aspects which relate to morality. Of course it would be possible to include almost every discipline, since anything *can* affect moral development. But centrally, we are obviously concerned with psychology and sociology in their various forms. There will be various factors or phenomena of *general* relevance to any particular type of teaching or practical enterprise, which the practical educator will need to bear in mind.

C. *Teaching and practical enterprises.* Here we are concerned with types of teaching and other practical experiences which might be thought relevant to moral development in the light of the aims (A above) and of the general factors which seem important (B above). We can distinguish further between
   (a)   The teaching of specific subjects — philosophy, history, literature, etc. — and other curricular methods; and
   (b)   'Social arrangement' or 'social experience' methods whose value lies chiefly in the social context rather than in the intellectual pursuit of knowledge.
   It is impossible, in practise, to distinguish clearly between (a) and (b), in any practical enterprise but more or less weight may be attached to either, and the theoretical distinction should be borne in mind.

In this book we shall be following this (very rough) pattern: the aims (A) I hope already to have introduced sufficiently; and we shall shortly proceed to B and C.

This rough taxonomy may at least save us from too much muddle. It is clear, for instance, that the disciplines as they stand may come into our purview in two quite different ways. Thus we want to know what psychology in general has to tell us that is relevant to fulfilling our aims: this comes under B. But we might also think that the practical enterprise of *studying* psychology, say, for pupils of secondary school age, would itself assist pupils' moral development (it might increase EMP, for instance): and this comes under C. Again, under A (analysis of aims) we need the philosopher to help us to clarify our objectives: if we wished to examine whether learning philosophy in Colleges of Education contributed to the student's moral development, that is now a practical enterprise and comes under C.

Much more might be said in a general way, but I hope I have said enough to show the reader what we are trying to do. Indeed, it might be thought that I have tried to spell out this general methodology at too great length and perhaps in too dictatorial a spirit — about which I am entirely unrepentant; literature on moral education suffers from excessive vagueness not only in its specific content, but (worse) in respect even of the general task which particular authors set themselves. Only too often, after the first few pages of a work, one wonders 'Is this author trying to tell us what "moral education" *means* — is he doing philosophy? Or is he reminding us of psychological findings (psychology)? Or is he giving an account of practical enterprises? Or is he just letting off steam about his own values, life, "awareness", society, and so on?' (The last is regrettably common.) Unless we are remorselessly clear-headed we shall only be blown around by the winds of educational fashion and our own fantasy. Moral education is the last subject in the world that ought to suffer from this.

References

1. See J. Wilson *Education in Religion and the Emotions* Heinemann, London 1971), Ch. 7, with references to Hare and Warnock.
2. See Wilson, Williams & Sugarman, *Introduction to Moral Education* Penguin, Harmondsworth 1968), Ch. 2.
3. *ibid.* pp. 44-45.
4. See R.S. Peters, *Ethics and Education* (Allen & Unwin, London 1966), Ch. V.
5. J. Wilson, *The assessment of morality* (NFER, 1973)
6. *Ethics and Education,* part I
7. *Education in Religion and the Emotions,* p. 105 ff.
8. On all this see for instance A. Kenny, *Action, Emotion and Will* (Routledge, London 1963).
9. This has been constantly under fire from philosophers over the last few decades: see for instance P. Winch, *The Idea of a Social Science* (Routledge, London) and R.S. Peters, *The Concept of Motivation* (Routledge, London), both fifteen years old.
10. *Introduction to Moral Education,* Ch. 4.
11. *ibid.* p. 403 ff. (for these distinctions as applied to the school). See also the discussion in J. Wilson, *Moral Education & the Curriculum* (Pergamon Press, Oxford 1969).

2 SOME PERSPECTIVES FROM ACADEMIC PSYCHOLOGY

Peter Tomlinson

To anyone well acquainted with what goes under the title of 'modern psychology', the range of its concepts, theories, and findings which might seem relevant to the various aspects of John Wilson's phenomenology of the morally educated person (see chapter 1) must be very broad. Since not all the potential readers of this chapter can be presumed to have such an acquaintance with the field, it is important to start by giving some idea of what I mean by 'academic psychology'; this, I think, is most usefully done by means of an historical introduction – albeit drastically brief.[1]

Although it incorporated a number of existing trends and could trace parts of its ancestry very far back, modern psychology as such is usually held to have got under way towards the end of the last century. In the broadest terms it can be said to have consisted of the embodiments of two emphases in the search for a scientific psychology, and it would probably not be too unfair to characterise these as being, on the one hand, more concerned with being scientific and, on the other, more concerned with achieving an adequate psychology. The former branch involved an emphasis on precision and experimentation, the sort of detached pursuit that could be respectably followed by university scholars – whence the 'academic psychology' of my title. The latter branch reflected the urgent need, in the applied setting, for a framework broad enough to allow conceptualisation of the seeming complexities of 'real life' psychological disorders: it was apparent in the work of Freud and a tradition that developed with reference to his views on the 'deeper parts of human nature'. Whilst there has been in recent years a certain rapprochement between the two movements, the distinction between them still seems sufficient to warrant separate chapters here on their relevance to moral development. I should also point out that the distinction is more involved than I have indicated, and will therefore receive further comment in chapter 5.

The academic branch began by attempting to systematise the study of mental phenomena, probably largely on account of their emphasis in traditional mind-body dualism. But Wundt's introspective method for analysing out the basic elements of consciousness and, with it, a large part of the concern with the mental, lost their place of honour as the new discipline was taken up outside Germany. In America the Functionalists' interest in animal intelligence, together with influences from physiology (Pavlov's studies amongst others) and biology (the theory of evolution) helped establish Watson's Behaviourism as *the* scientific form of psychology. Here, it appeared, was a truly objective approach that eschewed such woolly philosophical notions as 'the mind' and restricted its attention to observable, measurable behaviour. It offered well-established basic paradigms of learning, those of classical and operant conditioning, expressed in terms of stimulus-response connections, whose laws and application could be studied by objective procedures that made it as respectable a science as any other natural science. It is fair to say that this school and its conception of psychology as the science of behaviour dominated academic psychological pursuits, especially in North America, for the greater part of the first half of the twentieth century.

The other school of academic psychology with a comparable stature to that of Behaviourism was the Gestalt school, which had originated, like its Structuralist predecessor, in Germany, where mentalist traditions had proved more resistant. The Gestaltists were explicitly antielementist in approach, whereas the behaviourists dealt in atomistic stimulus-response ('s-r') bonds held together by association. Where the Behaviourists concentrated on the learning of publicly-observable behaviours, the Gestaltists' main focus was on perception.

By the 1950s and '60s the schools as such had declined, though their paradigms, especially that of Behaviourism, had stamped a lasting mark on psychology. The discipline had, however, extended its interests in various directions, had expanded its methodologies, for example in the area of multivariate statistics, and was acquiring a more realistic grasp of the complexities of its subject matter. If there was any single trend in the post-war period, it was the rise of cognitive psychology. In the area of human experimental psychology, whose content has traditionally consisted of such well defined and abstract topics as sensory perception, attention, and short-term memory, the predominant conception has become that of man as a skilled information-processor. The concept of skill specifically recognises improvement in efficiency with practice and the tendency for initially-monitored behaviour to become automatic. With respect to any particular activity this approach seeks to postulate a precise model of the 'apparatus' and mode of functioning required to generate the known facts and from which to derive further, testable hypotheses. Such models have typically come from communications engineering, and more recently from control theory and computer science.

Where broader, presumably more complex, problems are considered, as for example with the psychology of thinking, emotion, attitudes, intellectual development, and social interaction, the rise of cognitive approaches has been more noticeable, for the Behaviourist paradigm had simply legislated such sorts of question out of consideration. Thus it was not until the 1960s that Piaget's work on cognitive development was firmly registered in American psychological circles.[2]

Current academic psychology is a massive area of enquiry, whose subject matters and methodologies vary in a number of ways: involving organisms from humans to worms, aspects from the precise to the subtle, individual to social, fine-grained to large-grained and objective to subjective, and methodology ranging from the experimental-interventional to the correlational-descriptive. The range of topics with potential relevance to moral development and education is therefore large, as is illustrated, for instance, by the breadth of coverage offered in Derek Wright's excellent book *The Psychology of Moral Behaviour,*[3] or the realisation that reference to such dense areas as the psychology of communication and that of interpersonal perception and social judgement may be indicated if one wishes to deal just with what John Wilson terms EMP. Nor can one pretend that there is at present any single general principle or framework allowing integration of these various areas of academic psychology; like a recent president of the British Psychological Society we are still very much in search of a psychology that will offer a unified — if complex — understanding of the individual in his real life setting.[4] However, there are some signs and hopes for the integration of hitherto disparate aspects of academic psychology, and it is upon a sample of these that this chapter will focus. Apart from restrictions on the length of such a piece, this limited attention is also dictated by the fact that a large proportion of psychological research concerning aspects of morals has been directed towards children, often in their early years: such studies tend to consider aspects which may be thought less important in the age-range receiving attention in this book. In addition, the models employed in these investigations, even if they may form a basis for recommendations in terms of particular child-rearing practices, may have little to offer that is at all feasible in the context of higher education today. This point may seem obvious to some readers, but the applications of stimulus-response psychology are in general restricted to policies of manipulation, the more extreme of them going 'beyond freedom and dignity', as Skinner's title has it, to the objectives envisaged for the organisms under their charge. Such objectives do not seem, in any case, to coincide with the aims of moral education as conceived in this book; though in my opinion the issues in this area are by no means as simple as they are often made out to be.

With these points in mind, we now turn to various studies which may be described as being concerned with forms of moral and social judgement, but which might alternatively be considered as studies of personality in so far as the latter involves style of awareness and conceptualisation of any individual's situation. They have been chosen for the following features: (a) they involve the 'higher processes', that is to say, those aspects and functions which are held to be among the criteria for adult human personhood; (b) although in terms of the traditional intellect-will, thought-action and mind-body distinctions they might be thought to occupy respectively the intellectual, thinking and mental poles, they have implications for the respective alternative poles; (c) studies of students in higher education have been made within some of their frameworks; (d) the several approaches show an appreciable degree of convergence in their findings, as well as some differences; and (e) more precise understanding has been sought in certain of these approaches by the application of relatively better defined concepts and models of information-processing skill. These have come from studies of those more abstract and restricted human phenomena that have traditionally constituted the core content of experimental psychology, and it is encouraging that similar basic models seem to have been applied independently, and with some success, to these complex topics. Features (d) and (e) may also serve to give an idea of the nature and complexity of even a preliminary attempt at integrating hitherto disparate orientations in academic psychology.

Kohlberg's Work

It is the work of Lawrence Kohlberg that deserves first mention:[5] Kohlberg has taken the Piagetian approach to the study of moral reasoning, developing and expanding it in a number of ways, and changing certain aspects. His main method, following Piaget, is to present people with hypothetical moral dilemmas and to probe into their thinking about them: interest is focused not on the particular conclusion offered by a subject, but rather on the reasoning processes used to arrive at it. Of Kohlberg's dozen or so dilemma stories, perhaps the best known is the situation involving a man whose wife is dying from cancer and urgently in need of a particular drug; when all possible legal means have failed to obtain the drug, the man finally steals it. Another example of the dilemma and probe questions is the following:

Joe is a 14 year-old boy who wanted to go to camp very much. His father promised him he could go if he saved up the money for it himself. So Joe worked hard at his paper route and saved up the forty dollars it cost to go to camp and a little more besides. But just before camp was going to start, his father changed his mind. Some of his friends decided to go on a special fishing trip, and Joe's father was short of the money it would cost. So he told Joe to give him the money he had saved from the paper route. Joe didn't want to give up going to camp, so he thought of refusing to give his father the money.

Should Joe refuse to give his father the money? Why?

Does his father have the right to tell Joe to give him the money?

Does giving the money have anything to do with being a good son?

Which is worse, a father breaking a promise to his son, or a son breaking his promise to his father?

Why should a promise be kept?

Replies to the dilemmas are analysed in terms of some thirty aspects of moral thought deriving from the philosophical work of John Dewey: modes, that is, terms defining functional kinds of moral judgement (e.g. right, duty, obligation); elements or principles of judgement such as welfare, respect, and justice; and universal moral issues or values, that is, the application of the above categories to content areas or institutions, such as life, property, sex, and so on. A good deal of research has been done using these instruments, with suitable adjustments to the stories in the case of cross-cultural studies, and from the analyses Kohlberg claims evidence of a culturally universal, invariant sequence in general forms of moral reasoning. This sequence falls into three levels, with two stages at each level.

Level I is said to be *premoral or preconventional* in the sense that the level 1 person is egocentric in approach, interested only in concrete consequences for self: he or she may respond to cultural rules and evaluative labels but only in as much as they may be interpreted in the above terms. The orientation at the first stage of this level is termed 'punishment and obedience', which is to say that avoidance of punishment and unquestioning deference to power are valued in their own right, and not in terms of, say, respect for rules based on equality. The instrumental relativist orientation of Stage 2 is a hedonistic morality; as the term indicates, the justification of action is entirely relative to its instrumental power to satisfy one's own needs, regardless of others. Conformity to rules and the giving of favours may occur, but only as part of a social exchange which sees human relations in terms of a market-place totally dominated by the profit motive.

Level II is that of *conventional role-conformity,* in which maintenance of the expectations of others, the individual's family, group, or nation, is perceived as valuable in its own right, regardless of immediate consequences to self. The first stage at this level is termed by Kohlberg the interpersonal concordance or 'good boy — nice girl' orientation: the main motive being the desire to remain accepted by others. Hence there is much conformity to stereotypical images of what is majority or 'natural' behaviour, though intention may now be taken into account for the first time. The orientation at the next stage. Stage 4, is towards authority and fixed rules, towards maintaining the given social order for its own sake, as is implicit in Kohlberg's description of it as the 'law and order orientation'.

Level III is called the *postconventional, autonomous, or principled* level. Now there is a definite attempt to define moral principles and values which are valid apart from particular authorities or one's identification with them; on the contrary, such principles are not internalised and autonomous, and may on occasion dictate that one go against authority. The first stage at this level, Stage 5, consists in a social-contract legalistic orientation, generally with utilitarian overtones. This is a morality which recognises the relativism of personal values and opinions, and lays corresponding emphasis on procedures for reaching consensus and for changing laws on the basis of rational considerations. The most mature form of moral viewpoint is the universal ethical principle orientation of Stage 6, where right is held to be defined by conscience in accordance with one's own individual principles which appeal to logical comprehensiveness, universality, and self-consistency. Such principles are, as one might expect, abstract universal prescriptions rather than concrete moral rules like the ten commandments.

Kohlberg presents evidence that this sequence represents a cumulative hierarchy of cognitive complexity, whose stages are perceived as successively more adequate. Higher stages are shown not only to incorporate the logical features of lower stages, but to exhibit new features which allow their possessors to address problems unresolved, or even unrecognised, at lower stages. For Kohlberg, the core of each stage is a conception of justice — a 'justice structure' as he puts it — which organises patterns of role-taking in moral conflict situations, and it is the development of this core capacity that gives rise to the stage development outlined above. The question of what determines transition through the stages has been a crucial and controversial one in several cognitive-developmental theories, and this is particularly true of the Piaget-Kohlberg approach. The notions used by these writers are not always as simple or clearly defined as they might be, and it is certainly the case that they have usually been interpreted as placing heavy emphasis upon maturation of brain structures required for a particular level of intellectual functioning. Though they have not thereby clarified the maturation-environmental stimulation question in a completely precise and definitive way, Piaget and Kohlberg place central emphasis on, to use their terminology, logico-mathematical experience as the basis of equilibration. By logico-mathematical experience is meant a person's active interaction with his environment, in which he or she applies and checks the use of his various schemes of action and representation rather than just passively undergoing stimulation from without. Equilibration is the process of integrating discrepencies between, to put it crudely, what one expects and what one gets; it is a form of reorganisation fed by cognitive conflict, so that the moral educator will be interested in providing opportunities for role-taking or socio-moral conflict which may be integrated by forms of justice at or above a person's own level. This account is far from exhaustive, but it may suffice for present purposes.

Various investogators have studied moral judgement beyond the typical adolescent period, Kohlberg himself being responsible for a useful longitudinal study with Kramer[6] in which the responses of a group of adolescent males were studied at ages 16, 20 and 24-years, as were those of their fathers. The main conclusions concerning adults' moral judgements were that

> . . . the major change in moral thought past high school is a significant increase or stabilization of conventional morality of a stage four variety, at the expense of preconventional stages of thought. This stabilization of moral thought is not only reflected in the trends of stage usage for the group as a whole, it is also reflected in the trends of variability of stage usage within individuals. . . . there is reason to believe that adult age change is not only toward greater consistency of moral judgement but toward greater consistency between moral judgement and moral action.
>
> (Kohlberg and Kramer, *op. cit.*, pp. 106-7)

Development, in the sense of the structural reorganisation of forms of reasoning described above, does not seem to occur during adulthood. Instead there seems to be a process of social learning or adjustment producing an increased congruence between belief and social role. The more interesting finding with respect this present study, however, was that between late high school and the second or third year of college, 20 per cent of the middle class sample retrogressed in moral maturity scores:

This drop had a definite pattern . . . the 20 per cent who dropped were among the most advanced in high school, all having a mixture of conventional (Stage 4) and principled (Stage 5) thought. In their college sophomore phase, they kicked both their conventional and their Stage 5 morality and replaced it with good old Stage 2 hedonistic relativism, jazzed up with some philosophic and sociopolitical jargon.

(Kohlberg and Kramer, op. cit., p. 109)

Kohlberg claims, as his general developmental theory would predispose him, that this retrogression is functional rather than structural, since the retrogressors did not lose their earlier capacity to use Stage 4 and Stage 5 thinking and all of them eventually returned to a mixed Stage 4 and 5 morality by the age of 25, when their responses were next studied. And when they do return to this level, so Kohlberg contends, retrogressors do so with a more tolerant attitude which is less idealising of its own system. He further argues that development claim from his explanation of why retrogression should occur in the first place.

In terms of the psychosocial moratorium postulated by Erikson, in which new and non-conforming patterns of thought and behaviour are tried out: the establishment of such a moratorium requires something of a rebellion by those who are prone to guilt, as was the case with half of the retrogressors in Kolhberg's study. But it also seems to be the case that such a moratorium is to some extent invited by the freedom of the college situation, and the absence of conventional morality perceived therein. This point finds an echo in the work of Perry, discussed below.

Conceptual systems theory

This approach was originally presented by O.J. Harvey, D.E. Hunt and H.M. Schroder in their 1961 book *Conceptual Systems and Personality Organisation*; it has since been developed with emphasis on the motivational aspects of the theory by Harvey, and on the information-processing aspects by Schroder and Hunt, who have applied it, respectively, to the business and secondary school domains.[7]

Conceptual systems theory is a cognitive theory of personality, like the personal construct theory of George Kelly,[8] under whom both Hunt and Schroder studied. Starting from the viewpoint, often associated with the Gestalt psychologist Kurt Lewin, that behaviour can only be understood by taking into account both the person and the environment to which he is responding, it focuses on the systems of concepts on individual uses to analyse, organise and interpret his world.

Harvey, Hunt, and Schroder proposed that the most important structural characteristic of a conceptual system is its degree of concreteness or abstractness. A concrete system is one which shows fixed ways of perceiving and responding, whereas, in contrast, the person with an abstract system is able to transcend the immediacy of his situation, showing a flexibility which comes from the availability of alternative ways of conceptualising. In their original statement these authors viewed development in terms of progress through four hierarchically-ordered stages from concrete to abstract. The order was assumed to be fixed, but movement through stages was seen as depending on an interaction between a person's current stage of personality development and environmental conditions, some of which might facilitate progress at a particular point, others producing arrest of some sort. The stages were as follows:

Stage I: Unilateral dependence. The individual has maximally undifferentiated concepts and is sensitive to external control; he or she has difficulty with ambiguity and tends to view things in an absolute and concrete 'black-and-white' manner.

Stage II: Negative independence. At this stage the self becomes more differentiated from its world, but functioning is characterised by questioning of external control and the avoidance of dependence.

Stage III: Conditional dependence and mutuality. At this further stage, the individual separates himself from the outside environment and begins to build a relationship with it, with an effort to test concepts. Finally, at the most abstract level:

Stage IV: Interdependence. The individual has many concepts with which to respond to his environment and is now capable of an interdependent relationship with others involving continuous exchanges of views and feelings; there is an integration of mutuality and autonomy.

The main method used by Hunt and Schroder to measure an individual's stage or conceptual level has been the structural scoring of responses to a paragraph completion exercise having a number of sentence stems. In the Hunt version the individual is given three minutes to write at least three sentences on each of the following topics: 'What I think about rules . . .'; 'When I am criticised . . .'; 'What I think about parents . . .'; 'When someone disagrees with me . . .'; 'When I am not sure . . .'; and 'When I am told what to do . . .' Use of this instrument in various studies, in particular cross-sectional investigations on young people from 12 to 18 years led Hunt and his colleagues to add a Sub-I Stage 'characterised by very poor organisation, egocentricity, and immaturity' and to seriously question the usefulness of the motivationally-based characteristics previous postulated as aspects of Stage II and IV functioning. They also found that persons with Stage IV characteristics were virtually nonexistent. Hunt's conceptual level version views peronality organisation on a continuous dimension, with very general anchor points at what was referred to above as Sub I, Stage I, Stage II and theoretically though not often encountered in the 12 to 18 year range, Stage III.

Of the three original authors, Schroder has laid the clearest emphasis on the information-processing aspect of this conception of personality, focusing strictly on what he calls the individual's conceptual or integrative complexity. This has three aspects: (1) *Differentiation:* the number of elementary dimensions (stable, unique orderings of stimuli) in a cognitive structure; (2) *Discrimination:* the capacity of a dimension to distinguish stimuli; the more discriminating the dimension the wider the range of elements that can be described by it, the finer the distinctions it makes possible, and the longer the likely time-lapse before assignment of elements to categories; (3) *Integration:* the most important aspect of abstractness, this is the higher-order organising process by which a number of dimensions are used in interrelation to make a judgement. The complexity of an individual's integration rules in a particular domain is clearly of more importance that, say, his differentiation, since one may use subsets of one's armoury of dimensions in a concrete and simple way – even though this may become unlikely the more dimensions one has. Schroder *et al.*[7] outline various methods for measuring these various aspects of complexity, but like Hunt's, Schroder's main method has been the use of a paragraph completion test with a general manual, using similar topics. From this he derives Integration Index scores on a scale of 1 to 7.

Schroder obtains inter-rater reliability coefficients of ·80 to ·95 and Hunt ·80 to ·85 after training with their respective manuals. The differences in emphasis between these two approaches are indeed slight, in so much as the same set of paragraph completions, separately scored by Hunt's and Schroder's groups according to their own manuals, produced correlations averaging around ·80.

Validation of the concept of integration index or conceptual level as an important aspect of real life interaction has come in a variety of ways. Perhaps the most important studies carried out by Schroder and his group have involved complex inter-nation business-game and war-game simulations, in which it is possible to vary the amount of information input over time, the difficulty of tasks, and the cognitive characteristics of participating teams, and to monitor type and amount of requests for information, decisions generated, and degree of comfort or tension experienced. The wealth of findings from such studies indicate generally that cognitively complex individuals, as assessed by the paragraph completion method, do indeed perform better in complex situations. Hunt and his colleagues have concentrated on using the conceptual level approach to derive matching models for educational strategy, that is to say, to optimally match various aspects of the teaching environment to individuals on the basis of their differing conceptual levels. They have confirmed, for instance, that high conceptual level individuals profit more with low degree of structure, e.g. independent study, self-selected projects, whilst low conceptual persons perform better with a high degree of structure, e.g. concrete examples, clearly outlined examples, no discussion.

The last example, however, illustrated the use of a developmental model in the pursuit of goals defined in other terms; whereas integrative complexity and flexibility are presented here as worthy goals of moral education, having a degree of similarity to Kohlberg's explicitly moral dimension and, as such, possibly elucidating various aspects of the latter. How do the conceptual level theorists conceive of development through the stages, and what factors are thought to influence it?

Schroder believes that the learning of new categories and dimensions can be understood on the basis of the traditional learning principles of classical (Pavlovian) conditioning and operant (reward and punishment based) learning, including observation and language mediation. With respect to the crucial integrative aspect, Schroder adduces a variety of findings indicating the superiority of what he terms the 'interdependent environment' (as opposed to the 'unilateral' type); that is to say, one in which the person himself (rather than the training agent) generates combinatory rules and goals relevant to dimensions involved, one which provides feedback, i.e. the individual's monitoring of his own performance, and one which is intrinsically interesting (as opposed to extrinsically motivated by the rewards and punishment at the training agent's disposal). The last aspect, apart from constituting a tall order in some cases, indicates somewhat differing environmental conditions for transition across the different stages; in Hunt's terms, to proceed to Stage I, a person at Sub-I might profit from an environment in which the use of a relatively high degree of structure led to goals of interest, where such an approach would in theory tend to arrest a Stage I person at that level. Direct evidence is rare on the question of the antecedents of development, although a study by Cross[9] indicates that high conceptual level adolescent boys are likely to have more interdependent and anti-authoritarian parents than low conceptual level boys.

Here, then, we have the beginnings of one level of attack on the very complex topic of human information processing. The apparent similarity of this approach to that of Kohlberg has received some confirmation in a study by Sullivan, McCullough and Stager[10] of 12, 14- and 17-year-old Canadian high school students, whose Kohlberg scores showed an overall correlation of ·62 with their conceptual level scores, a reasonable correlation of ·34 remaining when the effect of their common dependence on age was partialled out.

Perry's Harvard Study

In 1953 the staff of the Bureau of Study Counsel at Harvard University, impressed by the variety of ways in which the students they were seeing 'responded to the relativism which permeates the intellectual and social atmosphere of a (their) pluralistic university', undertook to document the experience of their undergraduates over their four years of college. As Perry contends:

> Such diversity, as faced by a student in a college of liberal arts, would seem to be unique in Western society today only in its concentration and intensity. The increased mobility of the population at large, together with the new mass media, make the impact of pluralism part of experience in the society as a whole.
>
> (Perry, 1968, p.6)

As they set out to explore students' forms of experience, the investigators thought in terms of a dimension ranging from a strong preference for dualistic, right-wrong thinking, to an affinity for a much more qualified, relativistic and contingent style of thought. Starting from such conceptions and the work of Adorno and others on *The Authoritarian Personality,* they devised a measure called *A Checklist of Educational Views* in order to identify students along the dimension. Following up, by open-ended interview, students who scored at the extremes of the dimension — interviewing some of them annually through their four-year undergraduate careers — Perry and his colleagues gradually came to feel that they could 'detect behind the individuality of the reports a common sequence of challenges to which each student addressed himself in his own particular way'. They thus arrived at a stage development conception where they had started out with merely a notion of variation in personal style. They then proceeded to make explicit and precise the evolving sequence of challenges and responses discerned as the common theme in their interview data, to construct a manual for scoring position on this sequence, and to test this scheme in further four-year studies of larger numbers of students. These studies took place in the early '60s, and the scheme which these studies confirmed, is in very brief outline as follows:

Position 1: The student sees the world in polar terms of we-right-good vs. others-wrong-bad. Right Answers for everything exist in the Absolute, are known to Authority whose role is to mediate (teach) them. Knowledge and goodness are perceived as quantitative accretions of discrete rightnesses to be collected by hard work and obedience (paradigm: a spelling test).

Position 2: The student perceives diversity of opinion, and uncertainty, and accounts for them as unwarranted confusion in poorly qualified Authorities or as mere exercises set by Authority 'so we can learn to find The Answer for ourselves.'

Position 3: The student accepts diversity and uncertainty as legitimate but still *temporary* in areas where Authority 'hasn't found The Answer yet.' He supposes Authority grades him in these areas on 'good expression' but remains puzzled as to standards.

Position 4: (a) The student perceives legitimate uncertainty (and therefore diversity of opinion) to be extensive and raises it to the status of an unstructured epistemological realm of its own in which 'anyone has a right to his own opinion', a realm which he sets over against Authority's realm where right-wrong still prevails, or (b) the student discovers qualitative contextual relativistic reasoning as a special case of 'what They want' within Authority's realm.

Position 5: The student perceives all knowledge and values (including Authority's) as contextual and relativistic and subordinates dualistic right-wrong functions to the status of a special case, in context.

Position 6: The student apprehends the necessity of orienting himself in a relativistic world through some form of personal commitment (as distinct from unquestioned or unconsidered commitment to simple belief in certainty).

Position 7: The student makes an initial Commitment in some area.

Position 8: The student experiences the implications of Commitment, and explores the subjective and stylistic issues of responsibility.

Position 9: The student experiences the affirmation of identity among multiple responsibilities and realizes Commitment as an ongoing, unfolding activity through which he expresses his life style.

CONDITIONS OF DELAY, DEFLECTION, and REGRESSION

Temporizing: The student delays in some Position for a year, exploring its implications or explicitly hesitating to take the next step.

Escape: The student exploits the opportunity for detachment offered by the structures of Positions 4 and 5 to deny responsibility through passive or opportunistic alienation.

Retreat: The student regresses to a previously held position, usually 2 or 3.

The manual for coding the interview material was shown to be capable of generating a high degree of inter-rater reliability, and this was no less the case for the rating of excerpts from interviews, and condensed four-year reports. It is interesting to recognise, as Perry does explicitly, the similarity between this scheme and that of Harvey, Hunt, and Schroder, which was worked out independently during the same period; like these workers and Kohlberg, Perry found very few instances of the top level of his scheme among his subjects. Nor did he find anyone at the first position in the sequence; the contrast with Hunt's work, where the addition of a lower stage than those foreseen seemed necessary, is probably due to the difference in age and selectivity of the samples studied. Whilst Perry's work is mainly analytic and, indeed, is noteworthy in its explicit reflective awareness of the nature of the exercise, he is nevertheless willing to speculate on the variety of motives both towards growth and against such movement. Among the former: sheer curiosity, a striving for competence based on understanding, an urge to make order out of incongruity and anomaly (cf. Kohlberg's equilibration to settle cognitive conflict), a wish for community with humans looked upon as mature, for authenticity in human relationships, for the development and affirmation of an identity, and so on. Among the countervailing forces: the wish to maintain a self-identity one had established, often within the comfort of a home community whose values and thought patterns one was therefore loathe to abandon. 'Pervading all such motives of conservation', says Perry, 'lay the apprehension that one change might lead to another in a rapidity which might end in catastrophic disorganisation' — though he also points out that such a metaphor of opposing forces is adequate as no more than a shorthand characterisation of the complex self-regulating organism man constitutes.

Whilst, within this metaphor, the balance of forces seemed pervasively in favour of progress, the Harvard study is interesting for its consideration of the alternatives to growth — temporizing, retreat, and escape — and of their forms and occurrence at various points in the sequences. *Temporizing* involves an arrest in growth in terms of the positions in Perry's scheme, though in terms of underlying developmental processes it might merely be a slowing down. Temporizing may give rise to a resumption of progress, or, especially if the person adopts a passive attitude of waiting for something to change him, it may lead to one of the variations of escape.

Escape involves settling for a position (4, 5 or 6) whose implications for growth are either denied or rejected; it takes the form of dissociation or encapsulation. Dissociation, or the passive delegation of all responsibility to fate can eventually slide to a depersonalised looseness at Position 4. Dissociation is from the 'challenge of meaning' as Perry puts it: 'Its tone is depressed, even when pleasure is still possible in irresponsibility'. Encapsulation typically uses the relativism of Positions 5 and 6: some vestige of an identity can be maintained in sheer competence: 'Here the self is a doer, or a gamesman, and its opportunism is defended by an encapsulation in activity, sealed off from the implications of deeper values'. There is an important distinction between the commitment that constitutes a participation in and acceptance of a relativistic world and forms the higher positions in this scheme, and the above escape into commitment *from* such a world. Certainty is provided in the sealed off position, but the relativism outside it can be selectively employed to ground such stands as one wishes to take

Given the pluralistic, liberal, academic setting, the third possibility of *retreat* seems to have required some degree of fight. Furthermore, regression was typically into dualism, which itself defines the world in terms of us and them. Of these three alternatives to growth, the escape form seems of particular relevance in higher educational situations: this seems to be Perry's viewpoint, and from my own experience of present-day students, the challenge of relativism and the form of commitment seems one of the more visible problem tasks of life. There would be considerable profit, it seems to me, in systematically exploring the experiences of students in higher education today, especially when one considers that Perry's study took place in an American setting and that the intervening period has, as Wright and Cox have shown, seen various changes in the outlook of young people. Meanwhile, anyone involved in higher education would probably gain from a consideration of Perry's book, especially the fifth and sixth chapters.

Rokeach's Studies of Dogmatism

The major point of departure of Rokeach's work on 'The open and closed mind' was the studies of authoritariansim by such investigators as Fromm, Maslow, and perhaps best known, Adorno and his colleagues at Berkeley. Emphasising that it is the nature of belief *systems* and not simply the content of particular beliefs that he considers crucial, Rokeach considered that authoritarianism (aggressive conventionalism, uncritical submission to authority, stereotyping, concern with power, and so on) had been identified in a confused way with the form of it found on the extreme political right, as measured by Adorno and his colleagues' Fascism scale. Whereas, so he contended, there are aspects of authoritarianism, and especially such aspects of its cognitive style as rigidity and intolerance of ambiguity, which are to be found across the whole spectrum of variation in belief content: 'What about intolerance among Marxists, liberals, Freudians, Unitarians, academicians, and art critics, to name but a few?' Such a focus had also hindered the genera-tion of theory that might tie together in a general way the organisation of belief with the organisation of cognition.

Rokeach considered that belief systems and subsystems can be arranged along three continua: belief-disbelief, central-peripheral, and time perspective. With respect to the first of these, a system is 'open' as opposed to 'closed' insofar as: disbelief subsystems are weakly rather than strongly rejected as each point along the continuum; there is communication as opposed to isolation of parts within systems; and there is relatively little discrepancy in degree of differentiation of domain between belief and disbelief systems. The central beliefs of the open system tend to see situations as friendly rather than threatening; closed systems tend to evaluate people by reference to their relationship to authority whilst open systems deny this, and closed systems perceive the subsystems emanating from authority in relative isolation from each other, whilst open systems see them in communication, thus comparison, with each other. Finally, systems are open to the extent that there is a relatively broad time perspective, as opposed to a relatively narrow, future-oriented time perspective in the closed system. The most basic characteristic distinguishing the open from the closed mind is suggested to be the extent to which a person can receive, evaluate, and act on relevant information received from the outside on its own intrinsic merits, unencumbered by irrelevant factors — examples of which are unrelated habits, beliefs, and perceptual cues, irrational ego motives, power needs, the need to allay anxiety, and so forth. Rokeach's book *The Open and Closed Mind* contains a set of studies broadly confirming Rokeach's conception, using his Dogmatism scale as the main measure of openness-closedness.

These, then, have been selected illustrations of some psychological .approaches to moral and social thinking. They slow convergence as well as a good deal of divergence, which is perhaps a pointer to those considerable subtleties and complexities of this area not yet accounted for by such approaches — although they themselves can hardly be called simple.[12]

Skilled Information Processing

We now turn to a brief consideration of the concept of information processing skill and some proposals which relate its application at the level of traditional, fine-grained (or "moleculer") experimentation to explanation at the more complex (or "molar") level of phenomena so far dealt with in this chapter. It should perhaps be pointed out that this does not imply a restriction of all psychological explanation to grandiose reductionist integration, nor even an eschatological hope for one; it is simply fortunate for the purpose of this chapter that the information processing skill approach has been a very popular one in experimental psychology in recent years, and that it is a very flexible one, admitting of relatively broad application — as I hope the following pages will show.

A skilled performance is one that is accurate with respect to its intended outcome. It is expert, in the sense that skills typically require a measure of practice, with results being checked against effort, before such accuracy can be reliably reproduced in a smooth and rapid manner: initial performance succeeds only through step-by-step, often painstaking self-monitoring, practice and feedback lead to increasingly automatic production of larger and larger chunks of the task, whose performance as a whole becomes more and more accurate, rapid and smooth. The great impetus to the experimental study of skills by psychologists came during World War II, when there arose an urgent need to understand the factors making for ease or difficulty in the operation of elaborate equipment: the cybernetic approach which developed during this period stressed the organism as a system receiving and selecting inputs from many sources, combining them to produce from its possible response outputs that which met the requirements of the situation. The psychologist tries to set up models of such an information processing system, specifying as precisely as possible the nature of the basic functions, such as selective attention, short- and long-term memory, response choice, and the nature of the organismic structures involved in these: such models are designed to generate predictions concerning new situations, which can then be tested. In its search for precision, experimental psychology has tended to concentrate on relatively well-defined, simple skills, and models naturally tend to vary at least in detail, according to the skill under consideration. However, skill in the sense described above attaches to a very large range of activities: it need not be restricted, for instance, to manual skills. It is useful, as Sir Frederic Bartlett suggested, to treat thinking 'as a complex and high-level kind of skill'.[13]

An important concern of psychologists involved with models of skilled performance has been with forms and implications of limitation in information-processing capacity, and with the effects of various forms of stress, such as overloading such capacities. Such capacity limitation is, in fact, the fundamental aspect from the experimental tradition that has been taken up by a number of investigators seeking more precise understanding of the different — but converging — phenomena of complex social thinking outlined earlier. These ideas will now be briefly described.

With respect to the Piaget-Kohlberg conception of a hierarchical set of stages of thinking, it was Piaget himself who suggested, some fifty years ago, that the difference between the restrictive logic of the child and the more adequate adult system of thought was due to the child having a smaller immediate memory — it could keep less in mind than the adult. 'Loss of hold' errors have been noticed by Margaret Donaldson in her 11-year-old subjects, solving similar sorts of problems to those used by Piaget so long before, but this form of error dropped out as the children got older. In 1963 McLaughlin, apparently unaware of Piaget's original suggestion, showed how the age norms for digit-memory tests corresponded to the number of different classes distinguished simultaneously, which define, in terms of the algebra of classes, logics corresponding to those described by Piaget and his colleagues in children of varying ages. Recently, Pascual-Leone has proposed a somewhat similar 'mathematical model for the transition rule in Piaget's stages', in which he holds that that analysis of the various Piagetian tasks designed to indicate stage of cognitive development shows that those corresponding to any particular stage require a certain number of independent items to be taken into account, which in turn corresponds to the number of items a child can hold in mind as established by experimental memory tests (though Pascual-Leone himself would not agree to the use of the term memory). Such approaches postulate in common that a certain (increasing) information-processing capacity is a necessary though insufficient condition for the increasingly complex forms of reasoning. Recently Peter Bryant's work at Oxford has provided evidence of the important role of short-term memory with respect to Piagetian tasks. The work of Selman, Lee, Brooks-Walsh and Sullivan, indicates that Kohlberg's stages are, as he himself claims, increasingly complex forms of reasoning, requiring the application of structures assessed by the standard Piagetian tasks: there is thus strong indication that moral reasoning in general depends on basic information-processing capacity.

Turning to Rokeach's dogmatism concept, Torcivia and Laughlin have found, in a concept formation task, that high dogmatic subjects used less 'focus gambling' strategy than low dogmatics, whilst they did not differ in 'conservative focusing' scores. These two strategies differ in that they require respectively more or less novel information to be used as the basis for hypothesis: low dogmatics seem to be able to take more into account, and to be better at integrating information into their existing structures.

Basic variables such as short-term memory capacity have not been related to the conceptual complexity scheme of Harvey, Hunt and Schroder, but Schroder's research on complex simulation situations has definitely established the information-processing complexity component in their conception of social reasoning.

It might be wondered whether the cognitive approach does not tend to treat the various phenomena of moral judgement, personality style, form of awareness in college, and type of belief system, as forms of intelligence. It is true that Rokeach's dogmatism scores show no correlation with traditional intelligence test scores, and conceptual level shows only low positive correlations with them, as do scores on Kohlberg's moral judgement maturity. However, as Evans[14] has pointed out, statistical requirements have dictated the use of a certain type of item in IQ tests, so that the possibility of systematically different types of intellectual tasks is clear. Thus Rokeach is quite explicit that he is dealing with intelligence, even if not of a type measured by traditional tests. Kohlberg is dealing with intelligence from a Piagetian point of view. Schroder points out that objective item tests for conceptual level have never produced more than low, if significant, correlations with sentence completion scores, and have been consistently inferior in construct-validity studies. A full treatment of what we mean by intelligence must be left to the philosophers, but there is an important point to be made here, and it is that insofar as the moral educator accepts any of the stage hierarchies or the belief system analysis outlined earlier as descriptions of paths to his goals, the information-processing skills approach, whose relevance to them I hope to have shown, may offer some understanding and thereby a means to bringing about progress in their terms.

Before concluding, however, it is equally important to explicitly avoid any possible impression of having outlawed the affective-motivational side of things. Various aspects of motivation and affect can be represented in informational terms, and they certainly have their effects on information-processing: in traditional experimental psychology there is a great number of studies of various forms of stress and their effects, and at the molar level, one could point to the similar quantitative functions found in Schroder's studies. Such work underlines the essential interaction of value and fact, affect and cognition.

An attempt to deal with this work would, however, mean prolonging the present chapter to an extent which is not feasible. The reader will find some considerations concerning the motivational-emotional aspects of interpersonal awareness in the following chapter. Meanwhile, I hope that the foregoing will illustrate the degree of complexity involved even in current attempts at a precise understanding of man (a point to which I shall return in Chapter 5) and that its selective coverage will stimulate interested readers to pursue for themselves those topics which cannot receive more than passing mention here.

References

1. To anyone interested in following up this topic I recommend George Miller's *Psychology: the Science of Mental Life* (Penguin, Harmondsworth, 1962); M.A. Wertheimer, *Brief History of Psychology* Holt, Rinehart & Winston, New York, 1970). A recent introduction to psychology, easily accessible and highly recommended, is D.S. Wright, A. Taylor et al. *Introducing Psychology: an experimental approach.* (Penguin, Harmondsworth 1970).
2. It is interesting to note that British psychology never seems to have

succumbed quite so thoroughly to Behaviourism, though cynics might retort that this is due to a more general reluctance to believe that human behaviour may be systematically studied with any profit.

3. D. Wright, *The Psychology of Moral Behaviour* (Penguin, Harmondsworth, 1971).

4. H. Gwynne Jones, 'In Search of an Idiographic Psychology, *Bulletin of the British Psychological Society,* 1971, *24,* pp. 279-290. It may be added that, vast enterprise though it may have become, academic psychology has retained an emphasis on precision and certainty that has given rise to a predominantly mechanistic, individual and purist orientation. This point and its implications will be taken up in chapter 5.

5. References to Kohlberg's writings will be found in Wright, *op. cit.* A recent and typically lengthy contribution which illustrates the ambitious scope of Kohlberg's efforts is provided by his chapter 'From is to ought: How to commit the Naturalistic fallacy and get away with it in the study of moral development' in T. Mischel, (Ed.), *Cognitive Development and Epistemology* (Academic Press, New York 1971) Pp. 151-236.

6. See L. Kohlberg & R. Kramer, 'Continuities and Discontinuities in Childhood and Adult Moral Development', *Human Development,* 1969, *12,* Pp. 93-120.

7. O.J. Harvey, D.E. Hunt, H.M. Schroder, *Conceptual Systems and Personality Organization* (Wiley, New York 1961), D.E. Hunt, *Matching Models in Education,* (Ontario Institute for Studies in Education, Toronto 1971); H.M. Schroder, & P. Suedfelt (Eds.), *Personality and Information Processing* (Ronald Press, New York 1971).

8. For an introduction to Kellian views, see D. Bannister, & F. Fransella, *Inquiring Man: the Theory of Personal Constructs* (Penquin, Harmondsworth 1971).

9. H. Cross, 'The relation of parental training conditions to conceptual level in adolescent boys', *Journal of Personality* 966, *34,* pp. 348-65.

10. E.V. Sullivan, G. McCullough, & M. Stager, 'A developmental study of the relationship between conceptual, ego, and moral development', *Child Development,* 1970, *41,* pp. 399-411.

11. W.G. Perry, Jr., *Forms of Intellectual and Ethical Development in the College Years: a Scheme.* (Holt, Rinehart & Winston, New York 1968)

12. A useful set of readings on this area is: P.B. Warr, (Ed.), *Thought and Personality. Selected readings* (Penguin, Harmondsworth 1970).

13. A readable introductory coverage of the psychology of skills is provided by A.T. Welford, *Fundamentals of Skill.* (Methuen, London 1968).

14. G.T. Evans, 'Intelligence, Transfer, and Problem-solving', W.B. Dockrell (Ed.), *On intelligence* (Methuen, London 1970).

3   THE RELATIONSHIP OF DEPTH PSYCHOLOGY TO MORAL DEVELOPMENT

Douglas Hamblin

Words may obscure a problem rather than illuminate it. This is very likely when analytical psychology which embodies a 'talking therapy' is related to the wide field of moral development. The onlooker may feel that the words we use are heavily loaded with a significance which they do not possess. It is true that at times the depth psychologist has behaved as if he were permeated by a special wisdom and held revelatory insights which put him into the realm of the sacred rather than that of daily life. Yet it has become clear that at times we are only indulging in ritually closed interchanges of meanings with our clients, which may contain little more than the satisfactions to be found in mutual masturbation. These are hard words, but they suggest that therapists now appreciate the possibility that they may be practising a primitive word magic which has no meaning outside the therapeutic situation.

O'Brien (1972) found himself disconcerted by the lack of suspicion in his students. They rightly suspected the agents of capitalism and the prophets of politics, but 'they suspected one another too little, they suspected their own individual selves not at all'. The discussion in this chapter has been subjected to a heavily 'suspecting glance' in the hope of avoiding unjustified claims. It is based on the assumption that the depth psychologist has something to offer only when self-suspicion is blended with belief in what he does. The suspicion is not only directed at our claims, but at our procedures, for it is likely that many of them are not only very different from what we think they are, but embody contradictory and self-defeating strategies. Psychotherapy has no unique contribution to make to moral development. At the most it may help by clearing the emotional undergrowth a little, clarifying perceptions and providing the client with some belief in himself. It may allow the emergence in those in whom it was lacking of the capacity to make considered moral judgments, but it offers no prescriptions as to the content of the moral code. The argument which follows does scant justice to the complexity of modern analytic theory, being idiosyncratic and highly selective. The reader who looks for a complete account of depth psychology certainly will not find it, although he will find some attempt to isolate the processes which are common to most forms of therapeutic treatment and which impinge on the moral capacity of the client.

Psychotherapy is based on the acquisition of accurate insights, based on the therapist's accurate empathy with his client. The objective of the therapist is to facilitate change by raising the hidden significance of past actions and relationships to the level of rational examination. His efforts are directed towards helping those with whom he works to develop a knowledge of the way they see themselves; the way they deceive themselves and refuse to see how others see them; and the distortions thus caused in the way the client sees others. The therapist works on the basis of the belief that self knowledge can lead to self acceptance, which in turn may lead to new development and growth. It has been claimed that analytic psychology replaces the older doctrine of predestination with a newer determinism based on the unconscious and the inevitability of early experiences. This is a caricature of the real aim of psychotherapy which is to help those who use it to see that neither the unconscious nor the past need determine the present. The message of this aim is that it is possible in the present to reshape, redefine and redetermine the past. For the therapist no man is a prisoner of his past! If the process is successful, then a man can look forward to the future, facing it with that mixture of hope and anxiety which is our inevitable lot. He learns to look to the future without having to cast it into an inflexible form – which would be to replace one form of determinism by another, possibly harder to detect and more difficult to remedy.

The possibility of moral choice and development implies some model of personality. Each one of us holds some implicit model of the nature of man which influences our reactions to our fellows. It is the intention of psychotherapy to be life-enhancing rather than life-eroding, but in the past there have been two tendencies in depth psychology. The tendency in one group of therapists has been to assume that within a man lie dark urges of an instinctual type which have to be contained and directed to social ends through the process of upbringing and socialisation. Checks and controls from outside seem to be emphasised in this approach. Failure in the controlling processes and by the controlling agents indicates the need for therapeutic intervention as a means of developing self-management. In recent years a more optimistic view of the nature of man has come to the fore, which lays stress on the fact that inside a man or woman lie the potentiality for creativity and the possibility of future positive development. These essentially simple ideas of what is inside a man may underlie our technical phrases, and although they remain unverbalised because of their simplicity, they operate to structure our strategies to an alarming degree. The impediments to growth and responsibility, when they are external, tend to be more easily recognised by those who hold the optimistic viewpoint, whilst those holding the instinctual view of man recognise them more quickly when they are internal. A balance between these points of view is necessary, and we take into account also the way in which our own basic personality theory, which may be separated from our professional training, not only shapes our treatment, but what we actually perceive. Perhaps this is the point where we see that a depth psychology has to be related to the social climate. The instinctual approach seems more in tune with a society based on the Protestant Ethic of control and planning ahead, whilst the optimistic view, as a reading of Maslow (1954)[2] and Allport (1955)[3] would show, is of more relevance in the unpredictable and individualistic social ethos of today.

The dichotomy which has just been made is arbitrary, and, as suggested, it is more a matter of the relative balance between the approaches, than of an absolute division. Sometimes the differences are pseudo-differences, for in one the idea of fixation at an earlier stage is emphasised, whilst the other uses the idea of stunting. The educator wishes to be concerned, not so much with man as an acted upon and passive being, as with someone who is actively developing. Hence the second approach has more to offer, it presents a dynamic conception of identity. Each one of us needs to have some basis for evaluation in the flux and flow of interpersonal interaction, and depth psychology *can* aid the development of a sense of identity. Life appears to be full of comparison processes, but who are those with whom we compare ourselves, and who am I who makes the comparisons? Need I accept the evaluations of others as to what I am? Oppenheim (1966)[4] draws the attention of social psychologists to the fact that behaviour is a product of the way in which we perceive our environment. I would take this a step further by stating that our perceptions are themselves a product of our assumptions and inner needs. This is shown in the seminal work by Adorno et al. (1950)[5] which demonstrates the part played by the family in producing prejudiced behaviour and attitudes, but more important still, shows how unmet needs and inner fantasies determine perception. We behave in a certain way because of what we see, but we see what we need to see. Lazarus (1966)[6] has assembled some of the evidence and it is sufficient to make any teacher question himself about the nature of his evaluations of students.

The argument we are considering is that those versions of depth psychology which incorporate the positive idea of self realisation may have more to contribute to the decision making processes and autonomy that seem essential to moral development in higher education. The pace of social change, the ever-increasing unpredictability of the future, and the growing irrelevance of traditional guides and signposts for behaviour make the concept of socialisation suspect. Basically, socialisation is a way of inculcating the values of existing groups and individuals into the new generation. Yet is more true than ever before that conditions today are different from those of yesterday, and those of tomorrow will be vastly different from both. A clear sense of identity may provide the only stable anchorage in a world where uncertainty reigns and where gross ambiguities about the meaning of events have to be tolerated. This is not an argument for denying the existence of stable values, but one for recognition of the fact that values evolve, take many forms, and gain part of their meaning from the total social climate. This smuggles into the argument the idea of relativism, but this recognition also asks for acceptance of the fact that it is only those who have achieved the capacity to see themselves as they are, who can begin to attempt the task of understanding others and the world around them. Yet there are basic values, and the psychotherapist has a central place for the Christian injunction to love others as one loves oneself.

This alerts us to the need to look at ourselves as teachers, just as much, indeed more, than we look at the students. The therapist must supply what a student needs by adapting to him, which means giving love to those who cannot love themselves in the hope that they will begin to do this. We may find, however, that we are the unloved, and hence unable to give love to those in whom we claim to be facilitating development. This is the core of therapeutic interaction, yet we can destroy it when we attempt to incorporate depth psychology into a professional training. I have to ask myself if I am misusing my knowledge to condition students in a civilised way to reach a final point of convergence of viewpoints. This I then label as success whilst simultaneously deluding myself that my objectives are those of encouraging independent thought and the achievement of self realisation. It seems clear that I have to reject the concept of an inert man who has to be moulded into shape, but it also seems possible that the activities and style of interaction I use to stimulate responsibility can be inherently self-defeating. The student is attributed by me with the capacity for creating his own reality, but the pattern of interaction which I produce as a response to this capacity may be one which encourages identification. This is an emotionally-based process of merging with a warm and nurturant model, during which the person who identifies takes over the values and standards of the model. Identificatory processes may impose an identity or blur the boundaries between what is one's own self and what belongs to the selves of others. The creation of a warm and accepting climate can foster identificatory processes in which students can be caught and absorbed by the expectations of others in an identity-eroding way. Riesman (1968)[7] complains that many readers failed to understand that his inner-directed man is controlled by internalised figures which limit and structure his concept of what is desirable and possible for him. These figures are partially their possessor's own creation because he selects and interprets their values, but nonetheless they are imposed. It is possible to indulge in a circular pattern of first providing the conditions in which students can dissolve or discard earlier identifications, and then to encourage the students to replace them by others. In creating an accepting environment, we can ignore the fact that identity and opposition are looking-glass relationships. Love lacks meaning without hate, and equally we deny identity if we provide nothing to oppose in the leading situation. If we try to include depth psychology as an attempt to meet the developmental needs of students, we bring in new problems which cannot be evaded.

Earlier, mention was made of the necessity for an individual to learn to tolerate ambiguity and doubt without closing his mind to gain certainty, but there are many opportunities created for rigid interpretations when we adopt a more permissive approach to learning. This is not an argument against these new approaches. It is a plea that we do not replace overt authoritarianism or the tendency to see things in terms of black and white, by a concealed authoritarianism. Authoritarianism is only indirectly concerned with the authority structure; rather it is a cognitive style which acts as a filter upon perceptions. This is linked with the nature of person perception. Heider (1958)[8] is one of a number of writers who see person perception as a process of attribution of motives and intentions to others. This is illustrated by Heider's story of a man who enters his study and becomes aware of a trickle of sand on his desk. He then glances up and sees cracks in the walls and ceiling. His next step is to telephone the builder because he has inferred a fault in the foundation of the house. So it is with our perception of people. If we see a student behaving in a way which meets with our disapproval, we tend to infer a defect of character in that person. We may behave considerately, but we would do well to evaluate the basis of our judgement. Depth psychology argues for caution about the inferential step in person perception, because it sees the need in the judge for stability and order as a potential distorting factor. We want to predict, and to achieve this we build up networks of associations between events and behaviour, knitting these into a causal framework. We all do this, but therapeutic experiences reveal the way in which we react on the basis of this false psychological logic. This logic is often based on our needs and nature rather than the other person. Often we assume, without realising we are doing so, that a person who possesses one negative characteristic also has another. The relationship between intelligence and virtue is not inevitable, although some schoolmasters behave as if it were. Not only is the associational basis of our judgments doubtful at times, but so are the links between liking, approval and goodness, which are contained in a particular judgment. The therapist working in higher education may see this, but when he has to use depth psychology techniques as part of the training he gives, he may still be destructive. He may create anxieties, or through a situation of warmth and acceptance seduce students into accepting his point of view.

The student needs a suspecting glance. Most mature students who come into professional courses of training as counsellors have a sincere desire for change, but it is bewildering to find that they see it as primarily concerned with eliminating undesired parts of themselves. This may be a product of the myths about analytic psychology. There seems to be a confusion between the undesired and the undesirable which makes for this harsh view of the nature of change. It is anxiety-provoking to see that the undesired is not necessarily the undesirable or that the unwanted elements may be those which contain the potentiality for growth. To accept this is to accept the need to redefine change, and reorientate oneself. The reluctance to accept this need is sometimes a product of a devaluation of the inner life which is condemned as fantasy and therefore unrealistic. Sensitivity groups or other forms of therapeutic education may be visualised by the student as a ritualised means of casting out the bad parts of oneself; of expelling the immature aspects rather than allowing them to grow; as a painful process of confession and exposure rather than the reworking of inadequate solutions to basic developmental tasks. Those students who seem to gain from the therapeutic encounter report after leaving that their greatest achievement was a more flexible and adequate solution to the two great developmental tasks of adolescence as postulated by Erikson (1950).[9] They have gained a wider and more positive sense of identity and have advanced in their capacity to make a truly intimate relationship. They are then freed from their ties to adolescent experiences and can enjoy the present to a wider extent.

Depth psychology is concerned with facilitating a process of redefinition and reconstruction in the student based on his positive qualities. This suggests that many of them think of it as something which merely eliminates the unwanted, but the therapist refuses to accept these weaknesses as the most important thing about the student and will not define therapy in such negative and static terms. A helpful approach which has an affinity with education is that of Kelly (1955).[10] His construct theory underlines the active ability of a man to make his own social reality, construing it, validating the construction and then proceeding to develop it in a way which leads to more satisfying interaction. The importance of this process of construction lies behind the reliance on free association in therapy, which allows the client to see what is tied together in networks of meaning. The negative side was dealt with briefly in the paragraph on person perception, but the therapist wants his client to achieve some insight into the basis for his judgments. This opens the way for a revision of their significance with a possibility of a subsequent modification of behaviour. We must not delude ourselves about the efficacy of insight, for many people seem to know validly why they do something they do not wish to do, but still find themselves unable to stop doing it. Insight may be a necessary but not sufficient condition for the modification of behaviour, but it is equally likely to lead to confinement within a circle of shame without increased ability to resist temptation.

The self image is central in therapy and moral conduct, and there is a self concept of both student and tutor encapsulated in the transactions between them. All of us have an ideal picture of ourselves towards which we strive and an actual picture which is partially derived from the responses of others. At times students come to courses of higher education with the knowledge that they carry with them an ideal self which has been imposed on them by others, rather than it being a self creation. They gain the courage to discard it, but then react with over-sharp suspicion to those who try influencing them into making any attempt at real evluation of what is being presented. The ideal self is a problem for it can be used as a defence in many ways. It may represent a retreat from human frailty to perfectionist standards, but it also is the case that impossible targets and aspirations represent an evasion of responsibility rather than a dynamic striving after an unattainable ideal. It is a strategy which argues in a self-protecting way that no reasonable person could possibly blame the individual for failure in such an exacting task. In this way it can be seen that the ideal self is a residual part of a 'good boy' approach to morality in some students. Sometimes the distance between the ideal and actual self is great enough to cause depression. Therefore the student has to learn that he has the power to modify the ideal, readjusting it over time. The creative task of therapy is, amongst other things, to enable a student to see that he can create for himself an ideal which is his alone as a basis for constructive evaluation. This gives him a measure of inner control and helps to stop the negative comparisons with others which accompany a harsh ideal self. The modification of the ideal self is no easy task for it arouses acute anxiety. Not only is it more sharply delineated than the actual self, but it contains elements based on parental injunctions and cultural imperatives, which exercise a tight hold even on those who claim they have rejected them.

The therapist is not concerned with self esteem to the exclusion of other aspects of the self. Wall (1968)[11] showed the importance of the vocational, sexual, philosophical and social selves, but the educator can forget that these are affected by what he does, and that the student reacts to the educational situation through these selves. Within the individual there are conflicts between the selves. An able woman may not feel her intellectual competence, but display this aggressively, whilst this aggression is at variance with her sexual self where she sees herself as passive and dependent. In the philosophical self, a man may have a view of the world as one based on co-operation and sharing, yet simultaneously he is building up a vocational self in preparation for a business career where he recognises ruthless competition as the norm. The man may flaunt his dominance in the sexual role, but at the same time be painfully aware that his social self is permeated by a feeling of inadequacy. The male counsellor or social worker may find himself internally in conflict because he places a great value on tangible results, but finds that a basic requirement for his profession is the capacity for feeling and expressiveness which he associates with the female role. Self exploration must be concerned with these four selves and their significance in the future of the student, but we need also to assess their impact on the two great developmental tasks. Depth therapy can label people, diverting blame away from the system. Sometimes we realise that it is the system that should change rather than individuals. On occasions however, the desire to attack the system springs from the tutor's or social worker's inability to develop a good relationship with it because feeling and thinking are separated. Intimacy can be feared or called over-involvement and an unhealthy relationship, whereas the truly unhealthy relationship is one devoid of feeling and warmth. The taboo on tenderness is far from non-existent today. Students themselves desire good relationships, yet find themselves caught up into self-defeating patterns of behaviour due to the conflicting pulls of the four selves.

This leads our attention to the disquieting feature of the divided self and to the possibility that the educational system may reinforce these divisions. The divided self has been described by Laing (1960)[12] and Winnicott (1971).[13] It has been suggested that false conceptions of what may be the valuable parts of themselves exist in students, and much of the therapeutic work of T Groups or Encounter Groups is concerned with the gradual dissolution of the falsely imposed self. Caution, courage and integrity are necessary, for the capacity for self deception is always present in us. We can never be sure that the emergent self in the therapeutic process is the true self, for it may be yet another adaptation to the pressures of the current situation. Neither must we lightly assume that the true self is necessarily good, for there is the possibility that the negative view of human nature is sometimes justified. The most we can say of the true self is that it is a more honest revelation of the basic nature of a man, and one is forced back into belief that there is an inherent goodness in people which is a basis for therapeutic interaction. Courage is entailed in therapeutic interaction because the false self may be acting as a protective caretaker for an underlying self, and many of the activities and attitudes, which from the outsider's view appear to be sterile, are functioning to protect the hidden and undeveloped aspect of self from the real or imagined criticisms of others. To strip away defences is to risk premature exposure of a self that needs protection and nurture.

Worthwhile implications for moral development are found in this idea of the divided self, for it may account for the tendency in some of us to split our worlds into sharp divisions of good and bad. The divisions which exist within the psyche are projected on to the external world. If the inner self contains the creative elements, but the possessor of that self feels it is dangerous to reveal himself as he is, then this may explain why one often finds the equivalent of the old concept of *hubris* operating in underfunctioning able students. To achieve is to court disaster for such people. Varied reactions to the divided self can be found. The discrepancy between the inner and outer self or between the separated parts of the self may cause some to fall into acceptance of the approval motive as the source of their motivation, thereby denying the real identity in which academic achievement is irrelevant. Others may take their identity from their peers, too easily assuming that they are the victims of processing, failing to see the correspondence between their needs and the satisfactions offered in academic work. They then spend their time abortively, denying themselves in a self-punitive way.

The therapist hopes to provide the conditions through which a man can transcend his dogmatisms; admit both his strengths and weaknesses, and move to a new level of integration of inner and outer selves. In the course of therapy the realisation may develop that many alternative representations of reality exist, leading to the recognition that although some of these are displeasing and distasteful to him, this does not give him the right to condemn them. The therapist aids this realisation, but the criteria of judgement remain the individual's property. The experience of finding unseen facets of oneself calls attention to the possibility that there may be more in a problematical situation than the first look suggests. Two kinds of looking are required of us: the self-accepting one, which is then followed by the self-suspecting. The interaction of these, then, can lead to awareness that many of our hoarded facts about the nature of others and our moral discussions bear the same relationship to today as our discarded garments of childhood.

Moral development implies a permeability of the major dimensions along which an individual organises his world. Rokeach (1960)[14] has demonstrated the way in which closed belief systems create a dogmatism which prevents their holder from using new information as a factor for changing or replacing his belief systems. He showed that the dogmatist may analyse the problem accurately, but then lacks the capacity to reassemble the bits to make a more viable whole. He then retreats in confusion to his former position.

The self does not exist in isolation and we need to think of the self in relation to others. Many of us have a sense of separation from God, our fellow men and our selves. By denying feeling, educational experiences separate people from themselves. Alienation is a convenient term, although as a psychological term it is an emasculation of what was a radical criticism of society by Marx. Hegel (1949)[15] made a distinction that might well be relevant. He described culture as Spirit separated from itself, whilst morality was Spirit sure of itself. Hegel's certainty is both questionable and enviable, but it does seem that sooner or later we come to the unity of the outer and inner. There are crippling effects when we are estranged from others and from ourselves. The rub comes when we ask from what it is that we are separated. In a defensive strategy we blame the establishment, our parents or some other convenient scapegoat without seeing how futile this is. It is more painful to see that there are unbridged gaps within us, or that we are torn by inner contradictions. Higher education may well accentuate the sharp distinction between thinking and feeling and in so doing put greater distance between the self of the learning situation and the half-comprehended inner self. It is the positive step which causes alarm because of the heavy responsibility involved for oneself. I believe it was Feuerbach who saw this very clearly when he pointed out that a man can strip himself of all that is good and strong because he attributes it to others: parents, teachers, ideal figures and heroes. Is the price of approval in the teaching situation partially made up of this?

Moral development for the therapist is a process of moving towards a true self, and whilst it is accepted that true self may never be developed to its full, yet the search for it seems to be the core of moral development. This self discovery is intimately related to social inter-action, hence the development of empathy occupies our attention. We do, however, run into very grave difficulties if we equate psychologically healthy behaviour with moral behaviour without questioning this. Jahoda (1953)[16] has shown that we really do not know what psychological health is. We confuse it with an absence of disease, a state of happiness, successful arrival at a statistically derived definition of normality. If it is impossible to define positive mental health satisfactorily, then it is unlikely that we can trace its relationship to moral development. Not only can the therapist be doing, unwittingly, things that are profoundly immoral, but the very things we do that may be moral, may be misused by the client. To provide the Machiavellian personality who has been described by Christie and Geis (1971)[17] with increased skills in communication and interpersonal competences, is to provide him with a dangerous tool. His aim is that of deriving the maximal personal gratification from others, which means that he reduces them to the level of objects to be manipulated as he desires. The research shows that he is successful when he manages to disguise his objectives from others. To provide skills through encounter groups to such persons is scarcely a contribution to moral development.

If techniques are introduced into education which are based on depth psychology then unpleasant questions have to be faced. The emotional climate and the relationships with the associated dependencies open the way to subtle coercion and emotional blackmail. We are never free from the possibility of manipulation and the temptation to use illegitimate forms of influence under the guise of 'serving the best interests of the other'. I have been conscious of the moments when I offer a conditional acceptance, asking the client for honesty and openness, later realising that this was a latent request that he should define himself as deviant. Sometimes, despite my overt intentions, I have created a climate which made it hard for students to reject an attitude or behaviour pattern of which I approve. Therapy then becomes indoctrination. Concealed paternalism is also present when I attempt to hide or divert attention from the authority component, since it makes the student incapable of rejecting or opposing because the authority element is denied. Then confrontations and conflict, which are developmental, are avoided and my viewpoint cannot be rejected. A situation of cunning conditioning seems to be the outcome.

Empathy can be described as the ability to feel into the other person and then see the world through his eyes. It is the capacity to see the world as he sees it; to react in the way that he does; and emotionally to reverberate with him whilst still holding on to one's own identity. Descriptions of the empathic process appear in Katz (1964)[18] and Natale (1972).[19] From the perspective of morality, empathy may be on a higher level than sympathy. The latter implies a separation, possibly a sense of superiority, but certainly an accentuation of the difference between the giver and receiver of sympathy. Empathy encompasses the giving of compassion and suffering with the other or sharing his joy. Yet the therapist hesitates, asking when we delude ourselves. If our attempt at empathy is inaccurate, then it is merely an attempt to impose our own feelings and definition of the situation on those with whom we claim to empathise. Projection may contaminate our empathic attempts more frequently than it is comfortable to contemplate.

The current method of using depth psychology is through intensive group experience, and descriptions can be found in Bradford, Gibb and

Benne (1964)[20] Rogers (1971)[21] and Thompson and Kahn (1970).[22] The dynamics of such groups centre around the development of sensitivity to the signals sent by others and recognition of their feelings. The reception of feedback about oneself and making an adaptation to this occupies a great deal of attention. Perhaps it is useful to look at the negative side of this. The question of relationship between morality, adjustment and social competence again becomes relevant. If adjustment to others is an integral part of activity, does it contain a latent product which confounds us? The old question about the guardians in 'The Republic' can be taken into a new context. If a situation of mutual adaptation is created, it seems to mean that each is being guided by the others, but who then determines the direction and values of the group as a totality? It is possible to rely on some hazy notion of emergent norms or a sense of purpose which masks an unspecified belief that group forces are necessarily good. Not only does history suggest otherwise, but most of us become aware of destructive mechanisms of role sending such as scapegoating which damage vulnerable members. An outside observer might conclude that we often behave in such groups as if we thought catharsis always had a positive effect, never asking if it might strengthen negative feelings. It could be questioned. He might also think that we work on a model of a hydraulic man who has a predetermined amount of libido, which needs to be redirected if it is being discharged inappropriately.

It seems logical to say that it is the responsibility of the mature in the group to adapt to the needs of the immature, without asking if this means we are claiming to be able to distinguish between the mature and immature. Is a lack of knowledge of the way to behave in a learning situation or a therapeutic group necessarily immaturity? If we accept for the purpose of the argument that it is possible to distinguish between good adjusters and poor ones, then we need to question the propriety of encouraging the good adjuster always to give way to the poor ones. Let us ask what we are doing. In these groups it is possible to achieve a sort of equilibrium between the members which is then labelled as co-operative behaviour, but which may in fact be an uneasy truce or implicit bargain. We may fall into the opposite trap of over-valuing the expression of tensions and hostility because we connect it with development.

Let us be clear that group processes using psychoanalytic procedures are at least as likely to incorporate labelling activities as any other form of group interaction. The labels may be more powerful because they are loaded with emotive concepts such as that of 'infantile', which lead to guilt and shame. It is no defence to say that we do not use these labels, for students read and are aware of the implications without the therapist spelling them out. The onus is on the therapist to know the categories and the way in which he sees others, for much of the interaction centres around the interventions of the therapist and his constructs. If these are modified then we also change the nature of the interaction. Perhaps the easiest thing to forget is that there is a concept of self implicit in the transactions between the group members which is ratified by the experiences. In our zeal for acceptance, we may miss the point that it may not be constructive to confirm a concept of self which is the product of interaction within a specific group. I am reminded of the old story of the therapist who had a patient who announced that he was God. Refusing to be outdone, the therapist replied, 'All right then, I'll let you be God.' Do we implicitly play God?

Autonomy and choice must be linked with leadership and dependence. It does seem useful for the participants to see that leadership is the product of an exchange process. It is helpful morally to see the simple fact that leadership is only possible when there are followers, whilst the follower is not a passive creature of a frozen social matrix, but an alert participant deriving benefits from the follower position. Responsibility and hence blame cannot be moved to the leader alone. A student does learn that the basis of interaction lies in the creation of a system of expectancies, which are often unverbalised and are therefore responded to in a blind way. Simultaneously, he must see the self-eroding nature of rigidly crystalised expectancies, whether he applies them to himself or others. He then learns that he acts, not so much on the basis of rational thought, as on these underlying latent expectancies built into the transactions between himself and others. Evaluation of the process and the validity of his feelings of guilt which arise from failure to meet these expectations are crucial. He may then proceed to understand that at times his acts and feelings do not spring from the manifest views he holds, but from some unverbalised norm of reciprocity or a partially apprehended comparison between himself and others.

The leadership function has dangers for the therapist. Some react by remaining separate, providing feedback or interpretations of behaviour, possibly taking the position of the therapist in the story. The group may then attribute him with charisma and defer to his judgment. Rogers (1971)[23] by contrast emphasises the role of the leader as an involved facilitator who is able to express his care for the members. He facilitates a more honest expression of feelings within the group. This is a more positive position for it is based on the belief that all of us possess the capacity for caring for others and will do this in the right circumstances. Rogers' contention, that the leader should not 'withhold himself from personal emotional participation in the group holding himself aloof as an expert, able to analyse the group process and members' reactions through superior knowledge', avoids the potential arrogance of the therapeutic role. Instead it demands a humility, vulnerability and an openness which makes heavy demands on his sincerity. He has to be prepared to be hurt, to show this in a transparent way, and yet not produce guilt in those who have occasioned the hurt. The message seems to be that the therapist must be on the same level of interaction as the students and preserve an honest concern. The learning and therapeutic process is two-way.

The development of the capacity to care is obviously helpful, but the groups may also contribute to moral development by helping students understand the irrational nature of some conflict. A realistic conflict of interests can stimulate moral growth if it causes a re-evaluation of one's position. Unrealistic conflict is the creature of a need to release inner tensions and dissatisfactions which, for one reason or another, cannot be dealt with openly. It takes the form of displaced aggression and irrational attack, attaching itself to any suitable object. This usually means that the object of attack is unable to retaliate.

Our therapeutic endeavours run the danger of creating quasi-cults or systems of belief which have the attraction of religion whilst lacking the safeguards found in organised religious institutions. There are, as Rogers (1971)[24] suggests, those who learn the rules of interaction without assimilating the ethic. They then become the 'old pros'. They make those who cannot express their feelings frankly or who are hesitant in interaction feel guilty. As a result they are seduced into the dishonest or unwilling expression of feelings. A new tyranny of expectation is then the output from the therapeutic process. It is helpful to look at conflict in terms of Coser's (1964)[25] re-writing of Simmel's propositions. This draws our attention to the way in which members of a group react to the renegade and heretic. The renegade is one who after original adherence to the norms and values of the group, later finds himself unable to maintain this acceptance. His refutation of core values produces a deep sense of threat. The members of the group may then react by steadfastly adopting a closed position, refusing to examine his arguments and rejecting him. When presented so tersely, this sounds almost ridiculous, yet such reactions are part of therapeutic groups.

Our groups may contain some hidden idea of the *right* road to development, or if you like, to salvation. Let us consider the position of the man who accepts the goals, but differs about the method of attaining them. He is the heretic who causes conflict by proposing alternatives where the unspoken desire is that no alternatives should exist. He is rejected with the same consequences as before. It is a fact that these groups are likely to function very differently than we claim, once we look at the latent implications of the interaction. We can produce new forms of authoritarianism. Let me illustrate from my own work in counselling. Students are admitted to the course largely on the basis of personality qualities after certain thresholds in other qualities have been met, but once they enter they find themselves exposed to an ideology, which if accepted, causes them to view those who dissent from it (for example a heavily punitive teacher) in negative terms. They have become indoctrinated by an ideology of concern, and yet when they meet those who do not agree with them, their reaction is one of condemnation, rather than one of concern. They view that other person, with a quality marked by a lack of understanding, perhaps even with a lack of mercy, because he fails to conform to the ideology. This is rather a caricature, yet I find it is there, which means I am involved in a contradictory process. The therapist may well suspect that many of his activities produce similar contradictions. Those who use depth psychology would do well to remember that what we can do with a good conscience as the representative of an ideology, we may also do ruthlessly.

Trust as opposed to mistrust is the central theme of therapy. In a trusting climate there is not place for the bland and non-committal front, yet the very technicalities of therapy can give this impression to the student. If we talk of feedback for students, we may be failing to see that this is a more appropriate idea for computers or machines than for men. The absorption with the technicalities may block the development of a genuine dialogue, asking for honesty on both sides. The tutor's task may be that of accepting the messages of the student, which may condense to 'Will he accept me if I do reveal myself?' In this process of fostering the capacity to trust, it seems important that we learn to think in terms of personal psychological space. Part of our task is that of clearing a psycholigical space around someone in which he learns, not only what he is and what he can be, but what others are. Respect for this psychological distance is necessary and perhaps some of our well meant therapeutic interventions run the risk of ignoring individual differences in the preferred psychological distance. If it is disregarded, then the violation may cause a loss of identity or a protective reaction which leads to falseness and distrust. It seems that we may well need to look at the possibility of psychological rape contained in the penetration of an inner core of privacy.

This has been a negative discussion so far because so many have written so well on the positive side of psychotherapy. If we do achieve something, it is concerned with the achievement of identity and also with helping students to see that they are not the passive objects for therapeutic and educational procedures, but are participants. Depth psychology contributes to moral development only in as much as it aids a man to be truly himself. It is the construction of a pathway of communication, embodying symbolic and emotional exchanges. The fact that so many snares exist, which are the opposite of what we are trying to achieve, has led me to think of therapy as an ongoing process akin to the Hegelian concept of the dialectic. As such, it contains many possibilities for transformations. This is not easy to accept, for the Hegelian dialectic has a tinge of romanticism, as well as the inevitable quality of the river running down to the sea. Useful therapy is that which frees someone from the past, by allowing him to redetermine it whilst constructing his own future. One sees the relationship of identity and opposition and perhaps this provides a clue to the morality of therapy. It is a process of engagement and communication: new meanings are given to experiences and that which was separated becomes integrated. Opposites become reconciled and a growing synthesis, which is unique, emerges, which reveals to the participants a little more of what they are and can be.

Life itself is a process of exchange, as Mauss (1954)[26] has suggested. The depth psychologist is concerned with the exchange processes in interpersonal relationships, but his preoccupation is with the purposes and meanings of the exchanges, rather than with what is exchanged. This may be a corrective, because it leads away from the individual act to its significance as part of a total system of meaning and development. The developmental aspect, and it seems to me that moral behaviour is an integral part of development, lies in the capacity of the therapist to enable people to 'read' the meaning and purpose which is developing in their system of exchanges and communication and to face the implications squarely.

The depth psychologist cannot persuade himself that he deals with objectivity, for he, like anyone else, responds to others as he sees them and not as they are. Most of our messages to others are based on our own needs and are fundamentally egocentric, yet this is the beginning of the dialectical process which may lead to an integrated personality. We take the constructively suspecting glance, but avoid dwelling on guilt and shame. Kelly (1970)[27] said that to feel guilt is to know that we have lost in some way our grasp on the outlook of our fellow men, although a more fundamental step is that of discovering ourselves as we are for the first time. The therapist is concerned with guilt and shame only when they distort growth and prevent the discovery of creative ways of making restitution and reparation which repair damaged relationships or block the path to achievement.

Ours is a task which requires humility and acceptance of the fact that we can never afford to ignore the unintended consequences of our interventions. Perhaps the most that we do is to help students face uncertainty and tolerate ambiguities without retreating into a false certainty. Yet we are not alone in this for it is a major part of an academic training. Sometimes we aid them to accept their unmet needs for dependency and extend a helping hand which allows them to discard illusory forms of independence which mask isolation and a fear of relationships. At times they learn from their experiences in therapy that dependency is not weakness but a form of strength, thereby overcoming the basic mistrust which has permeated their relationships. The task we take on in therapy is one of reconciliation. This is achieved through the symbolic transactions and processes which reconcile the earthy and the spiritual, integrate the crudely physical and the intellectual, enable them to see the correspondences between what is high and what is low, and bind apparent contradictions into a new synthesis. Even if the instinctual view were to be correct, this would still be our basic task for the students have a chance of accepting the dark and discreditable side of themselves and dealing with it through their own resources, rather than relying on external checks and controls.

It is not only beauty that is in the eye of the beholder, but that cherished thing we call reality. The therapist knows that his client's idea of morality is as good as his own, whilst his ideas of reality and goodness possess no greater objectivity. I am painfully aware that I have lit no lamps to guide those groping in the dark, but it would be wrong to suggest that I have any to light. Rather the therapist must learn to live with the anxiety which follows perception of the uncertainty of the meaning of life, for we are aware that things are not what they seem, or as it has been better put:

"as in a theatre,

The lights are extinguished, for the scene to be changed.

With a hollow rumble of wings, with a movement of darkness on darkness,

And we know that the hills and the trees, the distant panorama

And the bold imposing facade are all being rolled away."

I would like to express my sincere thanks to Hazel Johns and Mair Thomas for reading and commenting on this chapter.

References:

1. C.C. O'Brien, *The Suspecting Glance* (Faber and Faber, London 1972).
2. A. Maslow, *Motivation and Personality* (Harper and Row, New York 1954).
3. G.W. Allport, *Becoming* (Yale University Press, 1955).
4. A. Oppenheim, *Questionnaire Design and Attitude Measurement* (Heinemann, London 1966).
5. T. Adorno, E. Frenkel-Brunswik, D. Levinson & R. Sanford, *The Authoritarian Personality* (Harper and Row, New York, 1950).
6. R. Lazarus, *Psychological Stress and the Coping Process* (McGraw Hill, New York 1966).

7.   D. Riesman, in *The Self in Social Interaction,* eds C. Gordon &
     K. Gergen (Wiley, New York 1968).
8.   F. Heider, *The Psychology of Interpersonal Relations* (Wiley, New York
     1958).
9.   E. Erikson, *Childhood and Society* (Penguin, Harmondsworth 1950).
10. G. Kelly, *The Psychology of Personal Constructs* (Norton, New York
     1955)
11. W.D. Wall, *Adolescence in School and Society* (N.F.E.R., Slough 1968).
12. R. Laing, *The Divided Self* (Tavistock, London 1960).
13. D. Winnicott, *Playing and Reality* (Tavistock, London 1971).
14. M. Rokeach, *The Open and Closed Mind* (Basic Books, New York 1960).
15. G.W. Hegel, *Phenomenology of Mind* trans. J. Baillie (MacMillan,
     New York 1949).
16. M. Jahoda, The Meaning of Psychological Health, *Social Casework,*
     34, 8, pp. 349-54.
17. R. Christie & F. Geis *Studies in Machiavellianism* (Academic Press,
     New York 1970).
18. R.L. Katz, *Empathy* (Free Press, Glencoe 1963).
19. S. Natale, *An Experiment in Empathy* (N.F.E.R., Slough 1972).
20. L.P. Bradford, J.R. Gibb & K. Benne, *T. Group Theory and*
     Laboratory Method (Wiley, New York 1964).
21. C. Rogers, *Encounter Groups* (Allen Lane, London 1971).
22. S. Thompson & J. Kahn, *The Group Process as a Helping Technique*
     (Pergamon Press, Oxford 1970).
23. C. Rogers, op. cit. 1971).
24. op. cit.
25. L. Coser, *The Function of Social Conflict* (Routledge & Kegan Paul,
     London 1965).
26. M. Mauss, *The Gift,* trans. I. Cunnison (Cohen and West, London 1954).
27. G. Kelly, in *Perspectives in Personal Construct* Theory, ed. D.
     Bannister (Academic Press, New York 1970).

4 SOCIOLOGY AND MORAL EDUCATION: THE CONDITIONS OF IMPARTIALITY

Maurice Broady

The role of the academic teacher contains within itself one of the major dilemmas of moral education. It would generally be agreed that the academic should not moralise: that he should not use his authority or his podium to dogmatise, still less to proselytise. He should not expect, and he certainly cannot require his students to accept his ethical views. His job is to teach, not to preach. This has sometimes led to the view that the academic should, and could remain neutral towards both his students and his subject. But neutrality is not possible. Every relationship with another person, to the degree that it entails some choice of conduct, embodies a view of how people ought to relate to one another. Even the effort to remain neutral, impossible though it is, is itself to adopt a moral stance. Therefore the teacher faces the dilemma that, while he is inevitably engaged in a moral relationship with his students, he is committed to the principle that he should not moralise at them.

The dilemma is equally apparent in relation to his subject-matter. This is so especially in the social sciences. Social scientists have frequently claimed that their studies are scientific, and therefore objective, and, consequently ethically neutral. Such claims are now coming to be recognised as masks which cover over the fact that conceptual structures as well as methodologies embody what Charles Taylor has called a 'value-slant', an orientation towards a certain set of value-assumptions.[1] Durkheim's work, for example, which was broadly concerned with the problem of social order, for all its claim to be establishing an objective science of society, was based upon a quite fundamental conservatism. Marx, on the other hand, in developing the concept of class conflict, presupposed an analysis which called in question the validity of the social order which Durkheim assumed to be worth maintaining. The sociologist who only allows quantitative data a legitimate place in the armoury of sociological methods is likely to take it for granted that those aspects of social life that cannot be quantified are less important, if not totally unimportant or irrelevant. For, as Max Weber noted, axioms which are adopted for the purpose of scientific research tend to be generalised into universal principles of much wider relevance, and thus to provide their proponents with *Weltanschauungen* as well.[2] Thus, the concepts and, in large measure, the methods which are adopted in the social sciences constitute what Raymond Aron has described as a doctrine, that is to say, 'a social philosophy as well as a system of concepts'.[3] How then can the academic teacher avoid moralising, given the inevitability of a value-commitment both in his personal relations and in his subject matter?

The question is particularly apposite in a discipline like sociology in which the sociologist's 'doctrine' also informs the political views which he holds as a citizen. The positivist tradition in sociology sought to maintain the view that sociology can and should be value-free. I shall argue that a sociology which ignores the problem of the sociologist's values, under the guise of value-freedom, and which therefore fails to treat seriously the values which govern human purposes, is likely to fall prey to social determinism. A sociology, on the other hand, which accepts the sociologist's values as unavoidable, and even as legitimate, but which does not attend to the constraints of scholarship, is likely to become nothing more than ideology.

Sociology satisfies the primary conditions of moral education only when it recognises honestly the value-premises upon which it is based and when it makes scrupulous use of the scholarly procedures that are essential if that value-commitment is not to degenerate into mere ideology. This calls for a kind of detachment-in-commitment: an ability both to be committed and yet to be able to stand apart from that commitment. This is the intellectual analogue of the demand that the teacher should be dispassionate about the moral engagement which he cannot avoid. It is clearly stated in Raymond Aron's phrase that the sociologist strives to be scientific not by being neutral but by being fair, or as I should prefer to say, impartial.[4] For impartiality is the antithesis of both determinism and of ideology; and it is the chief attribute of that independence of mind which is at the heart of moral education.

The paradox raised by Aron — how, if one is not neutral, can one claim to be impartial — is echoed, for example, by Sir Isaiah Berlin, when he cites 'an admirable writer of our time' who wrote: 'To realise the relative validity of one's convictions and yet stand for them unflinchingly, is what distinguishes a civilized man from a barbarian'.[5] Similarly, an introductory sentence from an essay by Alasdair MacIntyre: 'Since I intend to criticise some of Mr Wolff's positions very sharply, I ought at the outset to express both my agreement with and my sense of indebtedness to him'.[6] Both of these statements express the detachment-in-commitment which is the nub of impartiality. The one recognises the contingency — the '*relative validity*' — of one's own convictions, the other the indebtedness of one scholar, even in a matter of political theory, to one with whom he disagrees.

Sociology as a Teaching Enterprise

Two main styles of sociology can be distinguished. The dominant influence in contemporary sociology has been positivism. In this view, the study of the social world should be modelled upon the natural sciences. Man and society, accordingly, must be studied not by analysing the patterns of meanings or the ideas which men claim to have guided their actions and their purposes, but by considering those structural characteristics in society which have an existence independent of man's consciousness or will.[7] Such an approach allows comparisons to be made between institutions in different cultures and in different historical periods, comparisons which, it is believed, can help to establish causal explanations and thus laws, not dissimilar to those which can be adduced in the natural sciences.

Sociology of this kind has only limited relevance for moral education. It may well train a student in scientific scepticism and in the tools by which alternative explanations can be appraised. But in modelling itself on the natural sciences, it tends to undervalue the significance of the specific, culturally-defined situation, within which problems of moral choice arise. Furthermore, it eschews subjective knowledge and ignores philosophical questions, apart from problems of epistemology. Teachers committed to this kind of sociology are likely to communicate to their students two kinds of assumption. They tend to make a sharp differentiation between social science and the traditional humanities on the grounds that the social sciences are in principle susceptible of objective study while the humanities are subjective and therefore unworthy of serious academic attention. In this view, the most important use to which knowledge is put is in research. Students accordingly are thought of primarily as potential academic researchers, and the possibility that there may be spheres of political or civic activity in which their intellectual preparation may well be of even greater significance is ignored. Consequently, the presuppositions are lacking that are needed to support a curriculum attuned to the requirements of moral education.

This kind of sociology, furthermore, tends to be deterministic. By concentrating attention upon social structures; by regarding social structure as analytically separate from the individual persons who operate within it; by regarding these structures of roles and institutions as more determinate than people's feelings and beliefs; and by conceiving the values and purposes which a person holds to as simply the expression of a dominant value system in society to which he is constrained to conform by social sanctions and a process of internalisation; in all these ways, this approach to sociology is inclined to lead to a highly deterministic, or an 'over-socialised' view of man.[8] It takes no account of discretionary activity, nor does it allow for the possibility that men may purposefully determine to react against, and even to modify their own institutions. Thus, the student rarely sees any link between this understanding of society and the decisions that he himself has to make, unless, of course, he decides to take up a career as a professional sociologist. Worse still, he may well apply to himself this devastatingly deterministic outlook and either lose his capacity for engagement or come to the illogical, though understandable conclusion that the only alternative is to overthrow the whole social system and start again from scratch.

In the course of the last ten years, however, a reaction has set in against this conception of sociology. Influenced primarily by the Weberian notions that social action has to do with shared meanings and that sociology is the product of a particular, historical context which influences the problems selected for study, this reaction has led to what Alvin Gouldner has called a 'reflexive sociology', whose task would be 'to *transform* the sociologist . . . to raise the sociologist's self-awareness to a new historical level'.[9] The role of sociology is not to try to fashion universal scientific laws but to make intelligible the age in which we live. It is concerned with social values and human purposes and it seeks to be *engagé* and relevant to current issues. It thus reaffirms the value of human liberation and a concern with man's control over his institutions.[10]

A sociology of this kind is obviously modelled more upon the traditional humanities than upon the natural sciences; and since it is more attuned to purposive action in the world of affairs, it is more likely to be consonant with the objectives of moral education. Reflexive sociology, however, is exposed to the danger that, in admitting value judgements openly into play, it can easily become a mere ideology which finds empirically only that which would be expected from the value-judgements which it adopts. This is particularly likely, though by no means exclusively so, on the part of sociologists holding left-wing political positions.[11] Some sociologists of this persuasion appear to suppose that to have declared their values openly at the outset of an enquiry absolves them from the requirements of scholarly argument. This is surprising in left-wingers who are well aware of how their antagonists can be misled by ideological considerations; though it is less surprising when one considers how unwilling people are to apply to themselves the same strictures that they apply to others. But to accept that value-commitments cannot be avoided in the social sciences makes it even more imperative that one should be scrupulous to avoid simply confirming empirically that which his values would automatically lead him to expect. Commitment to values is not *per se* incompatible with scholarship, rigour and fairness. But it is clear that some sociologists believe that the simple affirmation of their commitments permits them to assert without effective validation what they wish to be the case and either to ignore or to repudiate whatever they find offensive to their values.

In a sociology thus inspired, the student is likely to become entangled in yet another form of determinism — that of a dogma. When dogmatism is inspired by right-sounding values, it is certainly appealing. A commitment to redistributionist social policies designed to alleviate the lot of the oppressed and downtrodden in our society can easily lead students — and their tutors — to be blind to the cavalier disdain, the sneering and the attribution of false motives with which some proponents of this view, with more social concern than intellectual scruple, seek to buttress their own positions and misrepresent those of their opponents.[12] But how could they possibly fail to see in the breaking up of Professor Eysenck's lecture at the LSE or in the refusal to give Professor Huntington a hearing at Sussex a reluctance to hear arguments that might question commitments held on ideological grounds? In such cases, moral concern and even certainty have come to dominate the equally important ethical requirement, the essential pre-requisite of scholarly activity, that the scholar should attend carefully to honestly-expressed divergencies of opinion.

The major characteristic of the dogmatist is an excessive assurance which so often reaches the point of arrogance. This is an understandable posture if one is able to believe that there is only one truth, that one has found it, and that that truth, without any further question, provides a solution to all problems. It is still more easy to understand it, if one can also believe that one's own version of the truth cannot equally well be challenged by the kind of criticisms that one levels against other such positions. That, indeed, is precisely the failing in the crude determinism and simple ideology into which sociology is prone to degenerate. For determinists assume that other people's behaviour and thought can be explained causally, while implicitly reserving for their own conduct an autonomy which they deny to others. Ideological sociologists similarly analyse other views as ideologically distorted while defending their own against such analysis by what can only amount to special pleading. In this way, the sociologist is able to avoid the perplexity of applying to himself the assumptions that he makes about others.

Karl Mannheim and the Sociology of Knowledge

In avoiding the *tu quoque,* in this way, the sociologist is able to ignore the issue of how it is possible to believe anything with conviction if one's own beliefs are subject to the same kinds of criticism that one applies to others. This *tu quoque,* so often evaded but so critical in moral education, is faced directly in the work of Karl Mannheim. Mannheim's sociology of knowledge therefore indicates some of the premises upon which a theory of moral education might be built.

In his essay 'Ideology and Utopia', Mannheim discusses the social determination of knowledge.[13] He considers three steps in the development of the problem. First of all, in what he calls the particular conception of ideology, we analyse our opponent's opinions ideologically by considering their origin in the individual's personality. We may suggest, for example, that a tutor has an authoritarian view of his relationship with his students because he is personally insecure and is therefore afraid of relaxing the formality of the hierarchical relationship which screens his insecurity from the world. A psychological explanation of this kind applies to this person in this case, and is not generalised to other people in the same situation. It also assumes some common criterion of what is to count as objectively valid knowledge.

The second step is a move to what Mannheim describes as the total conception of ideology. This constitutes a more radical critique of knowledge, since it recognises that bias is not simply to be explained in terms of personal psychology. It is the product of different social contexts which give rise not only to structural differences in the total outlook or *Weltanschauung* of a society as a whole but also to quite different concepts of validity. In this way, it becomes possible to discredit not simply a particular opponent but a class of opponents. Marxists, for example, brand bourgeois thought as ideological by seeking to show that it expresses a self-interest which is a function of their position in the class structure, and which is inevitably opposed to the interests of the proletariat.

But this, in Mannheim's terms, is only a special application of the total conception of ideology: special in the sense that it does not yet recognise that this kind of analysis can also be applied to *every* position, and not simply to that of the bourgeoisie. As Mannheim says: 'As long as one does not call his own position into question but regards it as absolute, while interpreting his opponents' ideas as a mere function of the social positions they occupy, the decisive step forward has not yet been taken. It is true, of course, that in such a case the total conception of ideology is being used, since one is interested in analysing the structure of the mind of one's opponent in its totality, and is not merely singling out a few isolated propositions. But since, in such an instance, one is interested merely in a sociological analysis of the opponent's ideas, one never gets beyond a highly restricted, or what I should like to call a special, formulation of the theory. In contrast to this special formulation, the general form of the total conception of ideology is being used by the analyst when he has the courage to subject not just the adversary's point of view but all points of view, including his own, to the ideological analysis.[14]

Courage indeed! Mannheim follows this argument with a chapter in which he considers whether a science of politics is possible: whether, in short, it is possible in the welter of conflicting views, to establish what is true and what false. Mannheim argues that we are not entirely bound by our intellectual inheritance, and that a degree of detachment is possible in relation to these diverse ways of thinking with which we are surrounded. Such detachment depends upon our becoming aware of the determination to which our ideas are subject. 'The opportunity for relative emancipation from social determination, increases proportionately with insight into the determination'.[15] This kind of analysis is precisely the task of the intellectual; and since, as Mannheim believed, generalising perhaps too readily from his own experience, the intellectual was less tied into the all-determining class structure than anyone else, he conceives it as the role of the *freischwebende Intelligenz,* the socially unattached intellectuals, to fashion some degree of liberation from the toils of determination. This is to be done by considering every view as emanating from a specific socio-political context and as being, for that reason, a partial and necessarily limited view. To leave it at that would be to accept a radical relativism, in which every view is 'right' in its own context. But that would leave unsolved the problem of the validity of our beliefs. What Mannheim argues for, accordingly, is what he calls 'relationsim', in which sociological understanding is used to consider each viewpoint in its context and, in the cut and thrust of an open-ended analysis of divergent points of view, to form a synoptic view which would be comparatively independent of the bias of any particular ideology. 'Consequently, (he concluded) our knowledge of "reality", as it assimilates more and more of these divergent perspectives, will become more comprehensive.'[17]

The intelligentsia is hardly as free of the class structure as Mannheim appears to have believed. On the other hand, it is the intellectual's task to analyse and criticise divergent opinions and to try to maintain some independence of judgement. To that extent, Mannheim describes his task appropriately. Nor does he ascribe to the intellectual any spurious, transcendental authority. For while the intellectual must continually strive towards some more comprehensive view, Mannheim disparages any tendency to set up 'the chance situation of the movement as absolute and eternal.' He appreciate that people wish to do so 'in order to have something stable to hold on to and to minimize the hazardousness of life'.[17] But there can be no total liberation:[18] only a 'relative emancipation', since no one can totally divorce himself from the social context from which he is trying to gain some detachment. No absolute, permanent synthesis is possible: only a dynamic synthesis 'which is reformulated from time to time'.[19] Hence: 'A total view implies both the assimilation and transcendence of the limitations of particular points of view. It represents the continuous process of the expansion of knowledge, and has as its goal not achievement of a super-temporally valid conclusion but the broadest possible extension of our horizon of vision'.[20]

Mannheim's approach seems to me to present some important clues for constructing a pedagogy which might avoid the dangers of dogmatism and ideology to which I have suggested the social sciences are particularly prone and which might thus encourage intellectual autonomy. Its major features are, first of all, that it recognises as its starting-point the diversity of thought in present-day society. Second, it recognises that ideas are not held *in abstracto* but that they are formed in a social context. Third, these ideas and beliefs are often in conflict with one another, and contend against one another for allegiance. Fourth, Mannheim refuses to accept that one is totally determined and affirms the possibility of judging at least the relative validity of different ideas and of transcending their limitations. Fifth, he postulates, though he does not describe, a method for making impartial judgements. And sixth, his methodology is concerned with the exigencies of purposive action in the world, rather than with gaining simply 'a schematically ordered bird's eye view' of the world.[21]

The Conditions of Moral Education

The idea that one might free oneself from determination by understanding the sources of that determination is, as Mannheim appreciates, paradoxical. It is no less paradoxical than the teacher's concern to avoid moralising in a situation that is inevitably morally-charged. The question thus arises, as to the conditions under which an education might be fashioned that would lead to an understanding and practice of this paradox.

In such a pedagogy, one must first of all affirm the paramount importance of language. That words are the first tool of the scholar is a point that needs continuous reassertion. For words are so much a part of everyday life and so self-evident that the evidence is usually ignored which shows that students often do not know how to use them effectively. In higher education, discussion centres upon teaching aids and techniques, while the central problem of the student's use of words is barely considered. In the social sciences, it is taken for granted that research techniques and quantitative methods need to be taught and mastered if the student is to command his subject, but it is invariably assumed that he knows how to handle verbal argument and analysis. Indeed, social scientists of a positivist cast of mind often give the impression that in an ideal world words would be replaced by a symbolic language of a more objective, quantifiable kind. But not only would this rule out of court areas of great importance in our understanding; it would also be inimical to moral sensitivity. For the very subtlety of verbal language, which makes it such a difficult medium for a natural science, is a positive advantage in spheres of human concern in which, however rational they may be, no final and determinate knowledge is possible and in which tone and style cannot be divorced from the content of what is expressed. It is precisely because language is ambiguous and can be misleading when it is not scrupulously used, that so much attention needs to be paid to learning to use it carefully.

In relation to impartiality, furthermore, a command of verbal language is essential. Bernstein's researches have shown the critical significance of formal, elaborated language code for purposes of conceptualisation and analysis.[22] Only with such a code is it possible to do more than describe what the case is. And since impartiality of judgement depends upon our being able to analyse and compare, it is essential for the scholar to command the kind of linguistic tools which make that possible. For while it is true that language may trammel men in its webs of taken-for-granted meanings, it is equally and paradoxically the case that language is also a vehicle of liberation.

Language, however, can be either passive or active. It is one thing to listen to a lecture or to a reasoned process of argument; it is another actually to construct a reasoned argument for oneself. We appear to accept this point readily enough, for we require students to write essays and do exercises. These are often done mechanically, however, and the student may gain little of any personal significance or relevance from doing them. Leslie Button has noted that we are able to 'entertain a body of intellectual knowledge, ideas and precepts without their seeming to penetrate our system of thought and feeling.'[23] The lecture and the library should therefore be complemented by regular seminar work in which the student is required to present arguments *viva voce* in the course of discussion.

The seminar, accordingly, has a very important role to play in moral education. Mannheim described it as a workshop and advanced for it a quite distinctive rationale.[24] In a section devoted to the relationship between social organisation and pedagogy, he speaks of 'purely classificatory knowledge', systematic and ordered, for communicating which the lecture is particularly appropriate. This could be supplemented by the seminar in which, as he explains, with Continental experience obviously in his mind, 'abstract possibilities are considered. . . on a factual basis'. As against this, there is the *atelier* or workshop, which is characterised by 'a relationship of mutual participation between master and apprentice', and in which 'subjective and emotional impulses and personal relations' are allowed their play in a 'creative collaborative clarification of the aim which unites them'. In the course of this collaboration, ideas and styles are communicated which affect 'the whole person'. This placing of intellectual activity within a personal social setting seems to have been especially well developed in our English tradition of higher education, at least in its Oxbridge variant which has been so influential in establishing our educational paradigms. In the Oxbridge college, for example, intellectual engagement and personal, social relationships are obviously intended to be brought together under one roof. If, under modern conditions, the tutorial is an extravagance, its virtues can be maintained, provided appropriate procedures are devised, in the seminar conceived as a kind of group-tutorial and not, as Mannheim's Continental experience led him to expect it to be, an impersonal and formal addendum to an equally impersonal and formal lecture.

In developing curricula, and in seminars especially, it is important to incorporate two elements which have their analogue in Mannheim's ideas. First of all, there must be a dialectic. By this I mean that divergent approaches to the same problem need to be studied. These divergences of view must be sufficiently sharp to require the student not only to understand them, but also to induce him to puzzle out his own opinion. Second, each argument must initially be studied in such a way that its author's reasons and justifications are properly understood.

This happens less frequently than one might wish. For academics, alas for Mannheim's confidence in their dispassion, are often dogmatists who espouse their doctrines and are committed to their paradigms with an overweening confidence and even naivety. A tutor must certainly have a position on matters of importance relating to his subject; but it is none the less desirable that he should expound the views of those with whom he disagrees as fairly as possible, if they are worthy of attention at all. Instead of this, however, academics are often biased and dogmatic. They tend to be *parti pris* and I fear that they encourage this tendency in their students by requesting them to 'criticise' rather than to 'appraise' what other people have said. By 'criticise' is meant to show how invalid a position is: whereas an appraisal also involves understanding what is proposed and why and then trying to assess it fairly — not necessarily in a spirit of neutrality —

by attending carefully to what is valid as well as invalid in the case. Students are apt to knock down, rather than to understand, simply because that is easier to do and requires much less thought and sympathy. However tough-minded this procedure may seem to be, therefore, it is weak in that it allows the student to avoid the strain of understanding the context and the reasons which justify and make intelligible views other than his own.

Dispassionate but critical analysis of this kind is essential if judgements are to be made that might claim some measure of impartiality; but it is not the same as making those judgements themselves. Appraisal is not the same as decision and students must be encouraged to reach reasoned decisions of their own about what they have been at pains to understand. Academic curricula sometimes place so much weight upon a student's assimilating information, that he never has an opportunity to express his own judgements or defend his own considered opinions. I have known departments in which the student was subjected to two years of lecturing before he was allowed to participate in a seminar; a practice that was justified on the reasonable-sounding principle that he had to know something before he could discuss it. Students certainly should not be encouraged to speak without supporting what they have to say with evidence and good reason, since to do so debases scholarship to the level of mere opinion. But to dissociate the lecture and the seminar in this way rests upon the fallacious assumptions to know is to understand, and that discussion can only usefully begin once the student has 'a grasp of the subject as a whole'.

On the contrary, knowledge is valuable and indeed it is only useful if it is understood. Understanding is helped by discussion; so that, if understanding is our aim, then formal learning — the gathering of knowledge — and the discussion of knowledge must proceed together. From the earliest moment, therefore, a curriculum must afford the student every opportunity to comment on and to appraise what he has read or heard said. He needs regular practice in advancing arguments supported by knowledge and good reason. Indeed, one might even suggest that he should be encouraged even though he may well be proved wrong, for, as A.N. Whitehead once put it, 'Panic of error is the death of progress'.

The Student's Reaction

Students' reactions to a pedagogy based upon principles of this kind are not always favourable. As T.S. Simey remarked many years ago, they are not inclined to face the rigours of intellectual activity with anything like alacrity;[25] and an ability to fashion ways of encouraging them to do so is one of the undervalued merits of the better-than-average teacher. Nor is this really a matter for surprise since our students, for most part, rarely seem to have had any systematic training in their schools in how to deal intellectually with divergent and conflicting views.

It is especially difficult for those who are professionally immersed in an academic (and perhaps also an intellectual) culture, to understand how different that culture is from that from which most of our students come. One of the most incisive comments on this was made by a very bright student of mine who said that the difference between the university and Woodford Green was that, at home in Woodford Green, 'argument' invariably meant 'quarrel'. The essential feature of an academic milieu at its best is that argument is free from the personal nastiness that results in quarrels. Academics, being human, do not always sustain that dispassion in argument which the non-academic world, our students included, attribute to them; and many a naive entrant to the academic profession has been shocked when his expectations of dispassionate argument have been rudely shattered. Nevertheless, in broad terms, the distinction is probably valid. That being so, though there clearly is tradition of free discussion in this country which has its most obvious, but by no means its most important expression in Speaker's Corner in Hyde Park, one can hardly expect there to be a general understanding of the idea that systematic argument is a vehicle for discovery, which is the salient feature of a rational intellectual tradition.

Nor is this tradition communicated, except in a cursory and fortuitous fashion, in the majority of our schools. My impression of teaching first-year students in seminars for the past ten years or so is that they mostly come from social backgrounds which, if not actively *anti*-intellectual, are certainly *un*-intellectual. They come up to university largely unconversant with any ideas of general import and equally unpractised in any regular or serious effort to consider concepts other than those with which they have been brought up. In the schools, it is hardly possible perhaps — except in some of the more advanced and less routine work in the sixth form — to consider divergent views and how to cope with them intellectually. Students must learn to walk before they can run; and in any case the timetable is governed by the rigid exigencies of the examination curriculum. The text-books, with their frequent over-simplifications, invariably confirm the student in his belief that there is but one view of a subject which does not allow of much divergence or disagreement, at least under the constraints of time that operate if the basic work and study is to be done.

For the average student entering university, so far as I can judge from my experience, even to hold an honest opinion consistently is difficult. Some of the more mature students recognise that their opinions are simply the product of their own social backgrounds, and they may well find this so disturbing that they resolutely seek to ignore the intellectual and personal problems which it so clearly poses. Alternatively, they react by reaffirming their own point of view uncritically, or – what often amounts to the same thing – they retreat into rhetoric. They may also react against their inherited views by cleaving to a radically opposed position, which assumes, equally uncritically, that the view with which they have been brought up or the institutions or the country in which they have been nurtured and of whose limitations they are so fully and critically aware, could not possibly be vindicated except by the most perniciously conservative, *status quo* maintaining ideologist, worthy only of their cynicism and contempt.

The new student, accordingly, comes into higher education fairly unsophisticated intellectually. He is usually capable of making a factual summary of what he is required to read, but he tends at first to be rather hesitant in responding to the question of what he thinks about what he has read. There are several stock defences against the demanding tutor. The student will complain that he is only new to the subject and cannot yet be expected to hold opinions. He may indulge in what might be called book-fetishism and reply that since everything has been said in the book, what else is there than he can add? Or he may comment not so much upon the substance of the argument as upon the writer's style, especially if he has studied literature at A level.

In general, however, given reasonable encouragement, a student will often overcome his initial reluctance to enter an opinion before his tutor and (no less a problem) before his colleagues. He can even be induced to risk offending them by commenting in turn upon what they have said in the seminar. But there remain a series of intellectual procedures which have to do with the use of language which he has to learn to command. These are essential preliminaries to the subsequent, more difficult work to which he will in due course be introduced. They are primarily intended to get him accustomed to using language accurately, and to validating what he wishes to say with good evidence and sound reasoning. The attentive tutor finds himself noting year after year, how difficult his new students find it to use language precisely. For instance, they are apt to miss the point of the question or, hearing it, to reply irrelevantly to what they *thought* the question was rather than to what it actually was. When asked to state succinctly what colleagues in the seminar have said, they will as like as not say what they think about the topic; or they will adopt the easier course of saying what the other students were talking about rather than what they actually said. If such practices are not corrected, the student will go on supposing that he has grasped the point, when he has only seized upon a general sense of what the point was about.

In particular, the first year student frequently finds it difficult to distinguish the content and the form of an argument. He will therefore let assertions stand for reasoned argument and, by failing to understand how a piece of writing is constructed he will find it difficult to judge what is significant and what is not with the assurance that is needed if he is to read intelligently and with speed. Furthermore, he has nowadays had so little discipline in the study and use of language that he is often totally unconversant with the idea of *le mot juste* and certainly could not have entertained Tegner's dictum that that which is vaguely said is that which is vaguely thought. If his tutor should comment on infelicities, still more on ambiguities in his essay, he may well reply in an aggrieved tone, 'But you *know* what I *meant* to say' or 'But it's only a matter of style'. He is usually quite insensitive to the point that the style is part of the argument itself and not a gratuitous extra; and is also surprised to discover that a misused 'thus' in an essay is a matter of logic which bears upon the validity of an argument and which cannot be lightly brushed off as a mere question of style.

These pedagogical details need very careful attention. Teachers in institutions of higher education far too easily assume, despite evidence to the contrary, that the student already knows how to read and write and argue. The ability to argue with independence and impartiality however, depends upon the student's having mastered the basic tools of disciplined scholarship. Academics need to consider a good deal more carefully the minimum intellectual competence which students might be expected to have gained at each stage of an education. By the end of the first year, for example, the undergraduate should at least be able to grasp the point of a discussion; express the point accurately and succinctly; comment intelligently upon what he has read or heard; and be able to validate his comments with evidence and good reason. In addition, by appraising his colleagues' seminar papers, for example, he should also have considered the criteria by which intellectual judgements are made. Finally, he should have learned to understand a couple of divergent views in his field of study, each in its own terms; he should be able to argue the case for, and to see the weaknesses in both; and he should have reached the point of being perplexed by the question, 'What is my view about all this'?

It is difficult to know whether students go through a regular series of stages in the course of their intellectual development, and until research in higher education begins to deal with this kind of Piaget-type question, we shall continue to know more about the development of children in junior schools than we do about our undergraduates. In the absence of research, one is obliged to rest upon what may well be fortuitous experience. Certainly, I have met many students who have said that one of the major problems they faced at the university arose when they began to realise that there were several views that could be taken of a particular question and when they confronted their own bewilderment at how to decide which view, or which combination of views they themselves were prepared to adopt. The second and third year curriculum, among its many functions, should aim to help the student to resolve this question. And since to resolve it requires an exploration of the assumptions upon which different views rest, it is essential that at this stage of the curriculum, the philosophical bases of the subject being studied should be discussed, so that these premises can be drawn out for more careful consideration.

The Teacher's Awareness

But structures of education are only one factor in the equation: the teacher is the other. This is particularly the case in moral education, which depends so much upon the use of verbal language and for which the seminar is so much better adapted than the lecture. The seminar — the group-tutorial — requires of the tutor a much greater discretion and flexibility than does the lecture. Discretion and flexibility, however, have to do with how freedom is used. For that reason, they cannot be described as pedagogical techniques which can be learnt and taught, as one can teach the technique, for example, of using a blackboard effectively. They are, on the contrary, expressions of how the person, who is also the teacher, understands the purpose of what he is about, of how he expresses himself as a person within the constraints imposed upon him by the requirements, and by his understanding of his role as a teacher.

If then, the teacher is to overcome the problem of how, given his moral engagement, to avoid moralising, he will only be able to do so if he has thought out a philosophy or a set of principles which he understands and accepts and which, because they inform his interpretation of his role and his subject, he spontaneously expresses. This is especially the case where moral dispositions are concerned. So that, if the teacher, ethically committed as he is bound to be, is to communicate what impartiality or independence of judgement is, he will do it not only by precept but also by expressing these virtues in his own conduct. There can be no successful deception: *le style c'est l'homme.* Discretion in this context has to do with how these apparent opposites are to be welded together dialectically into some coherent and personally significant philosophy of education which will inform the tone, and thus constitute the ethos of the educational structure.

This involves much more than having a grasp of educational techniques; more even than understanding the psychodynamics of the seminar, important and necessary though such understanding is. For that understanding must interlock with a moral disposition on the part of the tutor, who is himself the bearer and interpreter of the intellectual tradition into which he is inducting his students.

Though the tutor will express his view of education crucially in a disposition-in-action towards his students and his subject, it is in words that this can be expressed; and I wish to conclude by commenting upon some of the basic ideas that seem to me important in a tutor's orientation to moral education.

The first point to make is that independent judgement entails risk. To make moral decisions that are genuinely autonomous involves some degree of insecurity. Much educational practice is so stereotyped and routinised that risk and insecurity are largely avoided. But education is a matter of learning to make risky judgements under conditions in which the risk is limited to the student and in which others are not put in jeopardy by his decisions. The educational process, accordingly, must be conceived as an exploration both into a new area of knowledge and into the use of procedures for making soundly-based judgements about that knowledge.

Excitement in exploration is commonly said to be one of the benefits that accrue to teaching from the tutor's continuing engagement in research. No doubt it does so if the teacher is genuinely excited by what he is doing and if he is also able to communicate his excitement to his students in a context that is relevant to them. But he is very often unable to express his enthusiasm and excitement, even if his research still continues to excite him, because he is inhibited by the idea of objectivity and by the feeling that emotions are out of place in scholarship. In any event, he often considers teaching to be an activity of only secondary importance on which his own research has little direct bearing. Lectures, too, are so often drab and conventional expositions while seminars, in which the process of mutual exploration is of the essence, are regarded as little more than opportunities for commenting on somebody else's lecture or on one student's lonely paper. Indeed, the procedures for guiding seminars so as to engage students in a process of discovery are ill-conceived and little understood.[26] Education, therefore, far from being a liberator often operates as a damper upon exploration and an inhibition to intellectual curiosity and creativity.

Education conceived as being concerned with grasping a 'subject' also tends to militate against a sense of exploration. In its conventional interpretation, this concept of education is related to what might be called a bucket theory of the mind. The subject is regarded as a huge pile of data which the student is obliged to assimilate before he can grasp the subject. The student's mind is conceived, in empiricist fashion, not so much as a *tabula rasa* as a bucket into which these data must be shovelled. The tutor's function is then to dig into this pile of data and to transfer it into the student's bucket-head so that he can regurgitate it in the examination.

An alternative concept, much more consistent with the idea of education as exploration, is the notion that education is concerned with inducting the student into an argument within an intellectual discipline.[27] The discipline consists of a body of theory or generalisations supported more or less satisfactorily by evidence and reasoning, together with a set of methods by which the evidence is collected, assessed and related to the generalisations which it validates or qualifies or refutes. The heart of the matter is the argument; and the object of education thus becomes not an abstract grasp of a subject but the much more concrete and certainly more active ability to argue within the discipline.

This concept has a number of advantages over that of a subject. The chief of these is that it recognises more easily and without embarrassment that there is a personal element in scholarship: that academic activity is about people arguing, and testing by disciplined argument what begins by being personal and subjective opinions or hunches. That is also more valid epistemologically than the alternative assumption with which many students enter university and which often seems to be confirmed when they arrive, that knowledge invariably begins with the collection of objective data. It has the further benefit that it more readily legitimises the student's expressing *his* opinion, even though that opinion, too, must be tested by the standard procedures of academic argument. It is also much closer both to how scholarship is actually undertaken and to how moral decisions are made. For in both cases we are risking our judgement upon an opinion which, as far as we can judge, is better-founded than any other we might consider. Thus, to conceive education as argument rather than subject is more conducive to the demands of moral education.

A final brief comment also needs to be made about scholarship and politics. Clearly, moral education, concerned as it is with making independent judgements, is highly relevant in the world of affairs outside the walls of the university. But scholarship, however relevant or *engagé* it may be, should not be confused with affairs. For the conduct of affairs is chiefly a matter of deciding how to act effectively; while intellectual activity is primarily concerned with what can be validly thought. A good policy may well be the one that is the most feasible. The exigencies of politics may easily justify Lindblom's view, sceptical though it certainly is, that policy objectives have 'no ultimate validity other than that they are agreed upon'.[28] Compelling though such pragmatic considerations may be in the field of politics, scholarship is not primarily in that field. Nor is the scholar primarily a politician, however much his work has political connotations. For the university is a deliberative and reflective, rather than an executive, institution and its primary, if not its sole criterion, must be whether the argument is valid, not whether or not it is politically acceptable.

Certainly, the two worlds come together: 'there is nothing more practical than a good theory'. In government, one certainly finds the academic mode, while the academic is not uninfluenced by the politics of his institution, his profession and his career. But to ignore these distinctions is to absorb the university into the world of affairs entirely and thereby to damage the institutional autonomy which is one guarantee of intellectual independence. More particularly, it is likely to break down the critical distinction between scholarship and ideology, and in doing that one would be destroying the intellectual premiss upon which the virtues of independence and impartiality, and thus moral education itself is based.

References

1. Charles Taylor, 'Neutrality in Political Science' in Peter Laslett & W.G. Runciman, *Philosophy, Politics and Society* (Third Series) Basil Blackwell, Oxford 1967.
2. Max Weber, ' "Objectivity" in Social Science and Social Policy', in Edward A. Shils & Henry A. Finch, (Eds.), *The Methodology of the Social Sciences,* (Free Press, New York 1968), p. 69.
3. Raymond Aron, *Main Currents in Sociological Thought,* vol. 2, (Weidenfeld and Nicolson, London 1968), p.v.
4. 'Le sociologue's efforce d'être scientifique non par la neutralité mais par l'equité'. R. Aron, 'Science et conscience de la societé', *Archives Européenes de Sociologie,* vol. 1, No. 1, (1960), p. 19.
5. Isaiah Berlin, *Two Concepts of Liberty* (Clarendon Press, Oxford 1958), p. 57.
6. Alasdair MacIntyre, *Against the Self-Images of the Age* (Duckworth, London 1971), p. 280
7. As in Marx's phrase: 'In the social production which men carry on they enter into definite relations that are indispensable and independent of their will' (*A Contribution to the Critique of Political Economy*); or Durkheim's 'There are therefore ways of behaving, of thinking and of feeling which have this remarkable characteristic that they exist outside individual consciousness' (*Rules of Sociological Method*).
8. See D.H. Wrong, 'The Oversocialized Conception of Man in Modern Sociology', *American Sociological Review,* vol. 26 (1961), and R. Dahrendorf, 'Homo sociologicus ' in *Essays in the theory of Society*

Routledge and Kegan Paul London 1968), ch. 2.

9. Alvin W. Gouldner, *The Coming Crisis of Western Sociology,* (Heinemann, London 1971), p. 489.

10. See Gouldner, *op. cit.,* ch. 13 and Alan Dawe, 'The Two Sociologies', *British Journal of Sociology,* vol. 21 (1970) pp. 207-18.

11. Conor Cruise O'Brien comments: 'The intelligent rightist makes use of the Marxist insights . . . but for his own purpose as Guderian made use of de Gaulle . . . The intellectual left on the other hand — though with some notable exceptions — has a strong tendency to neglect its adversaries and to dismiss even their most influential writings, unread, with a sneer', in O'Brien *ed.,* Edmund Burke: *Reflections on the Revolution in France* (Penguin Books, Harmondsworth 1970), pp. 69-70.

12. See Maurice Broady, *Social Administration: some current concerns,* (An inaugural lecture) (University College of Swansea, 1972), pp. 19-20. The point is more fully elaborated in my unpublished *Lecture at B.S.A. Conference, Leeds, September 1972.*

13. Karl Mannheim, *Ideology and Utopia* (Routledge, London 1960), ch. 2.

14. *op. cit.,* pp. 68-9.

15. *op. cit.,* p. 43

16. *op. cit.,* p. 92

17. *op. cit.,* p. 78

18. See especially *op. cit.,* ch. 2, sections 5 and 6 *passim.*

19. *op. cit.,* p. 131

20. *op. cit.,* pp. 94-5

21. *op. cit.,* p. 155

22. See for example, Basil Bernstein's seminal article, 'Some Sociological Determinants of Perception', *British Journal of Sociology,* vol. 9 (1958)

23. L. Button, *Discovery and Experience* (Clarendon Press Oxford 1971), p. 2.

24. *op. cit.,* pp. 159-60

25. T.S. Simey, *Principles of Social Administration* (Clarendon Press, Oxford 1937), p. 157

26. Maurice Broady, 'The Conduct of Seminars', *Universities Quarterly,* vol. 24, no. 3 (Summer 1970).

27. This follows Richard Peters, 'Education as Initiation' in *Ethics and Education* (George Allen and Unwin, London 1966), ch. 2.

28. Charles E. Lindbolm, 'The Science of "Muddling Through" ', reprinted in Andreas Faludi *ed.,* A Reader in Planning Theory (Pergamon Press, Oxford 1973), p. 160.

5   USING FORMAL KNOWLEDGE IN EDUCATION

Peter Tomlinson

To expand slightly upon the title of this chapter, although I am offering
considerations relating to the use of the disciplines concerned with the
human being and his functioning that have featured in the first part of
the book, and psychology in particular, many of these points would be
valid with respect to disciplines other than those considered. In fact, it
might be argued that certain of them are general to the real life
applications of any formal knowledge system.

Basic to such applications are questions concerning the adequacy
with which the formal system describes and accounts for the phenomena
involved. Conscious thinking tends to occur when the path to some
goal is blocked: mental experimentation may turn up solutions where
manipulatory efforts may be too costly or even impossible. But it is
generally accepted, and the psychology of cognition is showing in
increasing detail, that our thinking capacities are characterised by a
variety of limitations. True, we can extend our various capacities,
including our thought capacities: but the various formal conceptual
systems which are the vehicles of the forms of extended awareness are
themselves likely to cover only part of what we are concerned with in
any one issue. There will therefore arise some need for choice amongst
alternative perspectives, at any rate until such time as one attains an
overall viewpoint that combines them. Here intuitive commonsense
views are taken as further important members of this series of
perspectives, because they fill in where explicit and systematically
validated knowledge runs out, any may even constitute implicit axioms
in otherwise reflective and well-defined intellectual frameworks.[1] That
they are themselves intuitive assumptions rather than explicit
hypotheses whose validity has been estimated by means of procedures
designed for the purpose does not make them any less important. On
the contrary, in not having been subjected to scrutiny, they may
precisely form the tacit assumptions which define a particular problem
and thereby the eventual solution or solutions offered.[2] They are also
important for further reasons, to which we will return later.

Thus, there is a choice, or set of choices, to be made when one seeks
understanding of the moral educational process. In other words, whilst
we can distinguish between value and fact, between prescription and

description, all decisions involve an interaction between these aspects, so that deciding what is relevant psychology or sociology involves value-positions like any other type of decision. The question of the value-positions of the people being taught is distinguishable from this, but also interacts, together with the informational and evaluative processing concerned, in what might seem the more neutral intellectual level of knowledge application. Maurice Broady's previous chapter on impartiality in social studies has dealt with this area in what seems to me an exceptionally clear way. Although the issues dealt with by him have not always been given the consideration they deserve by sociologists and those seeking to use sociology for some practical end, this lack of consideration is perhaps more likely to occur in the area of sociology than in the area of, say, psychology. In so far as the smallest unit in sociology is the individual person, then on the subject side, more or less close attention is likely to reveal the great individual variation in what each differing proponent might call 'common' sense, and in the range of 'normal' preferences. On the object side, the complexities of social interaction are such that various assumptions are likely to be made in order to make phenomena manageable: when reason arises to disagree with particular explanations, the assumptions, explicit or implicit, of the models in question are naturally among the first candidates for revision (cf. Thomas Kuhn's analysis of 'scientific revolutions').

Maurice Broady's discussion of these matters in relation to the teaching of sociology and the paths he offers towards a reflective and dynamic synthesis apply to psychology also, particularly social psychology, and still more, to the derivation of perspectives from both sociology and psychology. However, psychology seems to offer some difficulties and pitfalls as well as useful lessons worth discussion in their own right. Whereas Maurice Broady's chapter finds its anchor in the value aspects of social science teaching, the following discussion will emphasise the informational aspects: partly because this is the other irreducible feature in decisions concerning educational strategies, and partly because it seems to me that questions concerning the validity and scope of the application of psychological concepts are of particular importance. This importance, in turn, seems due in part to the nature of the topic and to the now obvious restrictiveness of the Behaviourist school, so long dominant in modern psychology, but also to the centrality of the concept of man in social science. For instance, it seems no accident that the foundation of the 'New Sociology's'[2] critique of positivist approaches is a relativist epistemology, and that its positive focus is upon what it seems fair to call a cognitive social psychology.

Bases for Action: What's the Use of Formal Knowledge?

In this section I shall discuss some attitudes and views concerning the application of social science in education, both explicit and implicit, offering a critique of some of them from what I shall propose as an open, higher-order or reflexive viewpoint on the relation of knowledge and reality. Of course, attitudes and perspectives in such a complex domain as this may differ in a large number of ways, but there is one dimension of variation that seems to provide a particularly useful framework. Analysis would probably show it to be quite complex, involving a configuration of simpler dimensions, which is probably why I find it hard to characterise it concisely yet adequately. It will be illustrated by presenting somewhat overdrawn versions of its two extremes.

These extreme positions I would label 'naive American technology' and 'negative British amateurism'. To summarise, the former refers to the tendency towards an overhasty, unreflected application of formal concepts and findings to produce easily ascertainable results; the latter to a chronic disinclination to accept that human activity can be reliably analysed or that formal systems built on such analyses can be of practical use. To anyone familiar with the debate concerning the specification of educational objectives, these positions will appear as poles extrapolated from the various viewpoints expressed: but they seem to have wider implications which will, hopefully, become apparent in what follows.

Naive Hard-Line Technology: The technology approach goes for practicality and lack of ambiguity, and as such tends to value the clear definition and power that typically result from a relatively narrow focus on one thing at a time. But these intellectual and practical aspects are precisely aspects and not separate parts: they interact. Hence, a felt need for clear results tends to dictate high definition of issues and procedures, which in turn leads to reduced focus, which in turn redefines outcomes in narrower terms. In traditional philosophical terminology, this is known as rationalism. A technology arises to the extent that a particular sphere of life is defined and seen in terms derived from the precise focus that enabled the formalisation of a particular system, and to the extent that instrumental procedures are designed on the basis of the relationships that have been discovered using that formal framework. The technology — or rather its use — is naive in so far as the limitations of focus are forgotten and the whole real life domain concerned is treated in terms of the framework: that is to say, things and people are perceived through the filters constituted by a particular set of concepts. The inherent dangers of this sort of technological approach to human activities — in education, for instance — are indicated analogously in the physical world by the different levels of destructive effects of various chemical technologies on the ecology. In the human sphere of education, we insist on the achievement of results, perhaps laudable 'in themselves', but at the cost of dehumanisation in other ways: the achievement of such low order results as rote recall at the probable expense of understanding and the certain cost of further interest qualify as a prime example.

To attempt to abstract individual causal influences from the circular interactive process referred to at the beginning of the previous paragraph tends to lead to chicken-and-egg questions that are as fruitless as they are puzzling, since we are faced with understanding a continuing process, not with a god-like task of inventing and priming it. So there are very likely a number of interrelated reasons why we tend to find proponents of a narrow and behaviourally-defined set of educational objectives also inclining to a relatively hard-line behaviouristic psychology which deals with what would traditionally be called the 'lower' or 'animal level' processes in man.[3] To anyone who lends any credence to the constructivist implications of recent cognitive psychology[4] and to the social psychological consequences of a cognitive approach, as seen in symbolic interactionism, for instance, the dehumanising threat of the naive technology approach is even more dangerous and insidious. For, to put it briefly, to the extent that the way people turn out depends on the way they define themselves, the use of a psychology which outlaws consideration of reflexive-conscious levels of action will tend to produce life that is merely a matter of habit and external manipulation, the unexamined life which, according to Plato, is unliveable. In characterising this extreme as American, I am not making an equally naive generlisation about American educational psychology, but merely indicating that if there is any systematic tendency towards one or other poles of the dimensions under discussion, in North American circles it is towards this 'over-optimistic applicability' end.[5]

What of the reactions and effects likely to be produced in trainee educational practitioners of one sort or another, by approaches tending to this extreme? Those who are eager for immediate skills to achieve concretely-conceived goals will surely tend to welcome it as a precise embodiment of an attitude they already tacitly hold. Their tendencies towards anti-intellectualism and the establishment of habitual orthodoxy will be strengthened. But those whose anxieties do not befuddle their capacity to assess how far what they are presented with makes sense of the issues will tend to reject the content offered, and perhaps the whole discipline from which it has been drawn. And not without reason, for that content is, after all, only what some supposed expert on the psychology or sociology of education has designated as most useful. Everyone, after all, is a lay psychologist, at least in as much as his or her interpersonal activities are underpinned by an unconsciously-assumed framework of psychological notions, and that they hold some conscious views about the nature of behaviour. The latter may range from an incoherent mixture of introspective viewpoints on choice with deterministic conceptions of instinct-bound motivation, to a relatively elaborate and consistent construction of a large area of human functioning — and if we accept Perry's study and similar evidence[6] we shall expect students in tertiary education to be highly aware, on the whole, of the complex relativities of human affairs. Unless the ideas we offer are at least relatable and related to such implicit psychologies, we should not expect those who hold them to accommodate themselves to any supposed improvements we may propose. An introduction to Pavlov and Thorndike prefaced with assurances about the safety of the apparent great leap of faith required to accept their applicability to complex human processes such as reasoning, is not likely to convert any but those anxious souls referred to earlier. And the ploy of ranging children with the sub-human species for which such models might be thought adequate is only likely to delay such a rejection temporarily.

A worthwhile psychological theory, as George Kelly pointed out, must be somewhat reflexive: that is, it must throw some sort of light on the activity of the psychologist himself carrying out such a typically human activity as theory building. Psychology is not devoid of theories concerning higher mental processes, nor of models that seek to integrate concepts originally developed to cope with diverse aspects of human action, as section (ii) will briefly indicate. Moreover, some of this material can be put to reflexive use in coping with the problem of introducing lay psychologists to formal psychology, as I shall try to show in section (iii). Meanwhile, let us consider the other extreme viewpoint regarding the use of formal knowledge systems in education.
Negative Amateurism: This extreme — and let us remind ourselves that we are polarizing the issues for the sake of clarity — is perhaps centrally characterised by its adherence to what it calls 'common sense' notions and the use of 'plain ordinary language' to express them, its negativism consisting in a refusal to accept that human activity can be fruitfully subject to systematic and precise analysis. This is a strongly individualist approach which denies any professional competence apart from that gained by experience. A romantic outlook seems to find this approach most attractive though its adherents are by no means all romantics, by which I mean roughly those who set more store by immediate emotional comfort than by ultimate efficiency. It is clearly the extreme toward which the great British amateur tradition leans, especially on issues of relevance to the social sciences, where one could cite many examples of a hypersceptical attitude towards explicit definition and theory.

Although this viewpoint often makes overt claims about avoiding the nonsensical reductionism of formal theories (all use of which is seen as a form of technological extreme) it does take stances on particular issues for which it must use an at least tacitly assumed set of psychological or sociological premises: as I maintained earlier, everyone can be considered a lay social scientist. But the arrogance with which formal approaches are rejected is well protected by an unwillingness to reflect and check on the possible shortcomings of its own assumptions. 'Muddling through' is thought likely — partly because of the possible social construction of success? — and is used as a rationalisation for carrying on as before. Questions of accountability tend not to be raised.

Any social scientist involved in the preparation of educational practitioners who leaned toward this particular extreme would surely be well on the way to arguing himself or herself out of a job. But in a system heavily influenced by the amateur 'infection-by-immersion' school of practice, one will find a good many administrators and 'educationalists' of this sort. An obvious danger in their presence is that such people will help perpetuate a vicious circle in which education attracts the anti-reflective and control-oriented and confirms them in these traits. A system composed of such people makes up the minds of those who are hesitant about its approach, and puts off those who see its narrowness. Less docile recipients, and the application of the sociology of knowledge to education by such people as M.F.D. Young will hopefully minimise the survival of tendencies toward this extreme. The viewpoint of Young and his associates is of its nature a higher-order or reflexive one but it seems worth pointing out that, whatever its merits or demerits, [7] the relativism it is seen to propound *can* all too easily become miraculous evidence for the canonisation of that individual preference each person likes to call 'common' sense: the legitimizing of a romanticism with all the unfortunate qualities it set out to combat. Though, having said this, I must immediately affirm my opinion that the questions raised here unavoidably require a reflective stance to which the relativity of particular first-order views will be apparent. *The Open-minded Approach:* Having indicated some of the problems of educational theory and practice by means of two exaggerated viewpoints, what can be offered by way of attempts at solutions? Firstly, although it may well be likely that we shall end up wanting to avoid extremes of one kind or another, it is not simply a matter of propounding a *via media* or compromise between the extremes (which, incidentally, some might think more typically British than the amateur romantic tradition I referred to earlier). For this would be to adopt yet another first-order viewpoint with our reasons left as tacit assumptions. Extremes touch, as the proverb has it, and the most salient likeness between the two considered above is their egocentric definition of matters in terms of their own particular set of constructs. This is made

82

possible by their failure, for whatever reason, to examine their own assumptions or to really try out alternative conceptualizations.

Thus, one has basically to try and step back to what I called above a reflexive stance, which attempts to take account of the various ways of construing the issues at stake. Perhaps this need is recognised in the inclusion, in educational training courses, of sections dealing with the philosophy of education. It is true that a reflexive, critical stance has been the traditional concern of philosophers of education, but it should be stressed that we need more than just analysis and criticism. We do not want to proceed to action blindly and without reflection, but, on the other hand, we do not wish to remain on the level of philosophical analysis. In more direct terms, we want neither technicians nor philosophers; rather we need flexible but capable practitioners. Thus the philosophy in educational preparation must be, and be seen to be, of instrumental value. It should enable student practitioners to analyse and criticise the various conceptual frameworks underlying particular techniques they may find useful, but we should also attempt by whatever means, to equip them with the skills of positive synthesis of what among the available alternatives is best in particular circumstances. The question of alternative viewpoints and their comparison within particular fields such as the psychology of education will arise in the next section. However, regarding relationships between such formal systems and everyday concepts as conveyed in ordinary language, which is what the philosophy of education is very largely concerned with, my own experience indicates that students are not untypically offered a range of knowledge and skills (psychology, sociology, etc. of education) and a separate exposure to analysis and criticism of them (philosophy of education) but with no attempt to initiate them into the formation of broader viewpoints combining both sets of insights. The acquisition of this sort of level of thinking would not remove their capacity to use particular techniques based on particular systems of ideas, but its relativist insights would allow more flexible and adaptive practice. Those responsible for such courses might reply that such worthy aspirations are unrealistic given the students concerned and the time available. One suspects, nevertheless, that the introvert-individualist approach so typical of the academic sphere has more than a little to do with the current state of affairs in education, and its emphasis on separate forms of knowledge.

In case the above be taken as calling merely for a slightly more complex form of rationalism than I criticised earlier, it should be made clear that getting beyond particular viewpoints and comparing them in their coverage of particular issues by no means implies that one thereby reaches an exhaustive and adequate higher-level account. In the area of human values and decisions such analyses are more likely to reveal large areas where we are either quite in the dark or where there is considerable inconsistency or even opposition between the available explanations. We are not bound to any dichotomy which forces us either to provide completely general explanation or rest content with intimate familiarity with an infinite number of differing individual cases. As Ruddock[8] points out, models have been much in favour in a wide variety of domains, following a retreat from general theory in the last decade. Indeed, in keeping with what I asserted at the outset of this chapter about conceptual frameworks and their limitations, one might say rather that attempts at explanation have recently been recognised as largely a matter of using models. Models are simplified patterns of symbols, rules and processes (Meadows)[9] devised to help think about and explain a particular domain or system: being avowedly focused in scope and purpose, they expect, as Ruddock puts it 'like a Marxian dialectic, to be transcended, discarded, or conserved in a new unity'. At any given point, then, we are faced with a variety of models of man, or more likely, a variety of models of various aspects of human functioning. What agents in the educational process need is at least to be aware of the purposes and consequent limitations of various models, rather than just being able to use their prescriptions cookbook fashion. Since their perspectives on human individuals will hopefully not remain limited to those foreseen and defined by such models, these agents should also assess the relationships between them, their degrees of translatability, of overlap in reference, their possible complementarity or opposition, and so on, so that far from an over-defined rationalism, one hopes for a sensitive rationality, that is, a stance which is clear about the limitations of the clarity of any particular model or set of models sometimes called 'commonsense' or, often presumptuously, 'naive', that a person brings with him to a particular issue, often unconsciously. They are important for at least three reasons. Firstly, they constitute an individual's more or less established way of thinking which will persist to the extent that no new perspectives are acquired. rather than by reference to psychological needs within the perceiver. On this view, of course, the alternative extremes sketched in the first two parts of this section would constitute obvious instances of closed-mindedness.

Before going on to briefly review and comment on the variety of approaches in current psychology, it should be mentioned that there is one set of models which are of particular importance: that is the set of models sometimes called 'commonsense' or, of ten presumptuously, 'naive', that a person brings with him to a particular issue, often unconsciously. They are important for at least three reasons. Firstly, they constitute an individual's more or less established way of thinking which will persist to the extent that no new perspectives are acquired.

Secondly, they have at least formed the basis of feasible interpretations of life for that particular person. Thirdly, they must be taken into account if the person is to be introduced to new ideas in a meaningful way. This connecting of new formal concepts to existing commonsense ones may be aided by the continual modification that models undergo, which in the case of commonsense views consists to an important extent in co-opting notions from formal systems: a process that can take place with increasing speed and impact in this age of mass-media popular exposition. Turning, then, to one formal discipline by way of example, what do we find in psychology and of what value is it in education, especially with respect to the value aspects of tertiary education?

Contemporary Psychology

In Chapter 2 I attempted to provide a selective illustration of some viewpoints from psychology which differed in some ways, but which all dealt with the processing of information of a social nature and which could, as such, be related to the information-processing skill concepts that are dominant in the main stream of experimental psychology. In these viewpoints motivational aspects are regarded as intimately related to cognitive, or informational aspects. But what of psychology in general? When we turn towards formal psychology, seeking insight and improvement in our educational practice — not least where we are training educational training agents themselves — what are the strengths and weaknesses we are likely to find? What are the emphases, and where shall we, for the time being anyway, have to 'use our (informed) commonsense'?

In what seems to me a particularly honest and well-argued article[11], Peter Warr, a psychologist at the University of Sheffield, refers to the increasing criticism from within and outside the discipline that academic psychology misses many of the essential aspects of life. According to him it is valid and useful to distinguish three dimensions-of-difference to characterise any given psychological undertaking, and thus any given psychologist's or institution's typical interests and pursuits.

These are:

(a) *The Mechanistic-experiential Dimension:* The mechanistic tendency involves emphasis on psychology's roots in the natural sciences, the deterministic nature of behaviour, the usefulness of machine analogies, and the value of experimental manipulation, probably within a behaviourist approach, whereas the experiential approach stresses, respectively, the uniqueness of human nature, individual choice and intrinsic motivation, and the use of a variety of methods of investigation according to the particular problem. This opposition between preferred models of enquiry is felt to be the major contrast between the two poles, but they will also give rise to interest in different ranges of topics. In particular, experiential advocates of the strongest variety stress a need for participation and self-examination by the investigator, and often claim to find a difference between the ways the mechanistic-minded view themselves and the ways they view their subjects.

(b) *The Pure-applied Dimension:* Pure psychology tends to involve studies set in a laboratory or otherwise standardised setting, with the investigator ideally as a neutral observer, whereas the applied study takes place in a natural setting, i.e. defined independently of the investigator, who may often participate in the activity under investigation. Perhaps a more important strand, however, is the immediate origin of the problem: the applied psychologist takes his problem relatively directly from a real life situation where the pure investigator studies questions arising entirely from psychological theory.

(c) *The Individual-social Dimension:* This concerns the extent to which the focus of study is upon an individual alone or upon a person as an interacting member of a group. There is a further variation in approach within social psychology which I would characterise, differing slightly from Warr, as a behavioural-cognitive dimension: this involves focus ranging from interaction sequences of behaviour, communication patterns, reactions in group situations, and so on, to the ways people handle information of a social kind.

The proposal, then, is that we may usefully represent any given psychological study in terms of these three variable dimensions, which we may assume to be continuous. Warr offers a simplified illustration of this possibility in a figure which is reproduced below. The middle frame

The Subject Matter of Psychology: A Three-Dimensional Representation

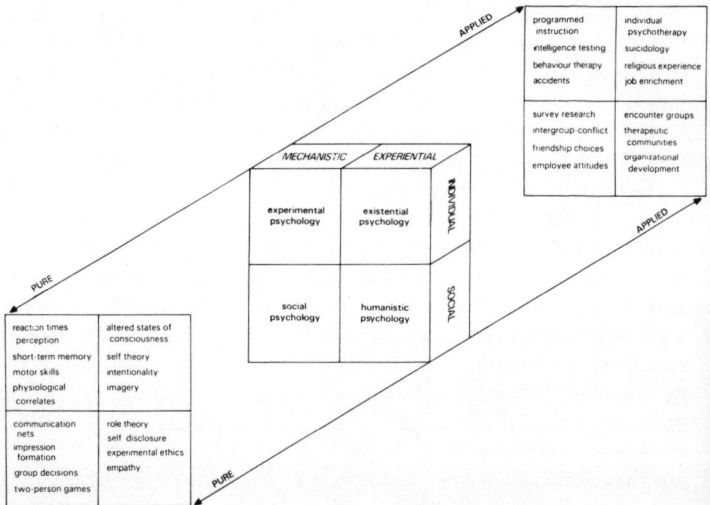

FIG 1. The subject-matter of psychology: a three-dimensional representation.

shows the crossing of the first two dimensions to give four quadrants representing main types of current psychology: as the dimensions are assumed to be continuous, these types are correspondingly thought to shade into each other. There is probably room for disagreement about the particular use of the labels 'existential psychology' and 'humanistic psychology', as Warr acknowledges in a brief discussion on this point: the schema is, after all, a simplified illustration.

Accepting this as a useful delineation of the potential field of psychology, we may now employ it to situate current academic psychology. Few will disagree with Warr's contention that 'we are predominantly mechanistic, individual and pure in our orientation' (p. 4), in which case they will probably also agree with his acceptance of current criticisms that academic psychology misses many of the essentially human aspects of life. For, as he argues, if the three-fold representation is valid, and if most academic psychology is located within a small proportion of it, then academic psychology is quite simply not covering the field: to repeat a point made in chapter 2, it would seem that academic psychology has been more concerned with scientific status than with dealing with its chosen content. Warr points out that in calling for greater 'humanness' in the sense of academic psychology ceasing to neglect areas of importance to us as human beings he is in no way characterising psychologists as inhuman or in-humane persons. In similar vein, I myself find the term 'humanistic psychology' somewhat unfortunate as it may tend to suggest that some set of investigators with particular approaches have 'cornered the market' in humaneness, or that some transcendental authority has assessed that group as the only students of human nature (cf. the Oxford Dictionary definition of 'humanist') worthy of consideration. Nevertheless, saying this in no sense belies my agreement with Warr's call for development 'towards a more human psychology' which consists of a shift of emphasis along the three dimensions concerned, to include, and hopefully integrate, what is known as humanistic psychology.

With all this in mind, educational practitioners might not approach psychology with very much hope of assistance: they might not be surprised, perusing tomes on educational psychology, to find either an academic stone-wringing approach which attempts to force meaningful prescriptions for the classroom or tutorial out of studies whose only connection seems to be that they involve a term that can be applied to both (e.g. 'learning', even if of a different sort and by a different species), or on the other hand, an atheoretical technology, that may be useful for the limited purposes for which it was developed, for example, ability screening, but whose role in the process of instruction, let alone its illumination of that process, seems non-existent.

Nor, when they consider the relative complexity of the educational situation, will they be much encouraged by remembering the maxim that there is a trade-off between generality and certainty, or put differently, the more you want to say, the harder it is to prove it. So that those more ambitious approaches, like the depth psychologies and their derivatives, which try to account for a greater range of the subtle and complex aspects of the human phenomenon, are correspondingly harder to validate, quite apart from the 'grave philosophical problems' Warr sees attached to a move towards the experiential end of his mechanistic-experiential dimension.

Nevertheless, if the picture looks black — and there is evidence that it does to some well-informed observers[12] — that seems to me unfortunate. Because for all the shortcomings discussed above, current psychology does offer the possibility of a more adequate and synthesised set of perspectives on human action than is indicated by not a few works offering psychology relevant to education. These procedures and concepts which the rapid developments over the last thirty years have given us also provide a substantial basis for further development and expansion. In particular, the central notion of skilled information-processing seems to offer strong possibilities of integrating aspects of widely differing scale, as I attempted to illustrate in the more focused presentation in Chapter 2, and to provide more easily for meaningful acquisition by virtue of its focus on cognitive aspects and of the consciousness-dominated outlook trainee educational practitioners bring with them. Hence, far from saying that Pavlovian approaches — to take a relatively extreme example — have no relevance to education, I am rather stressing their need to be seen as aspects within a framework that is more adequate and meaningful. Otherwise this impression of the irrelevance of psychology will cover up what useful insights I believe to be there.

Critically Aware Usage of Formal Knowledge in Education

My argument is that anyone seeking to utilise formal knowledge in education at the present time and for the foreseeable future should adopt a critical, open stance, realising that any particular formal framework is likely to apply only to a subset of the aspects of the problem area concerned. This means that more or less intuitive assumptions may have to be used, but — consequently — that one ought to be all the more open to revising such assumptions. These points have been given more precise illustration in the previous section, where the nature of current academic psychology has been briefly reviewed. On the positive side, it has been argued that one should try to attain some conception, albeit relatively vague, of the interrelationships of the various formal models and explanatory frameworks one thinks applicable to a particular domain.

These points seem to me to be of particular weight for anyone concerned with the value aspects of higher educational activities and wishing to inform their own participation through insights from the social sciences, for, as John Wilson indicates in the first chapter, the concept of moral maturity pertains to very many aspects of human existence. All the more important, then, to avoid any sort of reductionism, for that only fails to deal with issues which ought really to be seen as an integral aspect of the situation. It also tends to produce remedies whose extremeness easily achieves negative effects: casuistic precision at the expense of firm commitment and practice, or 'moral fibre' at the expense of authoritarian blindness, to mention but two typical oversimplifications in this domain.

Having argued that the insights of social science can only be fruitful within a generally aware outlook, it must be admitted that this does land us in something of a dilemma. Namely, that those who study questions in depth, the social scientists in this case, tend in the nature of such pursuits to specialise in particular approaches: the more attention one devotes to pursuing one topic in depth, the less one can give to others. Moreover, as we mentioned earlier, the premium in academic circles has tended to be on depth, making for narrowness of focus on particular questions within a discipline, let alone on disciplines within an area. Though of course from many points of view one might think this correct, since ultimately depth and differentiation are conditions of fuller understanding. On the other hand, those in the field, involved with multi-faceted problems whose aspects seem to be inter-related and to deny separate treatment, are perhaps under some pressure to quickly take up any promising ideas they discover in what will often have to be an all too rapid survey. There are thus less likely to critically analyse a given approach, and its integration with other concepts will tend to occur, if at all, at the level of unconscious assumption. This means that any limitations of the approach will be discovered only in practice, which may be too late from a number of viewpoints. It will not be surprising, when one remembers the limitations of social sciences in their current state — compare, for instance, the sketch of psychology in the previous section — to find this leading to the sorts of closed mindedness outlined in the first section of this chapter. These, in turn, seem to me to have something to do with the apparent lack of rationality in the determination of what educational innovation *does* take place.

Any remedy seems clearly to require the establishment of applied disciplines in which the problems of the field can be dealt with by people with critical, but thorough and up-to-date, awareness of a variety of 'pure' disciplines. It hardly needs repeating that the above rationale specifies not only the provision of educational studies and training for intending practitioners, but also that educational institutions should resist any imbalance of emphasis, in either of those two perennial directions (not unrelated to the extremes described in the first section): one tending toward the mere uncritical inculcation of practical prescriptions, the other to the investigation of abstract questions so detached from current practical issues that their importance may remain minimal for years. It also means that there will need to be some form of cohesive teaching approach, whatever particular methods are employed, by staff whose relative expertise in differing domains can be fused within the sort of approach outlined earlier: the present book represents such an effort in written form. Thus, recent attempts by educational training institutions to achieve greater integration between theory and practice are to be welcomed, as is the trend towards a training requirement for teaching at an increasing number of levels. However, the reader who is at all familiar with higher education, in Britain at least, may well feel that such a requirement will never be made at that level, and I would agree that teachers at this level seem to tend to what I earlier called the common sense, rather than the technological, pole where educational theory and its application to their own situation are concerned. Moreover, one would also have to admit the plausibility of an argument running thus: since science, as viewed by thinkers such as Thomas Kuhn, consists essentially in the systematic validation, revision, and replacement of explanatory models, starting with commonsense notions, and since the social sciences are not only the youngest of such endeavours but also to be thought of as having possibly the most complex subject-matter, then in these areas we should have the least expectation of finding formal improvements on 'common' sense, especially that of such above-average intellects as abound in tertiary education. Indeed, one might well go another mile with the protagonist of such a view, and admit that in a good number of areas of, say, psychology, our formal models are a good deal less powerful than those which underlie a great many people's everyday performance. It seems to me, for instance, that those psychological writers who set the scene for their works with an introductory foray against the views of 'the man in the street' not only indicate that their offering is unlikely to attain Kelly's reflexiveness requirement in any form, but are also liable to put off any critical and open-minded person who was otherwise willing to accept new insights from the human sciences. This would be a pity, for higher education, in its value and interpersonal aspects as well as from the viewpoint of teaching efficiency, surely stands to benefit from a consideration of existing psycho-sociological models and from systematic study of its own processes.

These points, which concern the employment of forms of first-order knowledge, and stress the interaction of a large number of factors, may tend to sound philosophical, which means 'vague and useless' to some people. I would suspect that such people might have had their (perhaps overambitious) expectations of philosophy violated by some particular contact with one of its forms, and would point out that they are being asked to keep the foregoing discussion in mind when considering any given 'practical' viewpoint, rather than to consider it as some sort of global replacement for such concrete material. A situation may be considered from perspectives of varying breadth, but we should not test views sketched from one perspective by criteria suitable only for another. Thus the earlier chapters in this part should be taken as introductions to areas which would repay further study. Some essential points may have been distilled by the writers, but were there space, there would clearly be more to say. Thus in chapter 2 I concentrated on the person rather than the environment of teaching methods, individuals and influences with which he interacts in the educational situation. Having given considerable weight to the commonsense conceptions people employ, having urged the usefulness of social science models and the potential reflexiveness of certain psychological insights, it would seem fitting to conclude by attempting to indicate, even if very briefly, certain psychological views which may inform the teaching of social science in the ways recommended above, so to make its acquisition more meaningful.

It may indeed seem that this term 'meaningful', together with its near relative 'relevant', is in danger of becoming an empty cliché through over use, particularly in educational and mass-media rhetoric; though this over-use might also be taken to indicate the importance currently attached to its underlying sense. The latter seems to be relatively vague: something is meaningful to me in so far as I see it having an appreciable effect with respect to my decision-making. It may be a relatively direct question of value, or it may pertain to the informational aspects. On the other hand, psychologists have dealt with what may be regarded as various more precise aspects of this concept, and some of these approaches have produced more or less common conclusions. For Ausubel[13] the term relates to the informational aspect; learning is meaningful when what is learned is related to the learner's existing cognitive structures, that is, the ways he sees and relates things. This presupposes two things: firstly, what Ausubel terms "non-arbitrary relatability" of the two sets of ideas, and secondly, an active attempt by the learner to relate them. Although Piaget[14] generally supports very different teaching strategies from Ausubel, he holds somewhat similar basic views about the development of thought and knowledge. For him it is a process of adaptation in which the organism continually strives to deal with its environment in familiar terms, to assimilate it to the various internal schemata by which it is known. To the extent that this active, hypothesizing approach meets something new and unpredicted, it may accommodate its forms of awareness. Thus Piaget, also, places great emphasis on the actively attending stance required for what one might reasonably call 'meaningful learning' (though he does not use the term 'learning' for this). And in the non-intellectual field of perceptual learning and adaptation[15] we find that 'feedback' is required for organisms to develop new systematic frameworks of perception: 'feedback' does not just involve perception in a passive sense, but the checking of what is expected as the effect of action against what actually is perceived as a result of it, any differences being related back to modify future expectations. Thus we have relatively broad support for the idea that effective learning requires a relating of new and old and, consequently, for the notion that, in informational terms at least, instruction must be learner-centred. The message for the teaching of psychology seems clear: whatever actual teaching strategy is used, one should try to relate to the ideas brought by the learners, what I have called above their 'commonsense psychology'. This conclusion leads straight to the possibility that people will differ in their ideas, so that group teaching would be of little use. It is a reasonable expectation that the more precise the issue and the less common the topic, the more individually variable will people's notions be. So that alternative methods may need to be devised on that basis, quite apart from the question of different teaching strategies with people of differing personality orientation.[16] However, there are a considerable variety of ways in which meaningful connections can sometimes be achieved without having to provide an explicitly varied set of alternatives for different individuals or groups. Ausubel's preferred strategy is the provision of a general, relatively abstract, outline of the material at the outset, an 'advance organizer' as he calls it. This is not just a summary condensation on the same level of analysis, rather the more general nature of its terms makes it likely that it will connect with ideas most recipients already possess. On this basis, one might introduce psychology via the models of man implicit in everyday language: a little analysis may indicate their shortcomings (and strengths) sufficiently to bring about more open consideration of alternative, formal conceptions.

An alternative strategy might loosely be termed the 'concrete topic' approach. Here one introduces a concrete problem which is likely to stimulate use of the students' existing notions. Actual procedures can range from a relatively directed discussion to group projects and syndicate work, but the common element is that there is a focus to which different conceptions can be brought. Student choice of topic has mainly advantages, but there are also some dangers. The most obvious is perhaps that the degree of emotional investment in an issue is related to likelihood of open and flexible thinking about it in a somewhat complex way: most work in this area would confirm that affective involvement tends to increase quality of thinking up to an optimum, beyond which increased affective arousal has a negative effect. Moreover, the optimum differs from individual to individual. This is likely to be of particular relevance to the value issues with which this work is concerned.

Two other points from the psychology of skill are also important here. The first concerns something I would wish to avoid, namely the possibility that emphasis on the cognitive or 'mental' aspects of morals might be taken as implying some sort of constant conscious monitoring, the sort of compulsive error-checking characteristic of the anxiety neurotic. The point is that skills become automatic with practice, and that judgemental processes can, as Bartlett saw, be treated as forms of skill. It may be that a good deal has to be processed consciously at the outset, but even a reflective stance can, like other general thought strategies, become habitual. If error checking, for instance, were always done in a completely conscious way, unless the task were extremely simple, there would never be any time for anything else: but as it can become automatic, other functions can occur, roughly speaking, at the same time. The second point connects with what was said above about meaningful presentation. Skills research confirms what we might expect, namely that to the extent that an activity is complex, that is, consisting of a relatively large number of sub-processes, and especially where there is a degree of inter-dependence among these sub-processes, then there must be practice at the whole task as such, rather than just rehearsal of the eventually discernable parts.

A procedure which embodies this insight, indeed, one which can claim recommendation from virtually the whole theoretical range of approaches mentioned, including behaviourist learning theory and the Piaget-Kohlberg cognitive approach, is what is variously called role-taking, role-playing, simulation, or sometimes, socio-drama. Because it is a method that embodies so many aspects and can be used to consider situations of potentially immense personal importance to participants, it should not be undertaken without an awareness of various stress factors and a capacity to recognise and handle their operation in practice. This usually requires some practical training as well as relevant reading.

In conclusion: we have seen that the application of formal knowledge in education, especially with respect to the moral aspects of higher education, is not without its difficulties and systematic pitfalls. But, whilst recognising current limitations, which were considered particularly in the case of psychology, it has been my contention that social sciences are developing models and approaches which offer valid insights into important human affairs, including reflexive judgemental aspects and their acquisition. I shall be content if the present chapter has succeeded in indicating that an open and critical, but also positive and integrating, approach to formal resources must be maintained if the moral aspects of higher education are to receive the attention they deserve.

References

1.   Cf. A.V. Cicourel, *Cognitive Sociology: Language and Meaning in Social Interaction* (Penguin Books, Harmondsworth 1973); J.G. Vulliamy, *New Perspectives in Sociology,* A.T.S.S. Monograph No. 2.
2.   See N. Bolton, 'The Phenomenology of Thinking', in *The Psychology of Thinking,* (Methuen, London 1972),
3.   Though its adequacy even with respect to animal behaviour is seriously questioned by ethology and recent physiological psychology.
4.   Cf. Bolton, *op. cit.*
5.   R.C. Anderson and G.W. Faust provide a clear example of this in their recent book *Educational psychology: the science of instruction and learning* (Dodd, Mead, New York 1973)
6.   See Chapter 2.
7.   Cf. R. Pring, 'Knowledge Out of Control'. *Education for Teaching,* No. 2, November 1972; M.F.D. Young, 'Educational theorizing: a radical alternative', *Education for Teaching,* No. 1, 1973.
8.   R. Ruddock 'The Need for Models', in R. Ruddock (ed.), *Six Approaches to the Person* (Routledge, London 1972)
9.   op. cit.
10.   Cf. Chapter 2.
11.   P. Warr, 'Towards a More Human Psychology, *Bulletin of the British Psychological Society,* 1973, *26,* pp. 1-8.
12.   Cf. for instance, W.K. Richmond's remark about learning theory on page 87 of *The Literature of Education: a Critical Bibliography 1945-1970* (Methuen, London 1972)
13.   D.P. Ausubel, *Educational Psychology: A Cognitive View* (Holt, Rhinehart & Winston, New York 1968)
14.   Cf. J.H. Flavell, *The Developmental Psychology of Jean Piaget* (Van Nostrand, New York 1963)
15.   Cf. I.P. Howard & W.B. Templeton, *Human Spatial Orientation* (Wiley, New York 1966)
16.   For instance, the work of Hunt on matching models in education: see ch. 2, footnote 7.

PART II

CONTRIBUTIONS FROM PRACTICAL EXERCISES; ACADEMIC STUDIES

6 PHILOSOPHY

John Wilson

I need first to explain what I mean, and do not mean, by 'teaching philosophy'. I do not mean inculcating a particular creed, faith, outlook or 'philosophy of life' — as it might be, Christianity, hedonism, Marxism, existentialism, and so on — into students, nor giving them 'a faith to live by'. This is a kind of indoctrination. Nor do I mean teaching students *about* various creeds and 'philosophies — giving them a sort of cultural shop-window tour of the sages of the ages. This is sometimes done (particularly in some European countries) under the heading of 'philosophy', but seems to me to fall more properly under history, or sociology, or 'history of ideas', or even psychology. I mean what nearly all professional philosophers at reputable universities in the U.K., the U.S.A., Commonwealth countries and some others mean by 'philosophy'.

It is hard to explain briefly just what this is, but perhaps the first and certainly a model case of it is to be found in Socrates' work. Socrates was concerned with the discovery of truth via the analysis of language and concepts. Such discovery is best carried out, not by lengthy speech-making or the construction of abstract 'systems of thought' or 'philosophies of life', but by a process of mutual criticism and argument. That is why it is well-suited to the dialogue form. The dialogue is not however about empirical facts, as with science or history or almost any other subject: it is about the very concepts we use. And one way, perhaps the only way, of getting clear about these concepts is by looking closely at the language in which they are enshrined: by asking questions like 'What do we mean by "justice"?', 'What is "authority" exactly?', 'Does "It's right" just mean "I like it", or is there something left out of this translation?', and many others.

In pursuing this subject the magniloquent and the grandiose are not commendable: polysyllables and jargon are to be eschewed. 'Everything that can be said at all can be said clearly'; and the difficulty of the subject is just *to get clear.* This requires, not so much academic brilliance, but the more pedestrian virtues of patience, seriousness, care, and a workmanlike approach. We have to thrust aside our own prejudices and fantasies, to take a step backward from our immediate concerns and discuss the language in which we talk about those concerns — to stop praising or decrying democracy, and ask what we are going to mean by 'democracy'; to stop asserting or denying the existence of God, and ask what the question 'Is there a God?' means, and what sort of evidence we could possibly use to determine its answer.

The pressures and obstacles in doing philosophy are psychological pressures. What one philosopher[1] calls 'the fat, relentless ego' keeps breaking in. She was writing about moral living, not philosophy; but my first point is precisely this. The kind of seriousness, extrusion of the self, concentration on public rules and public criticism, care and loving (one might fairly say) attention to truth — all these are necessities for the moral life as they are for doing philosophy. Philosophy is, so to speak, a model or paradigm case, for you cannot begin to do the subject at all unless you are prepared, at least to some extent, to give up your ego. This applies in some degree to all seriously-studied subjects but particularly to philosophy, where there are no simple or parrotted facts to fall back on, no rote-learned procedures, no mechanical application of rules. You have to attend to language and meaning all the time. This is a strain, and it is not without reason that many universities believe that philosophy ought not to be the only subject of study for most students since even the most able cannot really do philosophy properly for more than a few hours at a time.

Secondly, it is essentially a public and 'non-authoritarian' activity. It is true that occasional lectures, perhaps even note-taking, are useful in philosophy, and it is also true that some people are clearly better than others at it. But there is little room for 'expert' philosophers to stand up on a platform and 'tell you the answer'. For one thing there are no 'answers' in that sense as there are answers to sums or scientific problems, and for another, no 'answer' in philosophy is of any value in itself — the 'working' is everything. It is essentially caught, not taught and is more like — indeed, just a sophisticated version of — learning to talk than like learning the multiplication tables or how to do a scientific experiment. It is a sophisticated skill, into which students may be initiated: not a set of *diktats*.

This seems to me of great importance for moral development, if one believes (as surely one must) that education in this area must respect the student's autonomy. It is important that a person's moral principles be *his* principles, particularly in a pluralistic and rapidly-changing society, rather than second-hand injunctions which are not grounded in reasons which he understands and accepts. Philosophy — and of course particularly moral philosophy (but it must be remembered that philosophy is a homogenous activity and cannot be compartmentalised) — is one necessary method for ensuring this. Without an adequate and critical discussion of moral principles and judgements (and moral philosophy is in essence no more than this), how could a person hope to develop a clear set of values which are truly his own? Philosophy is, for this aspect of moral education, the only alternative to various forms of indoctrination, conditioning, brain-washing and other such methods. In this light, it is not surprising that philosophy (in our sense) flourishes only in liberal and democratic countries.

For — and this has to be accepted and, indeed, welcomed — philosophy is of course potentially dangerous: dangerous, that is to say, to any established order which relies on the suppression of thought and opinion. The teacher who said 'I think it very good for students to discuss freely and frankly', but added 'so long as they reach the right conclusion', did not seem to understand what 'free discussion' means in English. Philosophy follows, as Socrates said, 'wheresoever the argument may lead'; and if you follow reason and argument enough, it will soon threaten your own and other people's preconceived notions and vested interests. It is an alarming subject, if it is done seriously. But for that reason it is also a very important one. For either we try and tackle our anxieties, fears, fantasies and problems by discussion and by trying to get at the truth, or else — and how often does this happen! — we relapse into autistic thought and behaviour, acting out our own fears and desires without much connection with the real world.

Thirdly, philosophy offers a technique which gives us some hope here. Nearly everybody, at some period of their lives (perhaps when they are young, before the world crushes such desires,) is rightly worried about many important human issues, and wants to achieve more clarity about them. These issues may vary, and appear under different titles as society or fashion dictates, but they will certainly include religion, politics, sexual and other morality, etc. It rapidly becomes clear that the chief obstacle here is *confusion*. Unless (and this too happens only too often) the person finds the tension of uncertainty so intolerable that he forgets about truth and takes sides with some doctrinaire and partisan group, he will need above all a *method of dealing* with the confusion and uncertainty. In other words, if we cannot give him a technique and methodology for solving his problems, he will abandon his reason and humanity by putting his autonomy in the hands of some group, gang, metaphysic, or *parti pris*.

Fourthly, there is a more specific but no less valuable function which the practice of philosophy performs. One of the most important — perhaps the most important — attribute of the morally educated person is the ability and willingness to confront moral situations alertly and seriously, and *describe* those situations (including his own feelings) honestly and precisely (I have referred to this briefly as KRAT (1) in the first part of this book). For instance, if I see someone I meet in the street as 'a bloody Pakistani' or 'an alien', I shall act very differently from the way in which I would react if I described him as 'a fellow human being', 'a stranger', 'someone in need', etc. If I see a moral choice in terms of 'what's acceptable to my mates', 'what's fashionable', or 'what makes me feel better inside', this has very different consequences from seeing it in terms of justice, honesty, human interests and contractual obligations. Now what we 'see things as' depends very much on the language and concepts we have available, and our ability to criticise these and be conscious of them. This ability is precisely what philosophy seeks to promote.

Instead of saying just *anything* (and hence enabling ourselves to act in any way we please), we learn in philosophy to say the *right* thing: that is, to use only those words and concepts which do full justice to what is before us. We sharpen our perception of the phenomena via awareness of the words, and vice versa (this is why philosophy is not, as some think, 'just playing with words'). A lengthy discussion of, for instance, just what is meant by 'prejudice', 'anarchy', 'democracy', 'freedom', 'authority' and so on will at least make students aware that things are not as simple as they seem: that their original thoughts and (more important) feelings need analysis, revision, sophistication and improvement in the light of the facts. Without just and true description, no serious morality or politics is possible. For our own impulses always try to pervert and distort a true description.

Rather than extend such generalisations, it may be more profitable to give an example. At a fashionable university where I once taught, the students were very proud of 'breaking down class barriers'. A philosophical conversation — or, better, a conversation which led on to philosophy — went somewhat as follows:

A. We haven't got any class barriers here, thank God.

B. What do you count as *class* barriers?

A. Well, you know, people minding about what their fathers do, or accents, that kind of thing.

B. You mean anybody is just as acceptable as anyone else?

A. Yes, that's right.

B. But I don't notice you mixing much with the students that wear neat suits and cut their hair short and hold Conservative views. Or with the over-thirties — 'squares', don't you call them, people who aren't 'with it'?

C. Yes, but they're different from us, that's not the same thing at all.

A. Well, but it's a sort of 'class', isn't it, and don't you have the same barriers in a different form?

B. That's not what the sociologists mean by 'class': they mean things like parental occupation, income bracket and so on.

A. Maybe; and if that's all you mean by 'class barriers', then OK But there's an ordinary sense of 'class', that's to say a group of people in a particular category: like 'square' and 'with it', or 'young people' and 'adults'. In that sense, mightn't there be just as many class barriers as before — or maybe more?

B. It depends what you mean by 'class'.

A. That's right, it depends what you mean by 'class'. But different concepts represented by the word 'class' might be more or less relevant to what you're saying.

B. What's that supposed to mean?

A. Well, you want to recommend the abolition of some kind of barriers. Are you only interested in the particular kinds erected by such differences as parental occupation, income groups, etc.? Or are you interested in other kinds?

C. Any kind — we don't want a divisive society.

A. Then you need a broader sense of 'class' than the sociologists' sense. What's 'a divisive society' supposed to mean?

C. A society where people are put into categories.

A. 'Are put into categories'. I'm not sure I understand that. Aren't people *in* categories, like tall and short, fat and thin, clever and less clever, boys and girls, and so on?

C. Yes, but we don't want them to be divisive.

A. You can't mean that people shouldn't *recognise* the categories and the differences, that they should be blind to (say) the differences between black skins and red skins and white skins?

C. No, of course not.

A. Then this seems to be something about the way people *use* the categories, or have wrong attitudes to them; or perhaps also the way in which they make up improper categories and use them. Yes, I suppose there are two things here. You might say (1) there should be categories of black and white skins, but people shouldn't have certain attitudes towards them: and (2), quite different, that there shouldn't be a category like, say, earning more than £10,000 a year.

B. We mean, people are equals.

A. That's very mysterious, though. I suppose you don't mean they're of equal weights and heights or IQs and so on.

B. No, I mean they have equal rights.

A. But couldn't you have a society with everyone having equal rights, but still have class barriers? I mean, they might not be very *fraternal* to each other even though they all had the same vote or the same income or went to the same schools or whatever.

C. I think there's lots more here than we've thought about.

A. Well, let's list a few things:—

    1. Getting the right 'social' or artificial categories, those within our control like income.

2. Having the right attitude to these categories and the 'natural' categories like skin colour or height, both (a) granting equal rights to all of them, and (b) being fraternal, willing to mix in and share with people in other categories.

This is a very primitive example, not a 'model case' of a philosophy seminar. But it should help to show how philosophical thought, if only at an elementary level, can be made to arise from students' particular concerns, or even (as here) from chance remarks. What I want to stress is that — from the viewpoint of moral education, if not that of philosophy — it does not so much matter how good the pupils are at philosophy, or how much progress they make: what matters is that they are given a taste of it, shown its relevance, and made to realise *for*   *
themselves, by talking, that their own impulses and language stand in   **
need of criticism and revision. Only a small taste of this is required before most students come to appreciate the naivety of carrying banners reading 'Equality' or 'Down with class', and the naivety of politicians talking about these things on the television. Only a small taste of seriousness is needed to show up myth, fantasy, propaganda, mob oratory and confusion for what they are.

I am not, of course, saying that the work of philosophical writers is irrelevant to this process. But, in my view, it is best used when the pupil is already engaged in and committed to discovering the truth about a particular topic. Consider this conversation:

A. I'm an anarchist.

B. What do anarchists think?

A. We're against any kind of rules and authority, we think people should only do what they want to do themselves.

B. Well, here's one rule: the word 'anarchist' is normally spelled a-n-a-r-c-h-i-s-t in English. Would it be OK if people spelled it some other way?

A. Why shouldn't they spell it how they like?

B. Well, suppose I spelled it C-o-n-s-e-r-v-a-t-i-v-e, or F-a-s-c-i-s-t, would that be all right?

A. No, don't be silly.

B. So you think there are some rules that ought to be kept?

A. Only if people agree to them.

B. Oh, yes, but that's very different, isn't it? I mean, if what you're saying is that people shouldn't have rules imposed on them against their will by illegitimate authorities or tyrants, of course that makes sense.

A. They shouldn't be imposed by anobody.

B. Well, suppose we agree to play a game with certain rules, and that means agreeing to various penalties (being out in cricket, or going back six spaces in Monopoly, or what ever), and perhaps we have

an umpire or referee enforcing those rules which we've agreed to
— would you call that 'imposing the rules' on us?

A. In a way, but not really. The thing is, are the rules *their* rules?

B. Well, what can one say here except that they've agreed to them?

A. Yes, if there's a proper contract and they're given a chance to
agree or not.

B. This is a problem which worried a lot of political philosophers.
You might like to look at Plato's Republic, and more particularly
at what Locke and Hobbes and Rousseau wrote about the social
contract, and what Hume's criticisms of it were: and there are
some modern authors . . .

There is some hope here that after enough talk of this kind the pupil
will want to read what philosophers have said about the social contract,
because he sees that his initial interests relate to this. But it is essential
that he first sees that his initial interests, as expressed in the language
he uses ('I'm an anarchist'), will not do as they stand. Some philosophers
have drawn a very persuasive parallel with psychotherapy here: for in
both cases the teacher (psychoanalyst) can only proceed if the pupil
(patient) feels — or can be brought to feel — that his natural, uncritical
behaviour is somehow inadequate. Socrates reduced his victims to a
state of aporia — being at a loss, aware of ignorange and confusion —
not in order to humiliate them, but as a crucial first step.

Partly because of this, the proper teaching of philosophy is bound
up — more than the teaching of most other subjects — with the social
context in which it is taught and the personal relationships of pupil
and teacher. Ideally, it should be a discussion among friends. Small
groups are infinitely to be preferred to mass lectures: and the 'staging'
is very important. Arguably, it helps if the disputants are not too
formal, and have shared things with each other before in other contexts.
Anything which will loosen the participants up — even alcohol — may
help: not that we want loose thinking, but we want them to forget
about themselves and their neighbours except as engaged in the task of
examining language. They have to set aside their social manners, their
doubts, fears, anxiety about status or personal characteristics, and
anything that might get in the way of the discussion. In a sense, they
have to learn how to talk before they can learn how to talk
philosophically.

Teachers and lecturers will realise how difficult it is to initiate
students into the art of talking relevantly. Various devices may help.
One of the most useful, in my experience, is the use of a tape-recorder.
If the group discusses something, plays back the recording, and then
discusses *that,* and so on, the members rapidly become more conscious
and self-critical about what they have said and are now saying. Another
more obvious method which prevents the talk from floating too freely

is to concentrate on the critical examination of a set text – preferably a very short and economically-written passage, and certainly not (to begin with) some long philosophical tome. A third is to make the members formalise their views by stating them as briefly and economically as possible – in a five-minute lecture, for instance – or of course by writing them down, though this latter is dangerous since it leads only too often to the production of a 'literary essay' on the topic rather than the kind of tough-minded dialectic that philosophy requires. These early stages are crucial. The student that can genuinely and greatly profit by reading lengthy books or writing theses knows quite a bit of philosophy already: it is the earlier stage of initiating him into the skill that is both difficult and important.

Teachers of philosophy (again Socrates is a paradigm case) will be aware that there is often a 'transference situation', as I believe some psychoanalysts describe it, between pupil and teacher: that is, the personal feelings (often reaching a high pitch of admiration, hate, love, trust and distrust, resentment and so on) become important. In this respect the parallel with psychotherapy is also close. The pupil may come to see the tutor as a tormentor, a sage, a dispenser of 'right answers about how to live', and many other things. It is an open question how far these very real feelings should be made fully conscious and discussed between teacher and pupil; and, if so, in what context. They emerge, of course, in all forms of teaching and education, and for many students they are so strong as seriously to limit the possibilities of progress. My own view is that they should be dealt with in some context (otherwise we are merely playing at moral education, or scratching the surface of it) but that it ought to be clear when we are doing this and when we are doing philosophy (or any other subject). But awareness of these factors is essential for anyone teaching philosophy.

So much depends on the psychological state, and intellectual competence, of particular pupils that it is hard to lay down general rules. For example, many students may come for seminars or tutorials on existentialist philosophy in the hope that they will derive some psychological benefit. If a student comes and starts by saying things like 'Who am I?', 'What's the meaning of life?', etc. what is the philosopher to say? Of course he can reply 'What do you mean, you know quite well who you are, you're Jane Smith and you live in 13 Acacia Avenue' or 'Read such-and-such a philosopher and you'll see that these kinds of questions are only pseudo-questions; and now let's get down to some serious analysis of language – this is philosophy, you know, not a therapy group or an existentialist wallow'. But this seems a bit too tough-minded, or tough-minded a bit too early. As with any teaching, we have to begin by showing the pupil that his *feelings* are serious enough, understood and shared by the teacher, but that his *thoughts* and what he *says* need a lot more work. Indeed the ability to make this distinction itself, and to keep it clearly in mind, might be said to be the beginning of any proper philosophical thinking.

This is not to deny that with many students it may be beneficial to do some teaching or lecturing in a way which is, initially, very far removed from their immediate concerns or interests. We might start, for instance, by discussing in a quite abstract way the logical differences between various kinds of statements — analytic, synthetic and so on. These distinctions are then found to be useful or essential when we come to discussing 'real-life' topics like democracy or anarchy. Doctrinaire views about 'starting where the student is' or 'making philosophy relevant to his real-life concerns' are of no help; of course philosophy is not a game and is relevant — the question is how to make its relevance understood. Only a fool would suppose that this can be done by making up courses to suit the fashion of the day — 'the philosophy of guerilla warfare', 'the philosophy of student protest' and so on. Philosophy is philosophy: one can learn to philosophise about a great many things, but we must choose those things that will get the students to philosophise most effectively, not those things which are the most *prima facie* 'interesting' or 'relevant'. (Just as we want students to learn history — that is, how to think historically: not any particular history. If a student learns this best by doing ancient Greek history, well and good; if another student learns best by doing the history of the Communist revolution, equally well and good. We are concerned with the form of thought, not with giving him little packages of 'interesting' or 'relevant' cultural knowledge.)

I do not think it would be profitable to say much more than this here, though the reader might like to be referred to what I and other people have said about the teaching of philosophy[2]. I will try, somewhat against my better judgement, to summarise the 'moral effects' of doing philosophy, by way of conclusion: but I must first stress that it is only by actually doing some that these effects can be appreciated.

1. The student learns to suppress his own autistic feelings in favour of the truth.
2. He learns to do this in a public dialogue, in which (a) he is given no 'answers' but (b) he is forced, because it is public, to attend to criteria of rationality.
3. He learns enough moral philosophy to appreciate the right sort of reasons for moral thought and action, and the nature of the attributes relevant to morality.
4. He learns a style of thought (a 'skill', if you like) which offers him a way out of confusion and anxiety about the major 'problems in life'.
5. He learns to develop the vitally important human or moral ability

of describing his world accurately via language.

Finally, I would like to stress that, if even half of what I have been saying is on the right lines, it seems to follow that all students should do some philosophising. Nobody is incapable of this, and we all need it. Philosophy has for too long been regarded as the preserve of intellectuals, suitable only for 'advanced' or 'able students. Certainly some will be better at it than others; but those who are better at it are not necessarily those who benefit most from it — the reverse is more likely to be true. Even quite young children are capable of becoming more conscious and critical of what they and others say, of the language and concepts they use, and hence of how they see the world and act in it. Once we get rid of false pictures of 'philosophy' as offering 'answers to life', or as something that can really be only done properly in Oxbridge Colleges, it is not hard to see the nature and importance of the skills and methods it has to offer.

References

1. Iris Murdoch, *The Sovereignty of Good* (Routledge, London).
2. John Wilson, *Thinking with Concepts and Language and the Pursuit of Truth* (Cambridge University Press, London) *Philosophy* (Heinemann London). Bernard Williams' essay in *General Education*. ed. M. Yudkin (Allen Lane, Penguin Press, London). R.M. Hare, *Essays on Philosophical Method* (Macmillan, London).

7 LITERATURE

Gabriel Chanan

What reason is there to believe that the study of literature contributes to moral development? What is generally understood to be research in this subject is an investigation of the influences on literature, not the influence of litereature on people. The study of literature is conventionally justified by the excellence of the subject matter. The beneficial effect of contact with this excellence is a presumption resting on the converging testimony of individual readers. Since these readers are nevertheless aware of getting slightly different things out of the same works, just as we take away different impressions of the same people, it is virtually impossible to define *the* function or *the* moral influence of literature. To bring a student and a work of literature into contact is to perform an experiment in which elements on both sides are likely to be unknown and uncontrolled.

Traditional literature teaching tends to concentrate on the common, seemingly stable element, the work itself, and to subordinate experimental effects to approved critical analyses. In reality the text, however assured its place in the critical canon, remains the blueprint for an endless series of further experiments, and its significance cannot therefore be delimited. Teachers of English are liable to feel that they are custodians of a great tradition of moral (as well as imaginative and psychological) insight, and they may be tempted, on the basis of content alone, to affirm that literature develops people's moral qualities. If this confidence in 'good' literature is justified, so also must be apprehensions about the contrary effects of 'bad' literature. But there is no categorical dividing line – only one of quality, and quality is debatable. The most commercialized cheap novel shares all the *fundamental* attributes of literature – language, plot, character, imagery, metaphor, 'message' and so on. And while it would be easy to get critical consensus on the difference of quality between extremes, it is not so easy in the broad penumbra where minor 'literature' meets major 'entertainment'. Thus the question of literature and morality cannot be separated from the pursuit of literary criticism.

But for present purposes we need a new departure in literary criticism – one which would focus on the effects, not merely the properties, of literature. It would need also to traverse the boundaries between canonised literature and contemporary entertainment; and since it would be concerned with works which reached wide contemporary audiences (these presumably being among those with the greatest moral influences, for better or worse), it would have to abandon that dubious defence, the critic's (or historian's) 'fifty year rule': the withholding of judgement till the issue is safely in the past.

The new criticism would be concerned not only to discern 'surprising' qualities in the new and the popular but to recognise deficiencies — perhaps particularly moral deficiencies — in the old and venerated. By no means all great literature and art is unequivocally humanitarian in tendency. Modern criticism has selected humanism in retrospect as the distinguishing feature of much that we consider greatest in literature. But literature endures and revives and captures new interest for reasons beyond those sanctioned by any particular generation of critics. Whether because criticism cannot wholly control the production or effect of literature any more than psychoanalysis can control dreams, or because criticism itself differs so much from generation to generation and within each generation, the literature which endures embodies a great variety of moral attitudes. There is as much nourishment in the canon for, say, a temperament which glories in war as for gentler spirits.

Such a new departure (a social-research based criticism) could not replace, only extend, the old criticism. It would seek to discover, not to prescribe. But it would attempt to develop explicit criteria on which the important form of patronage exercised by the education system in its use of literary texts could be partly based. The cultivation of discrimination is not censorship: it makes censorship unnecessary. But if criteria of moral effect were developed, there could be no pretence that this covered all the functions of literature. It would merely govern the use of literature for that aspect of curriculum which was designed to meet moral objectives.

It is almost mandatory nowadays to say of any educational topic under review 'much research needs to be done'. Concerning the moral impact of literature this refrain rings particularly true. But English teachers are justifiably sceptical. Most educational research instruments show little of the psychological sensitivity demonstrated (whatever its other faults) by twentieth century literary criticism. It is no use drawing up a fifty-item tick-off questionnaire to investigate the impact of a body of work of which it has been convincingly and influentially argued that multiple ambiguity is the essence.[1]

It seems unlikely that we could ever prove that literature *necessarily* has a moral effect, or if it does, that it has an effect predictable from its intrinsic properties. It is possible to read parts of the Bible for titillation, or to be a Nazi and yet love art. These paradoxes should warn us of the danger of regarding art and literature as a total substitute for that moral development to which the present writers are concerned that it should *contribute*. The value of its contribution is dependent on the presence of other factors, principally reciprocity of human relations. Even if greatness in literature were synonymous with a humanitarian message it could only enhance, not replace, relations between people.

The question then is not whether literature has but whether it can have a moral effect; and if so, what are the propitious circumstances.

The elementary components of any morality are learned before and outside formal education, in the family, the peer group, the subculture and in society at large. Any moral 'investigation' of students must treat them as already morally aware and must be prepared to recognise when they are making moral judgements in perhaps an unfamiliar dialect, or through action rather than words. Any moral investigation must treat its respondents as partners in a dialogue, not as 'subjects' in an impartial research.

Until such time as research of the necessary quality is designed,[2] practical suggestions cannot rest on more than hope, intuition and personal conviction. Since this, however, is what literature syllabuses do rest on, it does not seem exceptionally rash to sketch out a few suggestions here.

The possible uses of literature in moral development must be as varied as literature itself. We cannot control the impact of literature. Our primary function is to make it accessible: to enable it to have its impact with, initially, as little interference from ourselves as possible. Our secondary function, dependent on the successful conduct of the primary, is to promote discussion of the impact and help the discussion to focus; in doing this we can ensure that certain kinds of question are raised.

Insofar as we want to use literature as a means of extending the appreciation of motivation and emotion, we will tend to focus of the concept of character. This concept is not equivalent to the term 'personality' favoured by psychologists and sociologists; its connotations embody something deeper. It is possible to have strong personality but a weak character. 'Character' also has the meaning, essential of course for this field, of the fictitious person in a work of narrative.

It is tempting to try to equate quality in narrative with the degree of complexity with which characters are depicted. But this is to attempt that complete equivalence of artistic accomplishment with humanistic moral standards which has already been rejected above. Questions of artistic quality are crucial to the present enterprise insofar as they coincide with moral sensibility, but we should not and need not make out that this equivalence is inevitable by definition. Literature offers a vast spectrum of character depictions at a variety of levels of sophistication, and we can move among these as need and interest dictate, without necessarily following any overall hierarchy of literary merit. Quality will of course affect us 'organically', through the author's effect on our imaginations, and it will be futile — simply unconvincing — to try to discuss a moral point on the basis of an artistically poor representation.

How, then, to structure an exploration of character through literature? The most natural method is the comparison and contrast of different works according to their styles of character-depiction. This in any case forms much of the substance of literature-teaching; but it is not often used as a major structuring element in the selection of texts and shaping of discussion. We usually tend to follow roughly historical lines, relating the literature of a particular period or sequence of periods; or idealistic-evaluative lines, selecting works according to their degree of 'greatness'. The treatment of character comes in as one of a number of artistic resources (others would be 'imagery', 'theme', 'plot' and so on) throwing light on the work. But there is nothing intrinsically less authentic about an approach based on techniques of character depiction than about a historical approach, or an approach which concentrates on awarding points in that sublimely absurd league-table which T.S. Eliot called 'the ideal order of art'.

Potential frameworks for exploration — best if loosely used, dispensible if they lead to rigidity — can be inferred from works of literature themselves. For each original work, as well as being unique, amounts to a sort of reinterpretation of its precedents and influences. If Harold Pinter's plays deal repeatedly with struggles of dominion and submission, have they not, in a sense, abstracted this theme from the foregoing tradition, in which master-mastered relationships are one of the most recurrent features over different periods and styles? If the tormented interdependence of Didi and Gogo in *Waiting for Godot* reminds us not only of investigations of marriage by Ibsen and Strindberg but also of the pathos of Laurel and Hardy,[3] does this not offer us some happily unusual routes for exploration? If Shakespeare has ceaseless recourse to mistaken identity as a dramatic means, is not the same true of all kinds of popular comedy, affording endless sources of comparison and contrast, all suggestive of morally pregnant questions about role and identity — and about why (psychologically) this particular representational device should be so tirelessly captivating to audiences?

Other frameworks might focus even more closely on types of narrative technique. One might postulate two poles in narrative writing, the one of introspection and author-centredness, the other of relative equilibrium between characters. One could investigate contrasts, or perhaps unexpected points of similarity, between, on the one hand, diaries, journals and first-person novels and, on the other 'broad social canvases' such as *Middlemarch* and *War and Peace*; or between characters, such as Shakespeare's, whose inner life seems almost always to be demonstrably related to their material predicament and others, such as Chekov's, whose inner life seems to inhabit a sort of freeplay area only loosely hinged to their objective problems.

Naturally, there would have to be cautions and qualification. But these would form part of the exploration itself. If we found, as we certainly should, that fictional characters cannot be rudely detached from 'plot', 'situation', 'structure', 'poetic unity' and so forth,[4] does this not help us to realise that to make sense of people in life we must also consider situation, interaction with other people, social climate and so forth? Of course, literature cannot simply be equated with life. Nevertheless, any observations we may make about character in literature can be regarded as at least sensitising us to the problems of understanding human beings.

As regards the arbitrariness of the suggested frameworks, one would try to ensure that students grasped that these were no more than 'hypotheses' at a certain level of generality, and that we would expect to be able to cut across them with other 'hypotheses', and then to introduce sub-categories, and then still to be able to find exceptions. No narrative work is exactly the same as another in its theme or structure since, at the most precise level, the theme and structure are the work. Thus our initial categories would gradually be rendered more and more crude by our accumulated examples. This progress from broad categories to sub-categories to exceptions and finally to the point where every example is an exception seems a worthy direction for the appreciation of literature to take. It is a pity that much literature-teaching works the other way, neutralising the individual work by progressively dissolving it into historical and stylistic categories.

A different objection that might be raised is that to put literature to extra-literary uses such as moral education is to make 'illegitimate' use of the texts. But it is hard to know what would be meant by a *purely* literary approach to literature, except one which somehow contrived to dissolve literature's engagement with its own inescapably representational subject matter. The moral approach is as valid a way as any other, so long as we don't pretend that it is the only valid approach.

What we are likely to find, however, is that since literature contains the most sensitive explorations of moral problems ever recorded, some of our explicit moral discussions around works of literature may be unequal to the subtleties of the 'illustration'. Literature can 'contribute' to moral development but moral development cannot subsume the whole content of literature, any more than history or psychology can. Literature is more modest in aim than all these pursuits to which it is such a near neighbour in its favourite materials. It does not attempt to explain, only to describe. But the best descriptions outwear the best explanations, and live to nourish new generations of explanation.

The business of literature is not primarily with *identifiable* emotions. The names of identifiable moods and emotions − 'anger', 'grief', 'horror' etc., − are essentially representations of ideal states; literature is always concerned to dissolve these relatively crude idealizations into precise descriptions, to show how real states traverse these categories. Of a play, novel or poem in which the expressed emotions fell neatly into categories such as 'wonder', 'grief', 'joy' and so on, one would say that this was unsatisfying as literature. It would have been neither meaningful nor satisfying for Keats to write, 'My heart aches, and a drowsy numbness pains my sense, as though of hemlock I had drunk' if it had been adequate for him to say 'I am sad' or 'I feel a mixture of muted anguish and melancholy' or some such thing.

The tendency for the writer to dissolve identifiable emotions into complex imagery teaches us something about emotions and that is that the more deeply we wish to conceptualize or communicate a feeling, the more we tend to concentrate on the eternal causes or precipitants of emotion and the less on trying to name inner states. This calls into question what exactly would be meant by the ability 'in practice to identify emotions and moods' in oneself or others (Wilson's 'EMP's above), since it may be that the more fully aware we are of people's emotions the less satisfied we are going to be with identifying them.

This specificity of description common to good narrative is a particularly good reason for making sure that any programme of moral development does include an encounter with literature. A besetting problem of all generalised moral statements is their tendency to vagueness. Unless related to specific situations, moral statements are apt to take the form (however eloquently disguised) 'good is good; bad is bad'. Faced with networks of unillustrated, unexamined phrases like 'a sense of responsibility', 'mature values', 'conscientious citizenship', 'capacity for harmonious relationship', 'moral courage' and so forth, one cries out for specific examples. For the specific behaviour which you would regard as showing a sense of responsibility, I might see as blind conformity; what I call a harmonious relationship you might judge to be romantic self-deception; what we both prize as moral courage might be estimated by someone else to be self-righteous obstinacy. One gets nowhere without a good deal of conceptual scepticism. Such scepticism is implicitly present in − is absolutely indispensable to − all literature of any stature. Literature is, if you like, a collection of specific examples; examples of *what* is the critic's problem; the narrator's concern is primarily to be descriptively specific, and the very absence of the easier kinds of names for human emotions and moral properties will help us to maintain our essential scepticism in the face of the abstract moral terminology which abounds in some of the other disciplines.

A second suggested approach for discussion of the moral aspects of literature is to focus on the explicit depiction of moral dilemmas. This is almost a cornerstone of modern literature and I am compelled to use the conventional let-out, 'it cannot be more than touched on here', without wishing to imply that if only one had more space one would be only too ready to do it justice. Formal limits are sometimes a blessing — they enable one to say a part when it would have been impossible to say the whole.

In the literature of our era, bewilderment has emerged as one of the foremost themes. Moral ambivalence has become an almost mandatory part of modern subject matter. In Henry James it expresses itself as the perfect counterpoint of 'optical illusions' — situations which permit of exactly contradictory moral interpretations. In Kafka it forms the sense of guilt which lacks any corresponding sense of having made a moral choice about which to feel guilty. In Isaac Babel it is the dilemma of revolution — the moral struggle which employs or releases immoral forces. In Joseph Heller and countless other authors it is the absurdity of war, the defence which seems to destroy the values it seeks to defend.

But it would be an evasion to conclude that our moral condition, as registered in the literature of our times, is one of total and unrelieved bewilderment. (It would also, of course, be an illusion to think that we could teach the literature of former eras as a means of transmitting a moral certainty which we no longer possess.) We should recognise that doubt of the correctness of one's moral judgement is a sign of moral seriousness, though no guarantee of finding an eventual certainty. What may appear to be a negative direction in modern literature, a preoccupation with mental breakdown, squalor, 'the absurd', is *at its best* a search for the organic base-line of morality, a search for the ground on which we must morally reconstitute ourselves. To have credence, any new morality must attempt to be free of the worldly-power bias, the institutional nature, in which previous moralities have lost their credibility. The modern writer at his best is attempting that very separation of morality from any particular power-bound moral code which the first chapter of this book advocates — but he has not found it easy. I emphasise 'at his best' because this is clearly untrue of a great many second-rate works. The problem for us, and for the student of moral education (teacher and student are on much the same footing here) is to distinguish works which embody a 'no holds barred' moral exploration from those, superficially similar, which embody mere moral bankruptcy. This problem could not be wholly settled by the teacher on his own, but would form part of the teaching/learning approach itself.

As regards contemporary and almost-contemporary works, we will not be able to deduce reliable guidelines as to moral content or seriousness either from critical acclaim or critical denigration. There is fashionable emptiness and unfashionable seriousness at both popular and minority levels. (But to rely on the works of former eras does not solve the problem either. If their morality is still relevant to us, it is also still under dispute. Different generations and schools of criticism agree that *Hamlet* is 'great', but not *why* it is great.) The plays of Harold Pinter, to take a vivid example, were first condemned and then acclaimed without in either phase much conscious consideration, as far as one can judge from reviews and criticisms, of their moral properties. They have been regarded both by admirers and denigrators as belonging to a genre of suspended morality, of 'absurdity', simply because they disdain the traditional language of morality and concentrate instead on the actual contours of morally-problematic situations. The *Caretaker* was regarded by many commentators as being morally reticent to the point of muteness. Yet, coolly read, it is a play about the charity of those who have little and the dignity of those who have nothing. Arthur Miller, on the other hand, is regarded by some of the trendier critics as old fashioned and not 'significant' because his plays are morally explicit on the model of Greek tragedies; yet if they prove to outlive scores of more shallowly despairing (as well as of shallowly optimistic) works it will not be the first time that a mainstream in literature has been mistaken for a backwater.

The teacher's function, if he adopts this approach, cannot be to settle all moral-criticial questions in advance. His main energies must be in the selection of works to provide apt contrasts in the moral sensibilities they embody, and in ensuring that the content of these sensibilities is fully exposed in discussion. The teacher's own, let us hope relatively mature, moral consciousness, will influence the discussion perhaps more by structuring it, by quietly bringing various moral concepts into currency with students, than by presenting explicit moral propositions.

One further tentative generalisation about modern literature may serve to link the two suggested approaches ('character' and 'morally problematic subject matter') and so permit the appearance of a conclusion to this essay: moral bewilderment and the sense of disintegration of character are closely connected. Dostoevsky, Kafka and others portray protagonists whose values are so shaken to the roots that they lose confidence even in their own concept of themselves. This close connection of man's self-concept and his morality confirms the underlying theme of the moral development scheme outlined in the first chapter above: that morality depends on one's appreciation of the autonomy of individual human beings, self and others. Any credible morality depends on acceptance of the notion that inidividuals have at least some degree of responsibility for their own behaviour. The myth that an individual has complete and unextenuated responsibility for his behaviour has been exposed by the modern recognition of the power of forces outside his consciousness – evolution, environment, history, culture and the subconscious. If, however, the sum of these forces amounts to a total determination of his behaviour, there is no room left either for character or morality – though 'personality' would still be visible. This is a feasible position to take, but if it were true, one wonders why the thought of it should depress us, make us feel somehow unrecognised. All these forces, including the most objective imaginable scientific statements are, *in their explicit form,* themselves the products of human consciousness. To attribute to them in turn complete responsibility for that consciousness may yet, so far from being the most relentless realism, prove as contorted a fantasy as some of the medieval superstitions which it supplanted.

If this has been a chapter of doubts, there seems little need of apology. We need to show more than that a particular subject or activity *could* be a basis for moral development or *could* lead to moral awareness. We have stated with regard to literature that it need not produce any moral effect at all. This surely applies equally to the other subjects represented in this symposium. We must not be satisfied to show simply that there is some connection between moral development and any given subject – that much does without saying. If we are asking what is or could be the contribution of a subject to moral development we must try to suggest the difference between those ways of teaching it which would and those which would not lead to moral enlightenment, and try to be sceptical about the 'would'. We ought to distinguish between moral objectives being inherent to some extent in the subject matters (which one may doubt to be considerable) and moral development as one criterion to which the teaching of various subject matters could be made to conform. We would then be in a position to start asking ourselves why we feel the need to establish moral development as a criterion of education, and how, as practitioners in an education system which exercises wordly power (over career prospects, mainly) as well as influence, we can sufficiently transcend our situation to apply such a criterion in good faith.

References

1. See William Empson, *Seven Types of Ambiguity,* (Chatto and Windus, London 1930).
2. The recently published Schools Council survey of reading, *Reading for Meaning,* has a second volume devoted to pupils' reading habits and responses. Although the researches reviewed in that volume are not, on the whole, specifically addressed to the *effects* of literature, they do provide a good deal of valuable information on tastes, habits and responses, which would provide an excellent basis for research of the kind suggested in this essay. Pat D'Arcy, *Reading for Meaning, Vol. 2: The Reader's Response* (Hutchinson Educational for the School Council, London 1973).
3. Critical analysis of films, as opposed to literature, suffers from difficulty of detailed access to the original. In the case of Laurel and Hardy, however, there is an excellent critical essay by Charles Barr which includes summaries of the films and copious illustrations. Charles Barr, *Laurel and Hardy* (Studio Vista, London 1967).
4. Perhaps the best explication of the unity of works of narrative is Henry James's essay 'The Art of Fiction'.

8 DRAMA

Roy Knight

That the study of drama may contribute significantly to the moral development of students has already been suggested in the previous chapter by Gabriel Chanan, and in other chapters in this section; and it is probably helpful to begin by examining why this is so. Those offering contributions on the study of literature and media-studies in film or television might well be expected to embrace works in dramatic form, and it is therefore not surprising to find Gabriel Chanan drawing his examples from Beckett, Ibsen, Strindberg, Chekhov, Pinter and Arthur Miller as well as Shakespeare, Charlie Chaplin, and Laurel & Hardy; or Gerald Collier inviting the study of Shaw's *St. Joan* or Eliot's *Murder in the Cathedral* alongside the films referred to in Chapter 13.

It is, however, interesting to note that of the four specific History topics chosen by James Henderson for more detailed consideration in Chapter 10, three have been extensively considered in contemporary dramatic forms (this is not significantly true of the Slave Trade, about which the novel has been, perhaps, the most eloquent forum). The moral issues of the Irish Question have been the mainspring for the work of Synge and O'Casey, and a majory influence in some of the work of Shaw, Beckett and Behan. The Port-Royal was a direct influence upon Racine's dramatic development, especially in his later religious dramas *Esther* (1689) and *Athalie* (1691)[1] not to mention his own short history of that institution (published posthumously in 1742), while it seems likely that the Jansenists were instrumental in securing the five-year suppression of Moliere's *Tartuffe* lest this attack upon religious hypocrisy should be misconstrued as satirising their own beliefs and practices. And the final example, Hiroshima, is that which is also considered in Chapter 11 by David Edge in the study of Science, noting that at least two plays upon the subject have been produced.[2]

This cross-reference is not merely coincidental: it serves to establish and reinforce the fact that frequently, almost inevitably, the dramatic form will enshrine and represent major issues of moral conflict; and that for the majority of people in many historical periods (fifth century Athens, western Europe in the Middle Ages, Elizabethan England, most of the Twentieth Century world through radio and television) drama has been the commonest art form in which audiences have been invited to witness and respond to matters of moral concern. This also accounts for the fact that censorship in the media of theatre, film, television and radio has been (and to some extent remains) more pervasive and persistent than in other literary forms.

It is not necessary to repeat here the discussion of censorship provided in the preceding chapter, arguing the abundant evidence that fear and suspicion of the immoral effects of literary work, often resulting in explicit censorship, inevitably presuppose that other works, or the same works viewed by those with different opinions, must have a moral influence upon their readers or audiences. Long after formal licensing of literature (and journalism) had been abandoned, the Lord Chamberlain's Office continued to exercise control over all stage productions; the certificate of the British Board of Film Censors is still necessary for the public exhibition of films, and by a historical accident which made them responsible for public *safety*, local Watch Committees continue to exercise *moral* control over film exhibition, with the power locally to override the industry's Certificate. A measure of television censorship is written into the Act governing independent television,[3] and the Board of Governors of the British Broadcasting Corporation undoubtedly do (though their Charter does not require that they should) exercise similar control over BBC television and radio productions. There is little enough research evidence of the effects (moral or immoral) of plays or films upon their audiences, but there is abundant evidence both general and specific (whether from vast investment in television advertising, or in public reaction to *Cathy Come Home* or *A Clockwork Orange*) to indicate public belief in an effect, and deep personal response to the moral issues raised.

Before proceeding further, it is necessary to indicate some of the areas of dramatic studies, in order to consider in what ways these may be the means of assisting the moral development of students. In higher education, the study of drama may (and sometimes does) include all of the following activities:

1. Experience of theatre or of other dramatic media such as film television or radio ('going to the theatre, or to the cinema', 'watching telly', and so on).
2. Study of play-texts (whether by lecture, seminar, tutorial discussion, or personal ('closed') study: such activity is indistinguishable in methodology from the study of any other literary forms such as poetry or the novel).
3. The production of plays (through rehearsals leading probably to performance, though some production workshops may not have any final performance in view).
4. Training in histrionic or production skills (speech, movement,

interpretation, costume, make-up, lighting, setting, direction and stage-management).

5. Creating drama (which may mean play-writing, but which also includes individual or group improvisation, and many non-verbal forms of drama such as mime and dance).

6. Theatre history (including theatre architecture, production and acting style, the social context of theatre, and the management structures of dramatic production).

7. Exercises and experiments (some of which will clearly be related to training (4) and creating (5) above, but these may extend into areas of therapeutic drama having very little connection, if any, with these other objectives of dramatic studies).

Of these seven areas, I do not intend to make any further reference to (2) since discussion of the literary study of play-texts has been effectively and relevantly covered by the previous chapter; and the study of (6), the area of theatre history, seems to have little connection with moral development other than as history or sociology, which are elsewhere dealt with. It is with the remaining areas, production, training and creating drama, related to theatrical experience, and with various dramatic exercises and experiments, that we shall be concerned.

In the earlier chapters of the first section, the authors have attempted to set the context, from the viewpoints of philosophy and the social sciences, within which we may attempt to understand and explore to what extent the study of various disciplines may contribute to moral development. John Wilson warns us against the dangers of educating students in the moral area where this process leads to an identification of 'moral' with 'in accordance with the values I personally favour'; and Peter Tomlinson, outlining a variety of psychological perspectives, draws our attention first to Lawrence Kohlberg's work in which 'the core of each stage is a conception of justice' which organises patterns of role-taking in moral conflict situations, proceeding from stereotypical images to more complex analyses of role and behaviour. Both these comments are immediately relevant to the study of drama, since drama immediately and inevitably places its students (and its tutors) in a role-playing situation. Drama is essentially representation: we are invited, indeed required, to assume roles, to investigate a situation, to solve a problem by pretending, by make-believe. This very process helps to remove the teacher and the author from the position of authority, from the danger of dogmatism. In most academic disciplines, the study-text (whether it is a historical or social 'document' or the expression of a critical viewpoint) will inevitably be viewed as *in some way* an 'authority', a direction of opinion, a conditioning statement; and the teacher, by his choice of the text, will be seen as another 'authority', either reinforcing or disputing the values and judgements of the original. The situation is, perhaps, less weighted in its structure in the study of any literary work, where the 'text' is a fiction: but even here, as Gabriel Chanan recognises, there is almost always an inherent suspicion that this piece of literature is one that the teacher likes/dislikes and that we are invited to share his response; and contains a moral viewpoint which we are invited to accept/reject. The process of studying literature places both teacher and student over against the work being studied: both are essentially dissociated from the work, and the first (perhaps the only) response must be one of judgement. But in the process of studying drama, teacher and student are associated with the work, must first get within it (must enact and interpret it) before responding critically to it; and even then probably exercising judgement over the enactment, over the interpretation rather than over the work itself. Thus, in the study of drama, only when we have made the work 'our own work', the situation or problem 'our own situation or problem', the reaction of the characters and their solution 'our own reaction and solution' can we begin to examine its values, its opinion, its moral stance and judgement. We shall then be examining the values, opinions, and judgement which we have ourselves, for the time being, adopted and advanced, arising from the situations which we have ourselves explored and experienced.

Another psychological perspective offered to us in Peter Tomlinson's analysis (Chapter 2) is the *Conceptual systems theory* of Harvey, Hunt and Schroder: and I was immediately impressed by how closely Schroder's analysis of the information-processing aspect of this conception of personality parallels the commonest process of studying and rehearsing a dramatic text: (1) Differentiation (2) Discrimination (3) Integration. As the individual develops a conceptual framework of growing complexity to analyse, organise and interpret his environment and his personal response to it (learning to understand and to *behave*), so the individual drama student approaches a role and its environment (the play), gradually developing a more complex conceptual framework by which the text can be analysed, the production organised, and the work interpreted (learning to understand and to *act out* the text). In processing the information (or data) of the text, the initial response is at the level of recognition of elementary stimuli (the persons in the play, the situations, the 'story') — this is analagous to Schroder's *differentiation*; as the capacity grows to distinguish 'stimuli',finer distinctions can be made with regard to motivation, depth of character, the linguistic structure of given roles within the play — *discrimination;* and the processing (study/rehearsal/production) may then reach the higher order of judgement and interpretation with regard to the complexity of relationship and behaviour, and the formulation of these new understandings into a view of the work as a whole — *integration.*

It is perhaps a little unfair to extend a precise and limited analysis such as Schroder's to a much vaguer process of realising a dramatic text, but I do so merely to reinforce the thesis that dramatic study is a process more directly concerned with personal response to and an analysis of uniquely experienced situations than many other educational or learning processes; and if such philosophical and psychological analyses of how people behave, and how their understanding and behaviour may be related to the development of moral views and judgements have any validity, then such validity may more easily be seen as transferable to dramatic studies than to many other disciplines. And I would wish to attend equally to John Wilson's distinction that moral *development* belongs to a learning process rather than to an *extending or toughening up* process: he says 'Coming to perform successfully in the moral area is more like learning to play chess or the piano, than it is like simply coming to have bigger biceps or more brain cells: it is something which we *do* and *learn* for ourselves rather than something which just *happens* to us'. Drama is the sequence of *doing and learning from doing*; not merely the response to something happening beyond us. Moral development is thus more actively assisted by the dramatic process since the required discipline of the subject is consonant with the very philosophical, psychological and, we might add, social processes by which we believe moral understanding and judgement to be formulated.

At this point, however, it is probably wise to tackle the inherent paradox in the dramatic situation: this is the paradox involved in identification with any dramatic role or dramatic situation, and a paradox implied earlier in this chapter by the reservation 'for the time being' in discussing the actor's voicing of beliefs or opinions belonging to the role, or his assumption of relationships and experiences pertaining to the situation and structure of the play. The assumption of or association with a part requires a dissociation from self, from one's own personality and behaviour; yet the successful creation of that role can be achieved only from one's own personality and experience. If this paradox were not allowable, then only an ennobled Venetian negro guilty of murdering his wife could attempt the role of Othello, and there would be even fewer candidates to attempt Hamlet. The process of stepping outside oneself in order to 'be' someone else, and then drawing from one's own resources, attitudes, values, judgements and experiences in order to achieve a greater understanding of the motivation of the character one is assuming is what we call 'acting'. If this process automatically resulted in greater moral understanding, then we could expect all actors and actresses to be 'greater' moral beings than those in other professions; and I have no reason to believe that such is the case: indeed, there is a sort of historic mythology about the profession which assumes rather the opposite. But we can argue —

and I would wish to do so – that for the teacher and student concerned seriously with moral development, this process may be exploited to provide greater insights into self, and deeper understanding of one's own attitudes and motivation. There is perhaps a distinction to be made here between the apprentice actor and the student of drama. Because the professional actor will, he hopes, spend a lifetime being other people, this professional pressure will diminish both the need and the opportunity for feed-back, and for transfer of training to the self-image; but the student of drama, whose study and training are essentially part of a process of self-education, may more easily be persuaded to exploit the feed-back element to increase self-awareness and understanding. In Chapter 3, Douglas Hamblin refers to Oppenheim's comment that 'behaviour is a product of the way in which we perceive our environment'; and he himself, discussing various applications of depth psychology, states: 'We want to predict, and to achieve this we build up networks of associations between events and behaviour, knitting these into a causal framework.' For the *actor*, the environment to be perceived, the causal framework conditioning his response to events and resulting in specific behaviour is the role he plays in the drama on the stage in the theatre; but for the drama student, the environment to be perceived, the causal framework in which he will behave is more likely to be the world in which he lives and behaves rather than the play in which he acts a part; what is for the actor a professional end will be for the student an educational means to a quite different (and more personal) end.

Nevertheless, it would be wrong to exclude or underrate the experience and value for moral development that may be acquired not merely through the study and production of plays but through the training in skills related to drama. So far, our discussion has been concerned almost entirely with those components in the moral area which John Wilson has classified as PHIL in the first chapter: the concept of person, and the use of this concept in forming relationships with others, thoughts of others, and actions towards others. Much of the training area of drama study is concerned to develop the EMP and GIG components of Wilson's classification.

Much of the work done in dramatic training, whether as exercises or related to texts and production, will be concerned with language, especially the spoken language and the translation of written language into speech. A great deal of emphasis has been laid upon the necessity for precision in the use and in the understanding of language if any effective moral development is to take place (see Chapter 6), but perhaps too much emphasis has been given in equating 'the use of language' with 'understanding the meaning of words'. Many, many circumstances in which moral issues will be communicated or moral

121

decisions required arise from the spoken rather than the written word (for from written reports of works originally spoken) — one can think of a variety of political, professional, family or personal situations. And in these cases, many dimensions of meaning have to be recognised which transcend vocabulary — dimensions of tone, inflection, emphasis, pace, volume and structure. At the very simplest level, the statement *'That's* wrong' (which the stress upon the first element) may be signifying a mis-ordering of experience, puzzlement in a situation ('There's something odd about this') or a variety of other objective judgements depending upon context; but as soon as we transfer the stress to the second element and say 'That's *wrong*', the statement begins to assume more subjective, and quite probably moral, overtones. Some social science researchers have begun to pay attention to this aspect of communication, which has long received investigation and experiment by those engaged in dramatic study,[4] and the more we are concerned with sensitivity to the meanings of language, the more training we need not merely in the ambiguities of vocabulary, but also in the variation of meaning and implication arising from qualities in spoken language that are inadequately communicated or incommunicable in written language.

But words are not by any means the sole communicators of meaning, of feeling, of opinions, of attitudes, or of judgements. This is recognised in folk-sayings such as 'Actions speak louder than words' or 'A nod is as good as a wink'; and only very slowly are we beginning to collect and analyse evidence of this greater variety of communication processes. Much of this interest arises from the popularization of zoological and anthropological studies; and subsequently from psychological research into aspects of social interaction. The actor and the director engaged in dramatic studies have of course always been concerned with gesture, with stance, with movement, with relative positions which communicate relationships and attitudes to an audience: dominance and submission, respect and contempt, affection and distaste, protection and rejection are a few of the many relationships which are as likely to be communicated by the body as by speech, or as well as by speech.[5]

What acting and production have always, to some extent, been about has been the observation and analysis of human behaviour in order to represent such behaviour effectively in dramatic representations relevant to life experiences; and this has been increasingly true during the last two centuries as naturalism gradually developed as the dominant mode of theatrical representation. What has now begun to happen, most obviously over the last couple of decades, is that the techniques used in drama for such observation and analysis are being taken over by the psychologist both to analyse and to condition human behaviour in a real-life as compared with a drama-fiction situation. Thus we can find many of the exercises and disciplines employed in sensitivity training used both by actors in their stage-training and by 'patients' in the care of depth psychologists, in group therapy and social interaction groups. More and more attention is being given to tactile experience, physical contact, eye-gaze situations, gestural communication, non-verbal sound, and exercises based on positioning, group arrangement, stance and movement.

None of this work, whether in drama or in group dynamics, can be seen as automatically supporting moral development; but rather as refining the tools by which moral development may be achieved. These, in John Wilson's terms, are the EMP and GIG components, especially EMP(1) and (2) (Cs) – the identification of moods and emotions in oneself and in others at conscious level; and GIG(2) (NVC) – the skill element in non-verbal communication with others. The components have to be recognised (in one self and in others); they have to be understood and interpreted; they have to be refined to reduce ambiguity; they have to be applied (KRAT) in the situations requiring moral assessment and judgement leading to action. The study of drama repeatedly presents the context in which such recognition, interpretation, refinement and application can and must take place.

The especial value of drama as a discipline is (again in John Wilson's terms) that it is not *autistic:* its concepts and/or its experiments 'are not divorced from the real world, but can be redeployed to give us genuine information which we would not otherwise possess.' Any work in drama, whether concerned with the creation or the interpretation of dramatic material, must relate the specific experience to the generic context. We must explore and understand the time and period (the historical context), the place and situation (the geographical and topographical context), the background, class and occupation of the characters (the sociological context), their motivation, attitudes and behaviour (the psychological and perhaps philosophical context), their vocabulary, language structure and other communicational processes (the linguistic context). I believe this to be true whether we are spectators, interpreters, or creators of the drama: the differences are likely to be of degree rather than kind.

There is a degree of audience involvement in any dramatic representation whatever the medium (whether theatre or film or television or radio) which is distinct from (and I believe more intense than) our involvement in reading a book or attending to a lecture; and this degree of involvement invites and often demands a disciplined response, sets in motion an active investigation, as complex as (though less intense than) that of the active participants in the representation. Whether we think of this in terms of Aristotelean *katharsis* or in more complex terms of perception psychology something happens not only *for* us but *to* us and *in* us. Those more directly engaged in the interpretation, the actors and director, will inevitably have carried their responses and investigations further, including response to and investigation of elements which have been rejected from as well as those which have been incorporated in the performance, the representation. Perhaps the highest order of response and investigation will be achieved in the act of creation by those not interpreting roles, translating a text into action, but creating roles and inventing a 'text' by the processes of improvisation. The value of this latter process has been recognised not only in the role-play exercises of psychotherapy, but also in the extensive use of improvisation in the rehearsal stages of formal dramatic production. Many directors, from Brecht onwards, have seen rehearsal not as working *from* a text, but as working *towards* it by improvisations, by the use of rehearsal texts distinct from the performance text, by demanding action in real-life situations prior to the creation of on-stage situations.

There is now wide recognition in professional as well as amateur theatre that drama does not inevitably proceed from the interpretation and presentation of *an* author's text. Group theatre in which the 'play' is created by actors and director working from original documents and/or personal experiences has been accepted as an equally valid way of creating and performing a play, and of providing an entertainment.[6]

It is not possible within the confines of this chapter to discuss work upon particular plays, and even if it were I doubt its relevance or help. Virtually every dramatic presentation, from a Sophoclean tragedy to a Whitehall farce, contains and exploits situations of moral conflict or decision. These situations may be at family level, at a social or political level, at a theological or philosophical level. How, why and whether these moral elements and implications are to be exploited, analysed and developed will be the choice and responsibility of the teacher, and of the students, engaged in the situation and the process. Sometimes the objectives of the process will be specific and explicit — if we are using dramatic method in direct attempts to secure moral development; sometimes they may be implicit, and arise as incidental moral discussions from more purely dramatic objectives. Either area presents a field for research.

Whatever experiments may be conducted, however research is established, the study of drama will offer unique contexts for the investigation of moral development. They will be contexts in which the content almost invariably relates to moral issues, and/or in which the skills are inevitably relevant to the awareness and sensitivity necessary for moral development; they will be contexts in which the dogmatic authority of the teacher has been significantly reduced or totally eliminated by the methodology of the discipline; they will be contexts which automatically enshrine some of the psychological and philosophical perspectives and models within which the investigation must be framed; they will be contexts in which the situations and subject-matter are often closely related to personal experience and behaviour in real-life situations; they will be contexts in which the individuals have come to terms with the paradox of dissociation through identification; they will be contexts in which the non-verbal components are likely to receive as much as or more consideration than the verbal components. This would seem to me to be a relatively rich field in which to work.

References

1. Sainte-Beuve, *Port-Royal* vol. VI Ch. 11.
2. See Ch. 11, note 15. It might be added that another examination of the scientist's moral dilemma is presented in Brecht's *Galilee*; and a more general example in Charles Morgan's *The Burning Glass*.
3. *Television Act, 1963* Section 3 Clause 1 (a) . . . 'that nothing is included in the programme which offends against good taste or decency or is likely to encourage or incite to crime or to lead to disorder or to be offensive to public feeling'. This clause has been invoked to prevent the showing of such diverse productions as a Denis Mitchell documentary containing a shot of a 'stripper' in action, and a *World in Action* programme about the costs of Britain's nuclear missile programme.
4. See for example two studies by J. Davitz, & L. Davitz, in *Communication* vol. 9 pp. 6-13 and 110-17; and as long ago as 1939, G. Fairbanks & W. Pronevost, 'An experimental study of the pitch characteristics of the voice during the expression of emotion'. *Speech Monographs,* vol. 6 pp. 87-104. Also: J. Davitz et al., *The Communication of Emotional Meaning.* (McGraw Hill, 1964) which deals with emotional communication in media other than speech.
5. This may be seen as originating with Charles Darwin's *The Expression of the Emotions in Man and Animals* (1872) and extending to Desmond Morris's *The Naked Ape* (1967) or Hans Haas's *The Human Animal* (1970). References to more specialised work may be found in Ray Birdwhistell's *Introduction to Kinesics* (1952); and in a variety of work by Adam Kendon, Albert Mehrabian, R.V. Exline and others; see Part Two (The Elements of Social Behaviour') in *Social Encounters: Readings in Social Interaction.* ed. Michael Argyle (Penguin Modern Psychology Readings: Penguin Books, Harmondsworth, 1973).
6. The best-known professional work has probably been that of Peter Cheeseman with the company of the Victoria Theatre, Stoke-on-Trent. For amateur work, see Peter Chilver's *Improvised Drama* (Batsford, London 1967) and Brian Clark's *Group Theatre* (Pitman, London 1971).

9 THEOLOGY

James Robertson

One of the common ways of exemplifying the relationship between morality and religion is to point to the fact that in the western world, for generations, the two were inextricably entwined. Religion formed the authoritative basis for promulgating the moral code commonly accepted in society. When, as a result of the advance of empiric science, mankind began to lose its traditional religious foundation for living, then consequently there came a breakdown in strict patterns of moral behaviour. This has led to a determined attempt to sever morality and moral development from religious roots and to base a fresh understanding of these human characteristics on the basis of natural reason.

This point is made now for an oblique reason, viz. that the popular climate of opinion is such that many are suspicious of any writing which would seem, however innocently, to establish afresh, connections between religion and morality, or between the systematic study of religion from a theological stance and the systematic study of moral development.

The basic question (formulated in Part I of this symposium for those writing in Part II) would seem to be this: *In what ways can the study of theology (religion), in higher education institutions, contribute in a relevant fashion, to the study and furtherance of moral development?*

It is interesting to observe at the outset that the way in which Part I has been expounded is heavily dependent on a model taken from the world of positivist science and modern technology. The *logic* of our task is (see page 14):

1. Establish our objectives.
2. Determine the sort of processes likely to achieve them.
3. Try out these processes in educational programmes.
4. Test whether in fact they work.

I am indebted to William Burton, Teachers' College, Columbia University,[1] who has pointed out how close this is to the 'Henry Ford Problem-Solving Method'.

1. Determine the optimum product description based on market analysis.
2. Design the machinery to produce the optimum product.
3. Organise the machinery in logical sequence for maximum

production.
4. Implement quality control procedures to prevent product deviance from standards.

He re-states this more simply as:
1. State objectives.
2. Design experiences.
3. Organise and implement experiences.
4. Evaluate.

This close analogy makes the point that the model used to construct the macro-curriculum of our higher education institutions (i.e. the spread of the disciplines taught therein) could very well determine whether or not theology (religion) is one of these disciplines. Where this study is to be found there is public recognition of its relevance to our understanding of the human condition. Where it is not found, one needs to probe and determine whether the reasons are accidental, or represent a limitation of the range of reality which has relevance for the formulation of objectives. This is perhaps the first contribution that the systematic study of religion makes to the spectrum of reality related to the moral.

In places where the study proceeds there are two further points to be made:

(a)   The study is not there *operationally* for moral development purposes. It shares this understanding of its role with the other disciplines. Therefore any illumination or help it gives to the process of moral development is a derived one.

(b)   It will have been noted how difficult it is to avoid circumlocutions or duplications in finding a title for the 'discipline' under discussion. Our institutions of higher education have a range of names: Theology, Religious Studies, Biblical Studies, Divinity, Religious Education. This transitional phenomenon is symptomatic of the way in which educational philosophy has made its mark on the traditions. Other factors have impinged, notably those coming from the secular humanist understanding of man, from the appearance of multi-faith communities in Britain, and from the recognisable predominance of the Christian tradition itself, in the culture as a whole.

These considerations set the context for a closer attempt to see the ways in which doing theology or studying religion can contributer to the study and furtherance of moral development.

It is illuminating to look first at the content of Theology/Religious Study courses in universities in England and Wales. Howard Marratt has done this inconnection with his background research for the report, 'The Recruitment, Employment, and Training of Teachers of Religious Education' (B.C.C., London 1971) Paragraph 98 records a simple analysis of 18 faculty courses in universities. Thus:

One subject degrees subject content	Compulsory	Optional (including further study)
Old Testament religion/theology	15	4
New Testament Greek texts	13	10
Old Testament history	12	4
Old Testament/New Testament English texts	12	3
Church history/doctrine (early)	11	8
New Testament theology	10	4
Systematic/historical theology	10	9
New Testament/classical Greek	9	–
New Testament: person and teaching of Jesus	8	–
Philosophy of religion	8	15
Old Testament Hebrew texts	7	12
Church history (another period)	7	9
New Testament introduction	6	–
Modern theology	5	7
History/study of (a) religion	5	3
Ethics	5	7
Comparative study of religion	–	5

The weighty emphasis on biblical, linguistic, and textual, historical and doctrinal studies would at first sight seem to indicate a poor correlation with the 'components' Wilson has listed as essential for 'success in the moral area'. But if we except the technical linguistic and textual studies, it is interesting to note that the content has running through it a 'people-in-community' thread which is of the very stuff that the 'moral' is concerned with. It is perhaps here that there is to be found one fundamental contribution of this discipline to moral development.

Further thought leads one to pick out several strands of relevance. First there is within the evolving community in space-time the very notion of person as precious and unique; of conflict between persons and between groups; of practical resolution in time of the same; of modes of communication direct and indirect, formal and informal; of real and spurious notivations; of growth in conceptual understanding; of the role of the morally sensitive in society; of obedience to vision and principle; of the power of mystery, myth and ideology in promoting particular choice and decision making. The list is almost descriptively endless.

Of course to make this claim of potential says nothing of the actuality of pedagogic success through the presentation of content. Nevertheless, the potentiality is evident.

If one looks next at the expressed aims of those designing theology/ religious studies courses in universities the information is slight. (cf. para. 100 *op. cit.*)

Categories of Response, from some correspondents (out of 18)

(a)	A study of Jewish-Christian tradition	12
(b)	A preparation of men for the Church and other professions	7
(c)	A grounding in basic theology	7
(d)	The development of critical/creative judgement	7
(e)	The study of *a* religion	5
(f)	Development of links with other subject interpretations	5
(g)	Personal interest of the student	5
(h)	Study of 19th and 20th century religious questions	3

Of these aims (b), (d), (f) and (h) are possibly the most significant for our present considerations, and we may consider them seriatim.

Theology and Preparation for Professions It would seem that this study is healthily undertaken by persons with a variety of eventual professional interests: e.g. ministers, teacher, social workers, personnel officers, etc. Very often, for the professionally uncommitted it is an attractive study because it is in fact different from what was studied in depth at school. It is interesting how part of the motivation seems to revolve round 'person-serving in community'. Perhaps this indicates a possible expression of an even instrumentality in regard to the 'I-other' feeling on which rightly so much stress is laid.

Development of Critical Judgement This hardly needs elaboration, for it is a dimension properly claimed by any discipline. Perhaps the only point to note is that the past hundred years has seen an emphasis on 'rigorous critical analysis' of biblical and traditional matters which is almost unparalleled in any other literature-faith-community area of human concern. Any student subjected to this sort of initiation must have every possibility of actually acquiring much of the KRAT (1) orientation which, as such, is an agreed pre-requisite of growth in the capacity to 'do' (OPU) ethics.

Development of the Links with Other Subject Interpretations There are two aspects of this to be noted. The first is already visible in the list on page 128. In doing theology one is calling upon the resources associated with (at least) the disciplines of languages and literature, history, philosophy, archaeology, anthropology and sciences. One cannot penetrate theological interpretation without uncovering to some extent the way in which other stances change the view. This surely makes for a strengthening of the GIG strand in moral development.

The second aspect relates to the steady increase in English universities of the use of theology as a subsidiary study, and of the concept of joint honours courses with theology as an equal partner. For example Hull offers theology with any one of history, music and drama. Here again the same links with GIG are joined to factors more commonly associated with EMP.

Study of 19th- and 20th-century Religious Questions We see the 'relevance' syndrome most vividly here at work and it is perhaps in these encounters that the moral issues become most personal. When those studying religion turn to questions of life, death, war, unity, ecological stewardship, obscenity, materialism, violence, etc. they come up against moral matters involving an understanding of, and feeling for, the predicament of man in society. They grapple with these both in simulated and actual context, and (despite the failures in personal choice and action) commitment is explored and achieved. But all these still potentially.

Loukes has written[2] 'All education proceeds by offering experiences of some kind; interpretation of some kind; and some measure, at the end of it all, of choice by the learner of what experiences and interpretations he will hold on to as elements in his own view or map of the human situation, with which he will find his way about the world. We consider a process educational, . . . when it offers a selection of experience that we consider significant or valuable; when we teach it for its significance or value; and when we enable the pupil to make some personal pattern from it, to be authentically himself within it.'

In this short description of the experience of doing theology at a university, we have tried to indicate its theoretical possibilities for an 'interpretation' frame of reference and for personal choice and decision making. Yet universities concentrate rightly on what might be called the 'pure' aspects of the area being studied. There are two other institutions which do theology or religious studies much more from am 'applied' aspect. These are colleges of education and theological colleges. Of course the 'pure-applied' antithesis can be on occasions misleading, but the distinction serves to underline two facets of the relation of theological studies to moral development in higher education. These are (i) the methods used in the educational process, and (ii) the character of the community which does the educating. This is not to maintain that these are not also significant in universities (and polytechnics). This is far from being so. It is only that a consideration of work in the other institutions will pinpoint the relevant factors more vividly.

A group of theological teachers in a report called 'Doing Theology Today' (C.I.O., London 1969) have some interesting observations and descriptions that merit a wider audience, and exemplify the thinking which animates these professionals. 'The same intellectual integrity, the same sense of the living tradition of Christian truth, and the same openness to contemporary questions must characterise the study of theology in whatever institution it is pursued.' They go on to isolate two factors:

(a) The need for the study of theology 'constantly to be brought to bear upon the realities of prayer and worship'.

(b) The need for 'careful integration of theological study with planned practical experience'.

For the purposes of this chapter one can quote two experiments related to the second of these factors (*op. cit.* p. 10)

(i)   'As an example . . . we would point to the courses arranged by the Chaplain of Littlemore Mental Hospital for members of the theological colleges in or near Oxford. Visits to wards are carefully planned and each visitor has to make reports on the conversations he has had; the day includes a seminar at the hospital, during which these reports are discussed in the presence of the Chaplain, and often also a lecture from one of the staff. Back at the college, further discussion takes place, and periodically an opportunity is found for those on the course to share their practical experiences and insights with the rest of the college. In such ways as these the practical work of each individual can be related both to his own theological study and to that of the college as a whole.'

(ii)   One of the same group of colleges describes (in a paper privately circulated) its Urban Ministry Project. 'Moreover, in practice pastoral care is more concerned with problem-solving than with enabling growth into the future. In the experiment, called the Urban Ministry Project, we include in the curriculum a carefully planned entrée to social studies so that the student may develop his powers of social perception about a community as a whole with its extraordinarily complex interactions, groups, interests, histories, traditions and institutions. We work, on the basis of this understanding, with a method of survey which includes not only basic sociological data but also detailed enquiry about the way in which we may begin to discern the implicit or explicit issues which provoke public and private anger, frustration and unease. In this process, we place students not in social casework agencies but in community work agencies, where, hopefully, they gain a much more comprehensive insight into the workings of a local community. This placement work is supported by rigorous analysis and by the development of a capacity for theological reflection. By the latter is meant the difficult task of exposing current issues to Christian perspectives about God, man and salvation and of exposing those perspectives to the current issues. As a result of this process of training — only briefly described here — we expect an attitude to develop in which the traditional clerical functions, part the subject-matter of specialist training, are now worked out reflectively in relation to the actual existent warp and weft of a society. In other words, the actual wishes and expectations of that society are treated much more seriously as areas which are ministered *in* rather than ministered *to*. With this mode of operation, we have to consider in a very open way how Christian convictions work out historically within a community. 'Theology no longer aspires to be a subject apart, prescriptive of conclusions in all other disciplines, not least science and history. Rather, is theology coming to be seen as a complex interweaving of various strands each of which is a response to a moment of insight, inspiration and disclosure, and each of which endeavours in a particular way to spell out a controlling vision of God, man and the universe.' As a result of this, much less is taken for granted both in church and society, and choices begin to emerge where they had not been thought to exist.'

Each of these instances makes the following educational point (*op. cit.* p. 10) 'But even more important than the choice of practical work are the conditions under which it is done. It is perfectly possible to do part-time or even full-time, work in factories, hospitals, or schools without ever being forced to ask onself fundamental questions or to relate any of the new problems encountered to one's theological thinking. One can simply accept the conventions and attitudes one finds there, and indeed one can gain a considerable sense of confidence and expertise simply by adapting oneself to the ethos of the particular institution concerned.'

Here we have in one minority group of higher education institutions an acute perception of the importance of the method in interpreting the experience, and in developing cross-references to various human activities where decision making of a moral kind is of the essence of the task.

Part of the strength of the colleges of education has been their pure-applied blend of learning the relatedness of theory and practice. Other contributions to this volume will be exemplifying this aspect of the total curriculum. But there is a need to make known how what were once called Divinity Departments have so changed their tradition that Religious Studies and Religious Education are now the more common titles.

Several trends can be detected which have a bearing on the purpose of this chapter, e.g.

1. There has been great experiment in terms of teaching method:

For example, see Chapter 13 of this volume for a description of one scheme. The actual class has become the experience and the interpretative guide.

2. There has been an innovating linking with many other disciplines in terms of thematic, interdisciplinary work.

3. The very debate round religious education in schools, its aims, content and methods, has been essentially a debate on a question of morality. No one can deny that potentially this has many of the marks of Wilson's 'moral components'. An examination of the vocabulary of the debate is indicative of the possibilities: readiness for religion, sensitivity to needs, freedom to make autonomous choice, openness, compulsory, indoctrination. The stuff is there to be used.

One interesting example of innovating enterprise comes from two units of work led by Rankin and Brown in Bishop Otter College, Chichester (quoted with permission). The first of these is a unit entitled, 'Reason and Revelation' — 'A Study of Religious and Secular Literature.' The students are given a booklet of eighty passages representing many types of religious and non-religious thought. These are chosen on five basic premises, and no references are given.

(i)   They are all expressions of thoughtful, intuitive people who are making an effort to express in their work something basic to man's thought and desire.

(ii)   They represent, as a whole, a catholicity of spirit, they speak from different environments, different cultures, yet without exception all the passages exhibit a similarity of pattern and depth of thought.

(iii) They were chosen with the aim of presenting different modes of thought from all parts of the world in order that one may gain some insight into many separate beliefs (or non-beliefs).

(iv)   The deliberate mixture of scriptural and non-scriptural texts was made with the intention of suggesting that the latter are as equally valid means of interpreting the meaning of religion as the more orthodox scriptural texts. Revelation should not be enclosed within the confines of a scriptural canon nor even within the religious language of saints and theologians.

(v)   The selection as a whole is an attempt to express the nature of man and his search for an understanding of himself and his place in the world.'

Students are invited to evaluate the passages and to make a crisp personal response. Several categories are offered for classification. Thus;

'(i)   Passages which appear to reveal something about the particular nature of a god or being outside the empirical world.

(ii)   Passages which appear to reveal something of man's search for a god or being outside the empirical world.

(iii) Passages where a god or a being is revealing or trying to reveal something of himself (herself, itself) to man.

(iv) Passages which refer to the power of religious belief.

(v) Passages which refer to the guidance of an ethical code.

(vi) Passages which appear to be a personal statement on religion by an individual

(vii) Miscellaneous — passages which do not appear to fit under sections (i)-(vi) — although their presence in section (vii) must still be justified.'

There is an interesting note at the end, viz. 'There is no right or wrong answer. The only justification for placing a passage under a particular section heading is the one you are able to give. If one can justify its position it is right; if one can't, then one needs to look elsewhere.'

Here is material offering an experience in choosing (cf. categories (i)-(vii) above) which combines the very strands of knowing, and feeling and deciding. The very rubric itself is an exercise towards an understanding of right and wrong!

The second example describes under the heading 'Concepts of Revelation and Themes of Belief' a year's study of Biblical material under the titles Myth, Word, Expression of Revelation, Law and Ethics, and, Interpretation and Exegesis. It is not only the section on Law and Ethics which offers the possibility of education in moral matters. The programme is set out in terms of Aims and Objectives, Method and Content, and Strategy. Some quotations from the sections are expressive of the authors' view of their developmental task:

"(b) To explore the nature of morality as an expression of the function of revealed law.

(c) To present a study of biblical problems related to modern society in the field of the nature of morality."

There is constant emphasis on 'acquiring criteria for evaluating'; on 'achieving understanding'; on 'understanding function'; on 'an interpretative elelement'. There is 'an exploration of myth in the personification of evil and its different role in different cultures' etc.

Enough has been written to indicate that in the hands of an able tutor there is real opportunity for ethical and moral development to take place.

Reference was made above to the community factor in the education process. Here it is exceptionally difficult to make an evaluation. However, it could be claimed that the educational institutions which overtly try to relate worship to the fundamental educational activity of the place are in a position to bring thought to bear on the KRAT(1) aspect of the themes being discussed. Indeed this is an aspect of the matter which requires an immense amount of study, at a more detailed level than anyone has yet publicly explored. Perhaps there is a particular challenge here to see how far the smaller 'religious' institution is both expressive of this dimension in human living and instrumental in deepening the same.

Running through every contribution to this section of the symposium is probably the notion that each discipline at its best equips the student with a fundamental language through which he learns to perceive himself, to relate with others and things, and with the meaningful transcendent for him. (Anyone doing theology in the Western Christian tradition will obviously use forms of words like creation, man and God.) Each discipline offers an opportunity to bring some order into chaos, to evolve interpretative categories, to find a satisfying 'human map' which one can share with others.

The religious contribution to this would seem to have certain distinctive characteristics which bear upon the symposium's theme, and this relation to the pedagogic problems in moral development will be obvious. (One writes now from the Western Christian position.)

1. The biblical tradition offers what might be called an extended classical paradigm of the human predicament between perception of the good and imperfection in achieving the good. It points to human learning in some things, and perennial failures in others.

2. Emphasis is laid on a gradual evolution of inter-human understanding, and this is coupled with the scandal of the discontinuous factor in human experience. The whole notion of 'gospel' or of 'revelation' pinpoints the predicament morally.

3. Even within one tradition there has evolved a variety of 'languages' of which the Catholic-Protestant divide is one example. Even within the one discipline the problem of communication between groups is manifest.

4. One illustrative concept which actually transforms any approach to a moral development theory is that of 'eternity' in relation to 'time'. Whether the concept is meaningful or not to all, does not alter the fact that where it is meaningful then the continuum we define as 'moral' is not only extended, but it is transformed.

5. Religion in general impels people to relate to a 'model', or 'exemplar' or 'ideal'. This has parabolic, imitative, mythological aspects to it which on a commonsense view would seem to relate to moral nurture.

6. No one can deny that the notions of belief, faith, and commitment in relation to decision and specific moral choices have a practical prevalence and lengthy history in the human grappling with the moral.

But of course one must reiterate that there is no magical direct cause effect link between the study of theology and moral development. All that one can say is that where theology is recognised as real, independent and insight-offering, then it provides one of many possible moral development 'mappings', and it relates to human experience and apperceptions out of which many moral men have been formed.

Perhaps a complementary study needs to be undertaken to perceive the ways in which the study of moral development further the doing of theology.

References

1. W. Burton, 'Behavioural Morality?' *Religious Education*' vol. LXVII, no. 4, 1972.
2. Harold Loukes, Article *Moral Education*, vol. 2, no. 1, 1970.

10   HISTORY

James Henderson

If moral development consists in learning the difference between right
and wrong and acquiring the capacity to apply that lesson, then History
is a terribly teasing teacher. For the aim in teaching that subject is to
make available the record of the growth of human consciousness, both
individually and collectively. Now the deeper the historian probes into
the substance of time past, the more he is driven to accept a paradoxical
conclusion, namely that the record reveals human beings making relative
choices in absolute terms. For example, some members of the Verney
family in seventeenth-century England fought for the King and some for
Parliament, and yet, viewed historically, their apparently absolute and
opposed choices within the dialectic of the historical process has only
relative validity; it was the glory and the misery of both, the Verney
Cavaliers and the Verney Roundheads, which conduced to the outcome
of the Civil War. Nor does this phenomenon stop the nearer we get to
the present day: Adolf Hitler must be viewed as an historical character,
but in his life-time he was evil incarnate to some and messianic salvation
to others. Already, a mere forty years later, the historians are quite
properly performing their function by refusing to make moral judgements
about his dictatorship. They can and should point to the hideous
inhumanity of man to man in Nazi Germany, just as they would with
regard to Nero's persecution of the Christians, but they can neither deny
that it existed nor maintain that the resultants of it were unequivocally
good or bad, for example the partition of Germany and the creation of
the Europe of the Six and then of the Nine. It simply belongs inextricably
to the overall conduct of man. The moral labels we tend to attach to
historical characters — St Francis was a good man and Judas a bad man
— stem inevitably from the projection of our own scale of morality on
to others in a distant past in which we ourselves are not directly
concerned.

   The poet, Wilfred Owen, realised and expressed the nature of this
paradox, of what it means to be aware of being involved in any human
encounter. Writing of soldiers on either side of the Western Front in the
First World War, he made the executioner say to his bayoneted victim:
'You are the enemy I killed, my friend.'

   That is why the first and easily the most profound contribution which is a study of History can make to the moral development of students is the inculcation in them of a sense of awe — awe in the face of human beings tragically committed to be always making relative choices in absolute terms. In the philosophical terms of John Wilson this means having feelings, full of awe, which pertain to knowing that there is a right thing to do, entertaining the desire to do it and yet recognising obstacles in the way of its performance. Arnold Toynbee has remarked most pertinently, 'the pursuit of historical curiosity is not just an intellectual exercise; it is also an emotional experience, and one of the emotions induced by it is awe.'[1] (Cf. KRAT (1)RA and KRAT(1)OPU). Professor Butterfield described this phenomenon as constituting the essence of 'the human predicament'[2] — a literally crucial one. Learning as richly and plentifully as possible from historical examples of this human dilemma is a vital part of the students' moral development in that it can help them to make choices here and now while recognising that in the not-here-and-now, in the perspective of History, their choices are inevitably partial ones. 'In history,' says A. L. Rowse, 'I isolate the element of dogmatic ideological certainty — particularly with regard to matters essentially uncertain in themselves — as responsible for untold human suffering. One side will burn the other for some highly disputable propositions, the other will hang, draw and quarter the first for similar reasons. Each of them will do it in the name of their exclusive (Author's note: my 'absolute') possession of truth — though a little later in history they find that these are no longer truths for which they killed, and are engaged in getting together ecumenically.'[3] Such recognition is the root of charity hence Bacon's invocation, adapting a passage from Lucretius:

'It is a pleasure to stand upon the shore, and to see ships tossed upon the sea: a pleasure to stand in the window of a castle, and to see a battle and the adventures thereof below; but no pleasure is comparable to the standing upon the vantage-ground of truth, and to see the errors and wanderings and mists and tempests in the vale below; so always that this prospect be with pity, and not with swelling or pride. . . Certainly it is heaven upon earth to have a man's mind move in charity, rest in providence and turn upon the poles of truth.'

A student capable of satisfying these three criteria, possessed that is to say of such a mind, would undoubtedly have progressed far in moral development.

The next contribution that a study of History can help in understanding the remorselessness of chronological sequence, of 'one damn thing after another' including the microscopically small life-span between birth and death of any one individual, and also the need felt for rescue from this otherwise impasse of futility, 'lighting fools the way to dusty death.'

Any such rescue operation necessarily involves commitment to a transcendental view of the nature of History in terms of the acceptance of History as that record of the growth of human consciousness already mentioned, the recognition of being within becoming, revelation within sequence. This point has also been pithily made by a poet, Emily Dickinson, who writing on the phenomenon of Spring's return each year answers the question of how one may indeed re-enter one's mother's womb, i.e. be reborn out of time into eternity:

> And Nicodemus' mystery
> Receives its annual reply

'The past,' wrote Simone Weil, 'is time with the dew of eternity on it.' The experiencing of time-transcendence in this sense is a condition of being able to tolerate the otherwise Sartrean prison of a mere sequence of contradictions.

Our claim then is that the study of History is conducive to a sense of awe, of charity and of time-transcendence: our contention is that without the initiation into the perception of the actuality of such qualities, a human being is deracinated and therefore withers.

'A person to whom the past is alien, who despises it or loses the memory of it, becomes alien to himself, and the same applies, *mutatis mutandis,* to society. What surer definition could there be of failure in moral development than individual or social alienation — the running sore of most of our present discontents.'[4]

The brief historical studies, which now follow, are based on personal experiences of undergraduates and post-graduate teaching. They are intended to demonstrate how the moral development of students can be fostered withour preaching at them or conniving at their evasion of the tragic element in human existence as revealed by men and women always making relative choices in absolute terms.

1. The Irish Question

The very title of this portion of History implies a particularly tough problem and a mark of interrogation as though compelling recognition of the fact that certain situations are of a kind which make them distinguishable from more normally prevailing human circumstances. Another example would be the German Question: in other words the 'human predicament' is sometimes and in some places more inflamed than at other times. For an Englishman or Irishman, Ireland is such a place, for an Arab or Jew it will be the Middle East.

Having established an historical perspective by sketching in the main features of Gaelic and Early Christian history in Ireland, it was then considered wise to establish the time-scale of the Anglo-Irish relationship by explaining the twelfth century English Pale, the Ulster Settlement at the end of the sixteenth century, the Battle of the Boyne (1690), the United Irishmen at the end of the eighteenth century, the rise and fall of Parnell, the Easter Rising of 1916, the Anglo-Irish Treaty of 1921, the emergence of Eire and Northern Ireland and Britain's contemporary involvement in Irish affairs as a result of the Civil Rights movement. Into this chronological framework there were then fitted the long-standing religious, political and economic issues, the 'four, deep, tragic notes in Irish History' according to Yeats (Four Bells), namely Catholic revolt in Queen Elizabeth I's reign, the Battle of the Boyne, the French Revolution in relationship to the United Irishmen and the dire struggle over Home Rule with Parnell's role in it. These have been summarised by Lady Gregory as 'hatred answering hatred, death answering to death through the generations like clerks at mass.'

The awe, charity and sense of time-transcendence postulated as the stimulus to moral development through the study of History was engendered by concentrating the students' attention on the Easter Monday Rising of 1916. In the first place they were exposed to Yeats' famous lines in which he commemorates the fate of the Irish rebels, who, after failing to capture the Castle in Dublin, then seized the Post Office, proclaimed a Republic but after a week's fighting were forced to surrender.

> I have met them at close of day
> Coming with vivid faces
> From counter or desk among grey
> Eighteenth century houses . . .
>
> I write out in verse —
> MacDonagh and MacBride
> And Connolly and Pearse
> Now and in time to be,
> Wherever green is worn
> Are changed, changed utterly:
> A terrible beauty is born.

What other examples of martyrdom, the students were asked, could we consider either in the past or the present? How much truth is there in the idea, as is suggested by T.S. Eliot in *Murder in the Cathedral* referring to Thomas Becket, that the martyr may be making his cause, whatever it is, in reality serve his own ego-interests? For what, if anything, were they themselves prepared to suffer martyrdom, and what is the nature of this 'terrible beauty' that the poet claims was born? Clearly, colourfully it was shown how a Resistance movement and a National Liberation movement may be intertwined, how the heroic

140

protest of 1916 failed at the time but prepared the ground for subsequent victory, but this, even then, only a partial one. The whole Irish psycho-historical process was then analysed into its constituent elements, religion generally (Roman Catholicism devout and fanatical and Protestantism genuine and bigoted), politics (the climax of revolt against centuries old foreign domination), economics (the cry of poverty-stricken underlings), culture (the Celtic Revival), personality (Leaders like Pearse and Griffiths, Collin and De Valera). Finally the following passage was set for the students to comment on:

'IRELAND EASTER BLOOD BATH'

A letter with this heading appeared in the Times of 7 April 1961, suggesting that the best explanation of the impulses of Irish history came from James Stephens, himself an eye-witness of the 1916 Easter Rising in Dublin:

'If freedom is to come to Ireland — and I believe it is — then the Easter Insurrection is *the only thing that could have happened* . . . If after all her striving it came to her as a gift, as a peaceful present such as is sometimes given away with a pound of tea, Ireland would have accepted the gift with shamefacedness and have felt that her centuries of revolt had ended in something like ridicule. The blood of brave men had to sanctify such a consummation if the national imagination was to be stirred to *the dreadful business* which is the organisation of freedom, but imagination and action have been stagnant in Ireland this many a year . . . We might have crept into liberty like some kind of domesticated men, whereas now we may be allowed to march into freedom with the honours of war.'

The students were invited to consider what the implications of this kind of judgement were. Did they agree with it? For example, did they go along with the deterministic notion implied in 'the only thing that could have happened'? Has the 'organisation of freedom' necessarily and always such a 'dreadful business'? How far had the proud hope expressed by Stephens in the 'march into freedom with the honours of war' been fatally besmirched by the bitterness of the Bogside? Co-operative and sympathetic examination on some such lines as these surely did not fail to contribute to the moral development of those engaged in studying it, however impossible to reckon its amount in quantitative terms.

2. Port-Royal

This second example, taken from the seventeenth century has proved susceptible to similar treatment: it also satisfies the terms of our criteria by offering experiences of awe, charity and time-transcendence. Establishing the historical context in this case meant sketching the main features of the age of Louis XIV, bringing into particular focus the religious issue of Gallicanism and Ultra-Montanism, the political issues of 'L'Etat, c'est Moi' and the cultural issue of life at the court of Versailles in contrast with the life of the Solitaries at Port-Royal des Champs. The skill of the teacher consisted in the way in which he conducted his students behind the figure of Cornelius Jansen — 'that dreary, old Dutch bishop' as Walter Pater called him — to the real heart of the matter. When stripped of the niceties of theological verbiage, this revealed itself as the perennial tension between Free Will and Determinism and the mysterious operation of that factor in human experience, which Christians call Grace. It was found necessary to persuade the students by means of many a telling example from the records of the time of what constituted the basic disagreement about how life should be lived — the disagreement which divided the world of Louis XIV and his mistresses at Versailles from the Arnaulds at Port-Royal. As that monarch bluntly declared 'On ne va pas de Port-Royal à Marly.' This whole exercise culminated in a study of Blaise Pascal — probably the single greatest forerunner of two centuries of apparent strife between science and religion, reason and faith. Students were then asked to compare two very different verdicts on Pascal, Nietzsche's highly appreciative one in the late nineteenth century and Aldous Huxley's early twentieth-century description of him as 'austere and morbid'. Above all they were confronted with such well-known Pascalian aphorisms as, 'Man is only a reed, but he is a thinking reed' or 'Thou wouldst not be seeking me, hadst thou not already found me' or 'The eternal silence of infinite space terrifies me.' They were challenged to think out the interpretations of those sayings, first in terms of their seventeenth-century setting and then in terms of contemporary philosophy and science. For example, what are the differences between past and present conceptions of the body-mind relationship? Do we recognise today the validity of the spiritual quest and, if so, in what form, and how does it differ from that of Angelique Arnauld, St Cyran and even that most human of mortals, Mme Chantal, who although capable of speaking of going into the country *'m'ennuyer pour l'amour de Dieu'* was all the same a fervent admirer of the Port-Royalist nuns? Or again, does the 'eternal silence' which terrified Pascal, terrify us in the age of space travel? The more thoroughly historical vistas are explored, the stronger becomes the convision that moral development is unthinkable without the historical dimension's support. As Freya Stark remarked, 'A man needs his strength as he lunges into the future like a boxer in the ring; and the punch of it is not in his fist alone, but in the whole body of his past that makes him what he is.'[5]

3. The Slave Trade

While it is possible to imagine a history syllabus, which does not include the Irish Question or Port-Royal, one without the Slave Trade is inconceivable. For that historical phenomenon stretches across three continents, Africa, America and Europe and spans five centuries of time: it reverberates from the past to the present and heralds the future. Students can be presented with it from at least three angles. Politically it can be viewed as an aspect of European Imperialism, an ingredient in American nationalism and, most recently, as the root of Black Power movements and much of modern African nationalism. Economically it can be regarded as an expression of entrepreneur capitalism in the three-cornered trade in manufactured goods, slaves, spices and other primary goods, which so greatly enriched the White maritime powers of the West. In human terms it has to be seen as an example of man's inhumanity to man, acted out in racialist terms. Three specific examples may be quoted, each calculated to demonstrate how History, if properly studied, is conducive to awe, charity and time-transcendence. These are, first, the appalling conditions on the slave ships with their high incidence of disease and death, secondly the paradox of the life of William Wilberforce, who inherited his fortune from the Slave Trade and then campaigned for its abolition, and thirdly the way in which a phenomenon of originally the late fifteenth century continued through the sixteenth, seventeenth, eighteenth, nineteenth and twentieth centuries until today its working-out comes within the compass of consciousness of us all, whether as the Civil Rights struggle in the United States or the giant force of Black nationalism in Africa.

The greatest contribution made to my own moral development by the study of the Slave Trade occurred during a visit to Ghana, where at the University College of Cape Coast I was asked to discuss the project method in history teaching with a group of local student-teachers. The first step we took in the exercise was to descend from the campus and walk along the coast to the fortress of Elmina, the oldest European slave-trade stronghold in Africa. Here we sat down on the ramparts, which now strangely enough housed the local black African constabulary, and engaged in a dialogue. First, I spoke to the students about how the Portuguese made landfall on that coast; then I invited them to speak of the indigenous population of West Africa at that time with its own internal tradition of slave markets; together we grieved over the ways in which the internal and overseas slave-trades came to complement one another. Then one member of the seminar spoke up softly:

'If it hadn't been for the Slave Trade and then the Christian missionaries, I would not be here now as a student-teacher, Ghana itself might no exist as an independent nation, Accra would not be the modern city it is.'

'Maybe,' said another, 'but if it hadn't been for the Slave Trade, my ancestors would have escaped transportation to the cotton plantations of the American Deep South.'

Then I, as an Englishman, replied, 'If it hadn't been for the Slave Trade, my ancestors would not have made their capitalist profits and so eventually contributed to the paying for my own education as a privileged White lecturer in history come to share his own learning with yours.'

The silence that followed these remarks seemed to make us all aware of being contained in the same 'human predicament'; whether then or now, historical circumstances compelled us to act towards one another as friends or foes. As a result of that shared experience of learning we had all grown a bit in moral stature.

4. Hiroshima

On 6th August 1945 an atomic bomb was dropped on the Japanese city of Hiroshima. There are at least four reasons why this event, undoubtedly a turning-point by any reckoning in human history, can provide appropriate material for the contemplation of the moral philosopher. First, because it was a tactic in the winning of the Second World War by the Allied powers; secondly, because it was a strategical move in the opening of the Cold War between the U.S.A. and the U.S.S.R.; thirdly, because it marked a significant stage in the development of applied science, and fourthly, because it offers an example of human inability or unwillingness to control the products of human ingenuity.

'To the moral philosopher it is a study in conflicts of loyalty — the compelling claims made upon a scientist or politician by his own instincts and ambitions, his friends, his country and mankind.'[6]

It is convenient to consider some issues which the Hiroshima occurence would quite naturally pose to any serious student of History and thus, by having his heart and mind cleansed by awe and charity, foster his own moral growth. For instance, have the conventions of traditional warfare become obsolete in the age of total war? Are any holds barred, and, if so, which? Did the case of Hiroshima raise specific problems for scientists as distinct from non-scientists, and, if so, do they continue to do so in this post-nuclear age? In what sense can the decision to drop the bomb be described as the decision of one man, President Truman, and how far should such a momentous judgement ever be entrusted to a single person? What conclusions may be drawn from the fact that a Christian priest invoked the blessing of God on the Hiroshima bombdroppers before they set out on their mission and that an American politician diverted the bomb from its original target of Kyoto because of that City's religious, though non-Christian, repute? Are we not here at the very heart of moral discourse?

Conclusion

The two propositions upon which the argument of this chapter rests are, first, that History is the record of men and women making relative choices in absolute terms at varying levels of conscious awareness, and secondly that the study of this process is conducive through the experiencing of awe, charity and time-transcendence to moral development.[7] Both propositions were then illustrated by the examples of the Irish Question, Port-Royal, the Slave Trade and Hiroshima. Our findings are that no direct moral lesson can be learnt from the study of History, that historians may expound the past but not exploit it in order to support any particular moral point of view. However, association with such exposition can nourish the student so that, without presuming to pass judgement on his forefathers, who were caught in the same predicament as he is of making relative choices in absolute terms, he acquires sufficient maturity to face the consequences for his own good and ill of taking inevitably immature decisions.

References

1. Arnold Toynbee, *A Study of History* (Thames and Hudson, London 1972), p. 495.
2. Herbert Butterfield, *Christianity and History* (Beth 1954)
3. A.L. Rowse, *Experiencing Today in the Past* (The Times' Saturday Review, 11 November 1972).
4. G'olo Mann, 'The History Lesson: On Not Knowing the Meaning of the Past', *Encounter,* August 1972.
5. Freya Stark, 'Lunch with Homer', *Encounter,* March 1968
6. C.J.H. Watson, 'The Bomb' Purnell's *History of the Twentieth Century* vol. 5, ch. 72 p. 2012.
7. Most of the foundations on which this view of History rests can be investigated in the following:
   J. Burckhardt, *Force and Freedom: An Interpretation of History* (Meridian Books, New York 1955).
   Goronway Rees, 'Between Hope and Nihilism: Chiatomonte's Paradox of History', *Encounter,* June 1971.
   Mircea Eliade, *Cosmos and History: The Myth of the Eternal Return*

(Harper Torchbooks, New York 1959).
C.G. Jung, *Civilisation in Transition,* Collected Works vol. 10
(Routledge and Kegan Paul, London 1964).
E. Erikson, *Gandhi's Truth* (Faber and Faber, London 1970).
Joseph Campbell, *The Masks of God,* part IV (Secker and Warburg,
London, 1968).
Anne Low Beer, in 'Moral Judgements in History and History
Teaching', *Studies in the Nature and Teaching of History* (Routledge,
London 1967).
J.L. Henderson, 'The Significance of the Past in Education', *The New
Era,* vol. 50, Jan. 1969.
J.L. Henderson, The Advent of the Psycho-Historian', *Teaching
History — The Historical Association,* Nov. 1972, vol. II, No. 81.

11 SCIENCE

David Edge

'The average scientist enters his career with no more preparation for the social and ethical problems he will encounter, than an Irish girl arriving at Euston Station.'   (J.R. Ravetz, 'Science: a World in Flux.')

Traditionally, the scientist is expected to pursue truth in his researches with single-minded devotion, oblivious to the moral, philosophical, political, religious and economic considerations which tend to sway other men. Nature, as interpreted by 'the state of the discipline', alone determines what the next experiment will be. And traditional scientific education exemplifies and perpetuates this myth: the honours science student pursues a syllabus in which the contents are 'closed' and self-contained, insulated from any wider concerns which he may bring to his chosen subject.[1] To study science is to be progressively introduced to a set of paradigmatic problem-solutions, and to acquire the skill of redeploying them in faintly atypical situations;[2] to become a scientist is to be initiated into the company of those who seek both to conserve and to develop the inner mysteries of their own speciality, with its particular techniques, subject matter, concepts and theories. This is an essentially *technical* matter, with its own rules and logic. It is 'pure science', and must not be 'contaminated'; any connections between this activity and its social context remain invisible to the student. He knows that his career will involve decisions and choices, but cannot guess that these could involve genuine moral dilemmas.

It is against this 'closed' training that Dr Ravetz protests, and he has written a book in which he analyses the need for a fresh approach.[3] For, in recent years, the inadequacy of innocence as a preparation for the social role of the scientist has become increasingly obvious. Alternative strategies, however, are not so easily devised. At the risk of pursuing the Irish Girl somewhat further than might be decently advisable, I do not think it unfair to characterise the standard responses to the challenge of preparing her for her impending fate under two main headings:

(a)*Technical*: from a survey of the job profiles of Irish girls in London, a repertoire of necessary skills can be compiled, from which a training syllabus might be prepared. This approach assumes that her future roles will include a number of well-defined *tasks,* for which special *skills* are required. These tasks may well include an ethical component, in that choices of action will be offered which demand a *decision.* But these decisions are themselves usually analysable in terms of a quasi-technical skill — in, for instance, estimates of economic gain or other satisfaction.

(b) *Moral:* this approach assumes that the possible roles and tasks are not only clear to the girl, and technically demanding, but that they can be classified on a moral scale. Some are worth doing well: others should not be undertaken at all. Preparing the girl to perform in a socially acceptable way then involves getting her to accept the *code* by which these tasks and roles are valued, and strengthening her *willpower* and *motivation,* so that she will tend reliably to choose the 'good' roles and tasks, and to 'resist the temptation' of falling for the 'bad'.

Here, in essence, is the standard prescription for the professional education of the scientific expert — that he must master 'relevant' technical skills, and internalise an ethical code to guide him in their application. The Swann Report's recommendations on the training of scientists for industry put more emphasis on the former, the protestations of the British Society for Social Responsibility in Science on the latter — but the form of the discussion remains the same. Two questions predominate: what technical skills are relevant?; and what ethical code is appropriate? Since the aim of all the parties in this debate is to enlarge the number of scientists who can be said to be acting, with a wider social awareness, 'for the common good', it may surprise them to learn that their approach has little to do with 'moral education', as it is understood in this book.

But can the study of science, given its traditional isolation, possibly lead to moral development? There are two common arguments that suggest that it can: I find them both inadequate.

1. The first argument emphasises *the values implicit in the practice of science.* As Bronowski argues, in his Pelican *Science and Human Values* (which is a classic of the lyrical approach to this subject), 'the practice of science compels the practitioner to form for himself a fundamental set of human values'. He lists them: 'dissent, freedom of thought and speech, justice, honour, human dignity and self-respect.' The implication is that the scientist will *generalise* these values through his whole life, so that they become 'part of his personality'. Bronowski admits, however, that these 'scientific' values do not cover *all* human values; as he says, some values 'are not generated by the practice of science — the values of tenderness, of kindliness, of human intimacy and love'. That these may be *overriding* values, determining when it is

appropriate to apply the other, 'scientific' values (or, indeed, that these two sets of values might ever find themselves opposed), does not seem to occur to him. A more tough-minded champion of scientific ethics is Anatol Rapoport.[4] Rapoport asserts:

"These, then, are the ethical principles inherent in scientific practice: the conviction that there exists objective truth; that there exist rules of evidence for discovering it; that, on the basis of this objective truth, unanimity is possible and desirable; and that unanimity must be achieved by independent arrivals at convictions – that is, by examination of evidence, not through coercion, personal argument or appeal to authority."

He submits that this 'is a respectable chunk of an ethical system', and argues that its uniqueness 'makes it a particularly suitable basis for a more general system':

"The bid of scientific ethics for universal acceptance rests on the claim of science to be the first instance of a universal point of view about man's environment and, moreover, a point of view not imposed by coercion or even by power of persuasion or dramatic, personal example but by its inherent, universal appeal to universal human experience, through being rooted in reliable knowledge.'

Rapoport sees the overriding value of 'the pursuit of knowledge' as 'the ethics of science', which 'must become *the* ethics of humanity'. Any potentially-conflicting values will eventually be superseded. This is the 'strong claim' of scientific ethics, and many scientists would assent to it. The distinguished Hungarian/American biochemist, Albert Szent-Györgi, for instance, is one of its more rapturous advocates:

'This new world opened up by science cannot be run without mortal danger by the old sentimental political methods, greed, lust for power and domination. It can be run only by the spirit which has built science itself, and if we want to stay alive we must rebuild our political and social thinking and institutions from the ground up in the spirit of science which is that of human solidarity and mutual respect . . . To solve a problem meet it with a cool head, with uncompromising intellectual honesty, unbiassed by greed, fear or hatred, collect data and try to find the best solution. If you have an adversary look upon him with respect as your associate with whom, together you have to find the best solution. If this spirit would prevail at the peace talks in Paris, peace in Vietnam could rapidly be achieved.'[5]

My experience is that science students recognise these values as implicit in their training. The assumption appears to be that the student will 'pick them up as he goes along'. However, it seems to me that this process can only be of value as 'moral education' *if* the values are made *explicit,* and the claims for them examined and *criticised.* This criticism can be conducted on at least three fronts:

(a) Inasmuch as Rapoport rests his claims to the uniqueness of science on such terms as 'objective truth', 'rules of evidence' and 'reliable knowledge', those claims can be explored via the *philosophy of science,* on the lines described in Chapter 6 (the debate initiated by Kuhn is very relevant here).

(b) The claims can be criticised on *purely ethical grounds,* by inquiring into the reasons as to *why* we *should* accept the proposed ethic, or by considering its application in specific instances. For instance, Mesthene, in an article[6] also intended to advance a kind of 'scientific ethics' (but of a quite different temper), cites the dilemma of the person who sees a man dash out of a house and round the corner, pursued a few moments later by a second man with a gun, who asks 'which way did he go? The relevance of a 'pursuit of truth' ethic to such a situation is, to say the least, obscure!

(c) perhaps the most pointed criticism comes from the *sociology of science,* and is that science is not, in fact, normally conducted in the ethical fashion claimed. In particular, the idea that the scientist is normally 'disinterested' in the outcome of his work, or that the scientific community as a whole conducts a completely open-minded programme of 'organised scepticism', cannot easily be maintained in the face of detailed studies. Where an appeal to a value (e.g. 'rationality') has some effect, it does so in a way common to the whole of society – not in a special 'scientific' sense. What *is* specific to science tends to be closely tied to particular technical issues, and hence cannot be generalised.[7]

In bringing all these matters to the attention of science students, we are asking them to reflect upon a process of socialisation on which they are actively engaged. Their immediate experience is directly relevant to the discussions, and their emotions are usually engaged, since they have begun to acquire the 'self-identity' of a scientist, and this includes beliefs about scientific practice. The combination of that experience with its critical exposure constitutes the possibility of moral development, as outlined in Chapter 1 – notably in EMP(1) and KRAT(1).

2. The second common argument concerning the moral value of the study of science claims that the *content of science has ethical implications.* This argument is at its clearest among the proponents of 'Evolutionary Ethics', and received its definitive summary in 1941, in this sentence of C.H. Waddington: "Science can provide a secure basis for ethics by discovering and exhibiting reality to be an evolutionary process, tending in a certain direction, action in conformity to which is taken as right conduct."

This claim has by now developed an extensive critical literature: particularly useful are the monograph by Flew,[8] and essays by Toulmin[9] and Quinton.[10] As in the case of the notion of an ethics of scientific practice, students find the claim sufficiently 'close to home' for profitable discussion: it is particularly useful to point up the way in which those advocating evolutionary ethics appear to be asking for *reassurance* rather than *guidance;* Flew, for instance, askes 'whether the putative direction of human evolution is being taken to be commendable as such, or only in so far as the actual direction satisfies some other standards', and Toulmin comcludes that 'the support given by Evolution to ethics serves as a source of confidence in our moral ideas, rather than as an intellectual justification for them' (still less, of course, as a *criticism* of them). This yields valuable lessons in the GIG domain (quite apart from its reflexive value) – and, if students find the theory of evolution somewhat passé, one can develop their enthusiasm for environmental conservation in this direction, by reference to analogous arguments advanced in what should perhaps be termed 'Ecological Ethics'.[11]

Consideration of claims of this kind can lead on to the discussion of moral topics on which scientific evidence has a more legitimate bearing. Flew ends his book, for instance, by emphasising the importance of 'seeing in an evolutionary perspective': the relevance of this notion to more mundane ethical problems offers scope for student views (and it can also draw attention to aspects of religious thought). Recent advances in medical science and genetics yields a rich crop of potential moral problems which, without modern knowledge, would not exist – and which require that knowledge for their realistic exploration. A particularly useful discussion of the issues raised by modern genetics can be found in a paper by Martin Golding.[12] this poses clearly the dilemma raised by the idea of 'our obligation to future, unborn generations' – and, in so doing, also clarifies one of the rallying cries of Ecological Ethics. Science students are well equipped to discuss issues like these; they can quickly appreciate the role of science (and technology) in helping us to predict the results of our actions more realistically, and also in more subtly altering our perceptions and valuations of the world.

So far, I have been describing an educational process in which those studying science can, on the basis of their experience, be drawn into a series of discussions, of 'primary reflections'. These could, of course, be merely 'paper' discussions of 'paper' claims, but I hope it does not require too great a feat of the imagination to see how the process can 'come alive'. When it does, the students are then in a position to pursue some 'secondary' reflections, of a more sociological kind, and to ask such questions as 'Why do scientists come to make claims like this, and the public at large to treat what they say with deference?', or 'What is the social basis which supports the values and beliefs of groups – including those of science students?' Such questions can lead to a self-understanding at a much deeper level than the mere display of one's 'emotions and moods'.[13] They can begin to expose the connections between science and the wider social system which supports it — connections which the traditional scientific education renders invisible.

Other parallel connections can also be made via the analysis of science as a specialised, differentiated activity within the political economy of advanced industrialised societies. Ravetz's book takes this approach, and elaborates it in considerable detail. Here, too, science students find potential moral problems of immediate concern, bearing on their own career choices. What are the ethical issues (if any) involved in choosing to work as a research biochemist for a drug firm, or in a secret, military establishment? Many students have troubled consciences on such matters, and we are failing them if we do not provide an opportunity for their hopes and fears to be both expressed and informed. Many, indeed, wonder whether perhaps the *whole scientific enterprise* might not, in the capitalist West, be devoted, implicitly and unknowimgly, to the preservation of false values.[14] These issues cannot be disregarded because the arguments are difficult (or 'left wing', or couched in obscure Germanic prose): they draw attention to some of the central moral problems of our time. Science students often have wind of them, even if their scientific tutors do not.

The strategy, then, that I have in mind for our Irish Girl is, in some ways, less inclusive in its aims than that outlined in Chapter 1 — but in other ways it goes beyond those aims. It is *less* inclusive in that it seeks to illuminate the moral dimensions *within the 'way of life' of science itself.* The New Left is fond of arguing that, in modern industrialised society, 'the moral is reduced to the technical': I am asking that we should rediscover *the moral implications of the technical.* Such a process, as I have pointed out, draws directly on the experience of the students: it can also draw on philosophical, historical and literary sources, in the manner indicated in earlier chapters. One major aim is to illustrate the potential *moral ambiguity* of the role scientists play in modern society — an ambiguity that is rarely even hinted at in the traditional training of a scientist. Dramatic instances sharpen the perception: there is ample historical and literary material with which to recreate the dilemma of Galileo (even if Brecht's play tends to simplification of the issues); or, to take a case which students find more 'real', and to develop James Henderson's suggestion of an exploration of the Hiroshima event, the tragedy of J. Robert Oppenheimer is open to similar discussion.[15]

However, I believe that this process by itself is inadequate. Although Gerald Collier argues, in Chapter 14, quoting Whitehead, that 'there is no moral education apart from the habitual vision of greatness', and that moral principles require 'vivid embodiment in convincing figures of above-average stature', it is my experience that science students tend to regard the likes of Galileo and Oppenheimer as somewhat exceptional: what they need is some *theoretical understanding* which *relates* the grand dimensions of Oppenheimer's anguish to the relatively trivial level of their own moral development as scientists – a *set of concepts* which are meaningful to the student in his own experience, which show him that that experience is essentially of a similar kind to that of the 'figures of above-average stature', and which can serve as a reliable framework for his own future learning and perception. It is here, I suggest, that we have to go somewhat beyond the aims of Chapter 1.

The science student is being socialised into the scientific institution, and if he is to make creative use of its implied 'way of life' (as opposed to merely passively accepting its 'rules'), he must be able to see that institution, with all its culture and values, as one among a range of other social institutions – to many of which he will owe at least partial allegiance himself. He will then be able to 'place' his 'emotions and moods', and those of others, in their social setting. This sociological self-understanding could be thought of as contributing to EMP, but it penetrates more deeply than that, eventually hinting at the bases of the expressed values and motivation of those who pursue science – or who argue for more effective 'moral education' (and who contribute to a book like this).[16] Some understanding at this level seems to me to be necessary in order to relieve the tension which develops when moral education of the kind we are advocating begins to show clearly that we all *differ* crucially in our values and attitudes, and that reasoning, as exemplified in straightforward 'moral discourse', *cannot by itself reconcile the differences.* (It is also, I believe, a necessary preliminary to a proper discussion of the views of the New Left theorists, who often give me the impression that they believe that the social basis of their position is comfortably opaque.) Suitable theoretical notions can clarify (or 'structure') social perception, and allow those involved to develop a more sophisticated appreciation of 'what's happening'. By talking, for instance, of value conflicts in terms of structural features of society (conflicts of *power* between groups, rather than of *ideas* or *'values'*), sociology can expose the more superficial notions of 'consensus', in morals and politics: this can lead to a more realistic expression of values, since those involved are no longer so puzzled by the apparent 'irrationality' of others. They also have the possibility of insight into *their own* motives and values, and so can more readily separate out, and concentrate on, the possibilities of rational decision and action in any situation.

To illustrate: one particularly useful 'relational' concept is that of 'role'. We find it so, for instance, in our discussions with students on the possible conflict of loyalties (and 'clash in values') which a scientist might anticipate in industry. The concept rebounds, as it were, to illuminate the university scene, and the current controversies over the status of staff and students within the community — and so the (abstract) study of an as-yet-unexperienced problem is vividly related to the present experience of students *by the use of theory*. Or again, take Mary Douglas' article (referred to in ref. 13). I have myself witnessed large bodies of otherwise 'rational' scientists reacting with outraged hostility towards Professor Jensen (because he challenged received opinions on racial differences), and towards innocent industrial scientists (over pollution of the environment, and the ethics of pharmaceutics). In all these occasions, reason has lost out to precisely the kind of social behaviour to which Douglas draws attention. There is no doubt in my mind that exposure to her analysis would not only increase the chance of a more rational approach to the problems in question, but also would lead at least some of those involved so to alter their appreciation of the nature and status of their professed values as to *alter those valued themselves*. The capacity for moral indignation should be cherished, but that does not entail that its direction should not be controlled.

The necessity for a theoretical understanding is heightened by the rapidity of social change in modern society. Perhaps my basic objection to what I earlier parodied as 'the standard prescription for the professional education of the scientific expert' is that it is *static* in its conception. Its basic assumption is that 'roles', 'tasks', and the contexts of both, are sufficiently stable for *their definition to be non-problematic, and to be specifiable in advance*. As Bernstein remarks, our traditional evaluation of courses 'places an emphasis upon attaining *states* of knowledge, rather than *ways* of knowing'. It has been said, tauntingly, that many experts are 'bundles of skills in search of jobs to fit them'. But if we are now aware that the *technical* skills required of a scientist and engineer are changing so rapidly that a routine training is inadequate, and the development of a more creative and flexible approach to problem-solving is necessary, how much more true is this of the development of ethical and moral 'skill'. Faced with a technical problem the expert has to decide, first, what *kind* of a problem it is, and what approach would be *appropriate:* he cannot merely impose his routine set of tricks on each and every 'problem' that appears. Similarly, in social situations involving ethical dilemmas, the perception of the *kind* of 'problem' which the situation raises cannot be taken as a 'given', confined to a limited range, and with a limited range of 'correct' responses specified in advance by some convenient code. The Irish Girl is not (and *could* not be) that knowing: her situation *confuses* her: she cannot deduce what 'problems' she is facing until she has effectively resolved them beyond recall: she 'doesn't know what is happening to her'.

154

Our notions of morality are similarly inclined to the static. It seems to me that the idea of moral 'skill' is derived metaphorically from manual skills. Behind the notion of ethical action which emphasises clearly-specifiable 'tasks' and 'skills', agreed 'success' and 'failure', and a moral component consisting of 'codes', and 'willpower' (and in which the 'good man' applies himself efficiently to the resolution of problems to predetermined 'good' ends, which he *imposes* on the situation), lurks the metaphor of, for example, a carpenter making a chair. Aristotle appears to have considered artistic activity in precisely these terms: the good artist is one who conceives of a 'good' picture, and then, as if guided by a blueprint, proceeds to realise that conception in paint. But does the artist work like this? I vividly recall, many years ago, seeing the film made by speeding up shots of Picasso painting on (the other side of) a translucent screen. One sequence, of some twenty minutes, was of the painting of a bull fight. It consisted of a large number of attempts, each one quite different, sketched in, filled out a bit, and then erased, to be replaced by a fresh image. The process could only be described as an *experimental* one; Picasso was trying out the capabilities of his ideas and materials, and modifying his idea of the final 'goal' as he saw the paintings develop. This seems to me a more realistic metaphor for ethics: it cannot be reconciled to a simple 'blueprint and skill' model, but emphasises the actor's *perception of a developing process,* and his tendency to *experiment* with more loosely-co-ordinated sets of ideas[17] (what Donald Schon has called 'typologies').

However, this still does not quite do justice to the Irish Girl's confusion, for she is likely to be faced with situations of which she can make, initially, *no sense at all,* where no obvious pattern emerges, and where she can find no typology to guide her experimental groupings. Worse: she may wonder whether it is worth trying to be ethical at all: why bother even to grope? It is in the context of radical uncertainties such as these that I would argue that theoretical analyses are of crucial relevance to the actors concerned. What we are concerned with here is their *perception.*

In any society, individual values are linked to social institutions: this is where we learn our values, and find their justification. But in a changing society, institutions can fail to change either adequately or appropriately, and so begin to fail in the task of maintaining the values they have traditionally professed. In this kind of situation, values become increasingly blurred, their application more problematical — until, eventually, the confusion is such that their coherence and validity is radically questioned. Since, at the heart of every institution, beats the notion that its values are congruent with, and sustained by (if not actually deduced from), the 'facts of the real world', the radical collapse is a matter of perception, of cognition. Previously, our values and our cosmology were 'all of a piece', and 'things fitted'. Now the 'information' escapes in a chaotic flood, the order and pattern of which we can no longer grasp. 'Reason' no longer has rules with which to operate. It's all 'one damn thing after another.'

Donald Schon[18] puts it like this:

"In all . . . domains of experience, transforming the system means passing through zones of uncertainty. I do not mean risk, the probability of some future event occurring, but the situation of being at sea, of being lost, of confronting more information than you can handle.

"The situations of crisis are the ones that provoke uncertainty. The most threatening changes are the ones that would plunge the system into uncertainty.

- I come to be truly confused over the behaviour of someone who, until now, has been close to me. His act appears hostile, but may be quite different. How am I to discover? How shall I respond to him?
- A psychotherapist who has been working with a patient suddenly finds himself confronted with behaviour that belies the hypothesis, the way of seeing the patient, with which he has been working — and there is, as yet, no alternative hypothesis in sight.
- A business firm begins to perceive that its product and its marketing policy are inadequate to the demands of the market. The market does not respond to the firm's tested strategies of recovery.
- A scientist, committed to a cherished hypothesis, encounters data which do not fit — and which present no clear alternative pattern.
- A scientific community — such as the community of physicists in the early years of this century, or the community of nuclear physicists in the last decade — find an entire conceptual framework inadequate to the data presented by a programme of experiments which cannot be discredited or abandoned.

'In these situations, there is not a lack of information. There is not an 'information gap'. There is an information overload, too many signals, more than can be accounted for; and there is as yet no theory in terms of which new information can be sought or new experiments undertaken. "Uncertainty" is a way of talking about the situation in which no plausible theory has emerged.

'For this reason pragmatism is no response. We cannot, in these situations, say "Let us get the data", "Let us experiment", "Let us test", for there is as yet nothing to test. Out of the uncertainty, out of the experience of a bewildering array of information, new hypotheses must emerge — and from them, mandates for gathering data, testing, experiment, can be derived. But in the first instance they do not as yet exist, and until they exist the method of pragmatism cannot be applied. The period of uncertainty must be traversed *in order that* pragmatism may become an appropriate response.

'The feeling of uncertainty is anguish. The depth of anguish increases as the threatening changes strike at more central regions of the self. In the last analysis, the degree of threat presented by a change depends on its connection to self-identity.'

In the confusion which accompanies social change, we need a *theory* (a set of analytical ideas, a frame for perception and learning) as a focus for *experimental action*. More than this we need some reasonable source of assurance that this endless experimental action is *worthwhile*. In other words (one might say) we need some 'metatheory' about *the role of theory and experimental action* — i.e. about 'being ethical'. Here, perhaps, is the fundamental, interdisciplinary focus of concern in contemporary moral education. We are now aware of the extent to which scientists are social *agents:* the education I have been describing is intended to assist them in becoming *knowing* agents. The Irish Girl will then be equipped, not with a 'kit of parts. tailor-made for some specific and well-defined role, so much as with a conception of what it is *to decide to play, and to modify, any role,* given her particular capacities and talents. This is the skill that Edgar Schein has defined as 'role-innovation'.[19] It requires KRAT: it also demands a radical reformation of scientific education.

I have been concerned only with the educational experience of future scientists. I have argued that this experience is 'closed', and that claims that it has its own implicit moral value are deficient. (This is not, of course, to deny that the practice of science can exemplify in a heightened form aspects of values that are already more widely accepted, for quite different, and sounder reasons.) I have further argued that the experience of those who practice, or who are being prepared to practice, science contains its own moral dimensions, ambiguities and dilemmas, and that these can be fruitfully made explicit; and, lastly, that the final transformation of this experience from a passive imposition and a limited exploration to an opportunity for fully self-aware learning and development (for 'moral education') rests on the acquisition by the student of a theoretical understanding of his experience and its social roots, without which he may find himself radically confused. Those who currently determine the course of scientific education are not, in general, equipped to help the student to reach this understanding. They are themselves handicapped by, and are perpetuating, the 'closed' education they received.

The matter is one of some urgency. It seems to me that the institutionalisation of professional expertise, and its problems is a changing society, make the spread of this theoretical understanding an important part of the ethical preparation of the expert in the modern world. It's what every Irish girl needs, in order to increase her autonomy, and her ability to respond as a person to the situations she will face, rather than be imposed upon by chance circumstances. The aim throughout is to 'clear the ground', so that reason can have a larger potential sway. It may be that the social history of the world is a record of the relative feebleness of 'reason', and of the transistory nature of its grander claims. But, in a world dominated by the sheer physical potentialities offered by science and technology, such a fatalistic view may be literally fatal, to us all. And I might add, as a slightly malicious footnote, that the cause of rationality in ethics is not helped at all by those fashionable linguistic philosophers who, by emphasising the integrity of total cultures, 'life styles' and languages (scientific, ethical, religious), deny the possibility of any communication whatsoever 'across the boundaries', and hence of any 'rational' approach to the resolution of conflicts – other, of course, than the technical.

References

1. For a most useful set of categories with which to analyse both curricula and their social setting, see Basil Bernstein, 'On the Classification and Framing of Educational Knowledge'', *in* Michael Young (ed.), *Knowledge and Control* (Open University, 1972). See also my essay 'On the Purity of Science', in W.R. Niblett (ed.) *The Sciences, the Humanities and the Technological Threat* (forthcoming).
2. For a description of this process, see T.S. Kuhn, *The Structure of Scientific Revolutions,* 2nd edn. (Univ. of Chicago Press; 1970).
3. J.R. Ravetz, *Scientific Knowledge and its Social Problems* (Oxford University Press, 1971).
4. Anatol Rapoport, 'Scientific Approach to Ethics', *Science, 125* (1957), pp. 796-9.
5. *in* E. Laszlo & J.B. Wilbur (eds.), *Human Values and Natural Science* (Gordon and Breach, 1970), pp. 48-9.
6. E.G. Mesthene, 'On the Need for a Scientific Ethic', *Phil. of Sci., 14* (1947), pp. 96-101.
7. For a more detailed exposition of these arguments, see S.B. Barnes & R.G.A. Dolby, 'The Scientific Ethos: a Deviant Viewpoint', *Archiv. europ. sociol., XI* (1970), pp. 3-25. See also S.B. Barnes, 'Making Out in Industrial Research', *Science Studies, 1* (1971), pp. 157-75, and several of the essays

in his reader, *Sociology of Science* (Penguin Modern Sociology Readers, Harmondsworth 1972).

8. A.G.N. Flew, *Evolutionary Ethics* (Macmillan, London 1967).
9. Stephen Toulmin, "Contemporary Scientific Mythology", *in* A. MacIntyre (ed.), *Metaphysical Beliefs* (SCM Press, 1970).
10. A. Quinton, 'Ethics and the Theory of Evolution', *in* I. Ramsay (ed.), *Biology & Personality* (Blackwell, Oxford 1965).
11. Statements of 'Ecological Ethics' are not so plentiful, but one useful essay is T.B. Colwell, Jr, 'Some Implications of the Ecological Revolution for the Construction of Value', *in* Laszlo & Wilbur (eds.), *op. cit.,* pp. 245-58. The topic is also related to recent discussions on 'environmental attitudes': see Yi-Fu Tuan's review of this literature in *Science Studies, 1* (April 1971), pp. 215-24.
12. Martin P. Golding, 'Ethical Issues in Biological Engineering', *UCLA Law Review, 15* (1968), pp. 443-79. For an essay review of recent books on medical ethics, see George M. Schurr, 'Array and Disarray in the Medico-ethical Front', *Science Studies, 2* (April 1972), pp. 191-202.
13. An example of a particularly pointed discussion of this kind, aimed at analysing the behaviour of environmental groups, is Mary Douglas' essay, 'Environments At Risk', originally published in the *Times Lit. Suppl.,* 30 October 1970, pp. 1273-75, and also in J. Benthall (ed.), *Ecology: the shaping enquiry* (Longmans, London 1972). This essay is also relevant to the point raised above, in relation to 'Evolutionary Ethics', of the use of science to add authority to a previously held moral position.
14. See, for instance, the readings from Marcuse and Habermas in S.B. Barnes (ed.), *Sociology of Science*
15. Documentation of the Oppenheimer case is now quite extensive. The edited transcript of the entire security hearings, *In the Matter of J. Robert Oppenheimer,* is now available in paperback form (MIT Press, 1970), as is Heinar Kipphardt's play of that name, in English translation Hill & Wang, New York 1968). There is also the play by Joseph Boskin and Fred Krinsky, 'The Oppenheimer Affair'(Glencoe, Beverly Hills 1968). Among historical and biographical works are: Haakon Chevalier, *Oppenheimer: the story of a friendship* André Deutsch, London 1966); Nuell Pharr Davis, *Lawrence and Oppenheimer* (Simon & Schuster, New York 1968); Peter Michelmore, *The Swift Years: the Robert Oppenheimer story* (Dodd & Mead, New York 1969); Abraham Pais, et al., *Oppenheimer* (Scribners, New York 1969); Michel Rouse, *Robert Oppenheimer; the man and his theories* (P.S. Eriksson, New York 1965); Denise Royal, *The Story of J. Oppenheimer* (St. Martins, New York 1969); and Philip M. Stern, *The Oppenheimer Case; security on trial* (Harper & Row, New York 1969).
16. See, for instance, Alasdair MacIntyre, *A Short History of Ethics* (Macmillan, London 1966; Routledge paperback, 1967).
17. This characterisation is close to that proposed by Mesthene ref. 6 although I can see no benefit in labelling this ethical style 'scientific'. There is no reason to assume that ethical and scientific discourses should proceed in similar manners, nor that the adjective 'scientific' should have an authority beyond its proper domain. Besides, beliefs about the nature of scientific method seem to be as variable as ethical values.
18. Donald A. Schon, *Beyond the Stable State* (Temple Smith, 1971).
19. Edgar H. Schein, 'Occupational Socialization In the Professions: the Case of Role Innovation', *J. Psychiat. Res., 8* (1971), pp. 521-30; see also his book, *Professional Education* (McGraw-Hill, 1972).

PART III

CONTRIBUTIONS FROM PRACTICAL EXERCISES: SOCIAL CONTEXTS AND EXPERIENCES

12 WORLD STUDIES

Robin Richardson

The study of contemporary world affairs features increasingly in the
syllabuses of secondary schools, and in the courses of institutions of
higher education. It takes place within the context of traditional
academic disciplines, including the social sciences, and also through
interdisciplinary approaches, in courses named 'international relations',
'international education', 'peace education', 'conflict studies', 'world
studies', 'contemporary studies', and so on. The purpose in this chapter
is threefold: first, to recall the broad contours of certain current
controversies both about world affairs in general and also the functions
of education in particular; second, to consider three main ways in
which world studies can be said, independently of such controversies, to
be of concern to the moral educator; and third, to review two clusters
of practical approaches which are currently being developed in many
educational institutions in Europe and the U.S.A. — games and
simulations, and the idea of community education.

First, then, it is crucially relevant for moral education to recall that
there are certain fundamental differences of opinion at the present time
amongst educators concerned with the study of world affairs. For the
various phrases — 'international understanding', 'world studies', 'peace
education' and so on — are not, or not only, just a question of accident
or locality or taste. Frequently, though not always (indeed not often)
explicitly, the variety of nomenclature in educational institutions
corresponds to a variety of moral values and educational assumptions
in the world at large. Certainly it can be very tempting — and perhaps
sometimes it can also be rather tactful or tactical — to obscure these
controversies beneath a veil of language whose recurring threads are
phrases such as 'the unity of mankind', 'the brotherhood of man', 'one
world', 'global perspective', 'survival of the human species on this
planet', 'world community', 'spaceship earth', and so on. But there are
times — and this chapter would seem to be one of them — when some
clear distinctions, including perhaps some painful ones, need to be made.

For the sake of clarity, though certainly at the risk of caricature, two
principal clusters of views may be identified. Two over-used but
adequate typifications for naming and separating them are 'liberal' and
'radical'. The 'liberal' position, in this context, first began to grow strong

in Europe and the U.S.A. in the late 1940s and early '50s, and in its early days was characterised by firm opposition to the prevailing orthodoxies of the time. It can be said to have two main aspects. The first of these is concern with, as the phrase is, world order. The goal is a system of supra-national laws, framed and enforced by supra-national institutions (for example, a world government), with the primary purpose of preventing open warfare between nation-states. At a period of history when memories of the Second World War still steeped the minds of all adults in the developed world, and when the major landmarks of that world were Berlin, Korea, Suez, Prague, Cuba, such concern with world order was understandable, indeed perhaps inevitable. 'Mankind must put an end to war', ran the much-quoted and well-turned phrase, 'or war will put an end to mankind.' Such language, focusing on the need for supra-national institutions to ensure the survival of the species, received an additional strengthening in the late 1960s and early '70s, with influential books such as *The Limits to Growth* and *Only One Earth*. Talk of nuclear warfare now gave way to talk of depletion of natural resources, and of pollution and over-population, as the recurring aspect. But the same basic 'liberal' assumptions about law and order, and the same basic mental models of world society, remained.

The second main emphasis in the 'liberal' view of world studies is on the need for changes in the content of courses in schools and colleges, changes which will, it is hoped, lead to changes in attitudes and loyalties amongst the young. In greater detail, the characteristic reference is to some or all of the following: 'an understanding and a tolerance . . . for the innumerable traditions and patterns of behaviour found throughout the world';[1] understanding and knowledge of the United Nations and its specialised agencies, and of other forms of 'transcendence of nationalism and growth of supra-national organs of government';[2] 'modifying the consciousness of the average man, so that he thinks of himself as belonging . . . to humanity as a whole';[3] changing the individual's aggressiveness, and the individual's national prejudices and stereotypes; evoking sympathy for the peoples of the Third World; imparting knowledge about global resources, for example the resources of the oceans. Underpinning such concerns, and frequently explicitly cited, have been those famous words from the preamble to the Unesco Constitution: 'since wars begin in the minds of men, it is in the minds of men that the defences of peace must be constructed.' A primary focus, that is to say, has been on the importance of changing attitudes and objects of loyalty amongst individuals. The 'liberal' position, as very roughly sketched here, seems to be increasingly orthodox and influential in educational planning, particularly in Western countries.

The 'radical' critique of the 'liberal' position is by no means that the

163

latter is wholly wrong; but rather, that it does not go deep enough in its preliminary analysis, hence that its prescriptions, both for the world at large and for education in particular, are at best treating symptoms rather than causes, and at worst actually aggravating the trouble.[4] At the political level, the radical stance has been greatly strengthened by certain world events and processes of the last ten years, particularly events and processes in the Third World. At the educational level it has similarly been most clearly articulated in places where there has been a confrontation between the values of developed and developing countries, or where there has been a clearcut social conflict within developed countries.[5] There are four main aspects of the radical position which it is relevant to emphasise here. First, it is said that to speak of the governments of nation-states as the main actors in the international system is to be misleading, indeed obscuring; a more accurate focus is said to be on the behaviour of dominant social and economic elites.[6] Second, supra-national laws to prohibit direct manifest violence *between* the élites of different countries are said to be of fairly slight importance compared with the need for greater justice, hence a redistribution of power and property, *within* these countries. For, third, as evil as direct violence, which hurts or destroys physical life, is 'structural' violence, which limits the realisation (in both senses) of man's psychological potential.[7] Such structural violence is said to be a characteristic, in varying degrees, of all industrialised societies, and to be the primary characteristic of the various institutions which regulate relationships between the developed countries on the one hand and the countries of the Third World on the other. Fourth, the radical position holds that one of the most potent agents of structural violence is a country's educational system: thus, an implication is, if 'liberal' changes in the content of the curriculum are not accompanied by 'radical' changes in learning methods and organisation, little or nothing of importance is being achieved.

This latter argument, that education is characteristically an agent of structural violence, is linked not only to certain political views about the social order but also to certain philosophical views about the nature of knowledge. Roughly and briefly, the argument is as follows. The final experience of a scholar working on the frontiers of knowledge is, it is said, of ultimate mystery and ignorance[8] — of the relative and temporary status of empirical propositions, of the intricate and unavoidable ways in which 'reality' is unknowable apart from selective human senses and from the ordering human mind, of the shocking ways in which many significant constraints on human freedom are invented and fashioned by human beings themselves, not, as most human beings however tend to suppose, by 'God', or 'fate', or 'nature', or 'history', etc. But education is always organised, the argument continues, in such a way that only a carefully selected and rigorously initiated (hence 'reliable') minority are ever permitted access to this final shocking mystery. Thus only a minority achieve 'liberation' from the alienated state in which human beings cannot distinguish between the man-made and the truly objective: only a minority, that is, develop the capacity really to generate new knowledge, or really to understand and change man's social world. It is personal liberation of this kind, not loyalty to supranational institutions created by dominant élites acting together, that the radical seeks to encourage at the individual level, and which he understands to be a crucial aspect of moral education with regard to world affairs.

For the majority of people, the radical continues, education is by no means liberating, but enslaving. For the majority, education does not involve encounter with irreducible mystery, or with the notion that reality is changeable. On the contrary, the argument runs, education involves primarily the initiation into certainty — 'these are the established facts, these are the laws, these are the standards'. And the educator, in this process, is basically no different from a medieval catechist — he is employed by the dominant economic élite to impart, and examine with regard to, 'right answers'. Such right answers crucially involve docility, deference, trust, obedience, dependence, these being the attitudes of mind most required in a situation in which political power and economic wealth are unequally distributed.

It is not appropriate, in this particular place, to seek to commend either the liberal or the radical position at the expense of the other. (If the radical comment is then that such timidity at the actual crunch is precisely a sign of liberation at its most flabby, then so be it.) Certainly to pursue the controversies here would be interesting and relevant. But it is also interesting to consider certain broad generalisations about the moral dimensions of world studies, and certain broad practical approaches, which can be made independently of the controversies. With reference to the moral dimension, three main points are relevant. First, it can be said that world studies offers, to liberal and radical alike, a vast reservoir of illustrations and case-studies which can be used to vivify abstract moral issues, and which can highlight the various factors, partly in human personality and partly in political and social structures, which inhibit or encourage the qualities outlined by John Wilson and Peter Tomlinson in the first part of this book. This approach to world affairs is similar to Gabriel Chanan's and Gerald Collier's view of literature in other chapters here, when they approach fiction for delineations of character and moral dilemmas; or to James Henderson's view of history when he seeks to dwell on examples of 'men and women making relative choices in absolute terms at varying levels of conscious awareness'. Whilst certainly literature and history have a much richer

165

texture, the case-studies drawn from world affairs may have a greater immediacy. Then secondly, it is through the study of certain issues and factors in the world at large that a student may develop certain qualities and skills within himself. For example, by studying concrete examples of 'open' and 'closed' minds in operation, and of the social institutions which stand in dialectical relationship with such minds, the student may himself come to develop the qualities which are said to characterise openness: readiness to consider new evidence — a rich variety of sources for one's beliefs, a rational and tentative attitude towards authority, tolerance of relativity (particularly the relativity of one's own perceptions), and respect for opponents as persons.[9]

Such development, if it happens, is partly unconscious, but partly also a matter of conscious choice. Other relevant examples of it include the following. A study of constraints imposed on human freedom by man-made social and political organisation may help a student to perceive more clearly the external constraints on his own personal situation, and in that sense to become more free of them. A study of the ways in which differing subjective interpretations can arise and be perpetuated, and can lead to objective conflict, may help a student to distinguish more clearly between image and reality in his own perceptions and relationships. A study of the notion of 'respect for persons' and, in contrast, of various forms of 'structural violence', may help a student to have and use a livelier sense of what counts, and of what does not count, in a consideration of other people's interests.

The third main way in which morality and the study of world affairs can intertwine lies in the fact that for many people the events in newspaper headlines and TV newsreels are perceived not only as empirically true but also as a kind of symbolic drama, similar in certain respects to religious myth and to fiction.[10] It can happen, for example, that a relationship in the public and distant world — say, between guerrilla fighters and a strongly established government — is unconsciously perceived to be similar, in its basic structure, to a relationship in the private world: the relationship between child and parent, perhaps, or student and tutor, or spontaneity and discipline within the individual self. It then happens that a person's stated views about the public world, and his expressions of anxiety and hope and so on, may be construed as, amongst other things, statements about his own everyday relationship and sense of identity. Thus talk apparently about the public world of nuclear warfare, for example, may really be about a sense of threat from close, or close-ish, friends and relations. Talk of the need for a strong world government may be expressive of an attempt to deny personal ambivalence and personal capacity for destructiveness; hostility towards foreigners may be related to fear of things much closer home; talk of pollution and depletion may refer to a sense of impotence and despair vis-a-vis the productive activities of a previous generation. And so on. Both the 'liberal' and the 'radical', as sketched briefly here earlier, need an interest in the ways in which the public and private worlds can thus intertwine.

In the measure that public news has indeed these characteristics of myth, the language about it may be seen not only as expressive but also as exploratory. A person may 'use' world affairs, that is to say, rather as a potter uses clay, or as a composer uses sound — a medium to work in. He manipulates the events of the public world into patterns, and hopes thus to order his private feelings and experience. It follows that more accurate and sophisticated understanding of the real external world — its complexity and variousness — may contribute to a more competent self-understanding and integration. In John Wilson's terms, such knowledge of the outer world (GIG) can lead to greater self-awareness (ALLEMP) and greater self-confidence (KRAT).

In the light of such considerations about the moral dimensions of world studies four broad generalisations can be made about the practical design of learning experiences. The first is that most teaching is, and teaching about world affairs par excellence is, an enterprise with profound political implications. In the measure that the situation does not invite and welcome both teacher and student to recognise this, then in that same measure it is likely that the students will have at best an *illusory* opportunity to develop significant moral skills and insights. Second, care needs to be taken in order that students do not, justifiably or otherwise, perceive the situation as one in which they are being nudged towards certain 'correct' answers. Third, the situation needs to capture some realistic sense of the immense complexity, multi-layered and multi-tongued, of the 'world affairs' which are the subject of study. And yet, fourth, there needs to be a trustworthy framework in which risks can reasonably be taken: the risk of discovering further, for example, and as one (radical) text puts it, 'that there is no such thing as objectivity, only degrees of subjectivity; that whatever you say something is, isn't; that one's definitions, assumptions and metaphors determine what "facts" one will uncover; that the world is in constant process of change and we can never see it all; that each of our senses is a censor, and so is each of our sentences . . .[11]

A recent practical development with regard to the study of world affairs, particularly relevant in the light of the four points outlined above, is that which is evoked by the phrase 'games and simulations'. The range of activity is enormous, and includes: working, and highly realistic, models of the real world; but also abstract allegories which have no direct correspondence (that is, no correspondence on the surface) with everyday life; elaborate exercises lasting several days,

167

perhaps using a computer, a telephone system, a printing machine; but also simple little adaptations of snakes and ladders, dice games, and even bingo; role-playing exercises, in which participants try to put themselves in other people's shoes; but also various kinds of party game or psychological experiment. It is not possible to weigh up the pros and cons of each kind of activity here. But a number of potential advantages can be identified, and are perhaps well expressed as a series of hunches, as follows. First, it may be that participants respond with greater pleasure and interest than usual because they find that they themselves are taken seriously as sources of information and imagination. The exercises depend on, they do not appear to devalue, people's everyday and commonsense perceptions, memories, impressions, ideas. In these circumstances it is perhaps easier to use exploratory language of one's own, and to pay serious attention to others. Second, it may be that also at the imaginary level simulation exercises give a satisfying sense of personal worth and importance — people feel, contrary perhaps to their more usual feelings, that the world's at their feet, in their hands, that it can be re-made by human intention, and that veils of mystification can be torn down without danger. This sense of competence may stimulate confidence in one's own ability to make sense of man's social world, and may provide motivation to master increasingly more sensitive models and concepts. Third, it may be that simulation exercises, or at least some simulation exercises, offer an optimum balance between direction on the one hand and freedom to make one's own meanings on the other. Hence participants perhaps have a more rational attitude to authority (neither unduly obsequious nor unduly sceptical), and take responsibility for their own learning. They are likely also, in this frame of mind, to enquire into the mental models and assumptions built into the simulation, and to choose rationally amongst them.

The argument, then, is that the many-faceted world of simulation is, in principle, relevant to the study of contemporary world affairs, particularly when it is the moral aspect of such study which is under focus. It can, that is to say, offer a secure but stimulating arena for the consideration of moral dilemmas and theories; it can offer a distinction between experience and interpretation, such that the student is freer than usual to make his own choices of interpretation; it can offer opportunities for language about public world affairs to order and re-order personal identity and everyday relationships. It *can* do these things — or anyway so the speculation is. Whether it actually does so in practice is likely to depend as much on the activities which follow an exercise as on the coherence of theories which underpin them, and therefore also on the care with which it is first planned, as on the exercise itself. The intention here has been to recall what the main considerations might be, both before and after the actual event.

Let us turn now to consider one further recent development in teaching and learning about world affairs. It is entirely different from simulation in its surface appearance but similar in the way in which it can combine simplicity and complexity, and the student's own feelings and interests on the one hand and the wider world of public affairs on the other. At its most elaborate it has four separate stages. Each is in principle separable from the others, such that they could be undertaken in any order. There is nevertheless an obvious temporal sequence, and that is the one which will be described here. First, students make an active study of certain aspects of their own local environment, — for example some issues in social history, some current controversies and anxieties, some of the main constraints and opportunities being experienced in a particular place and time. The study is active, in the sense that it involves lively interaction between the students and the objects of study (the latter being, indeed, not objects at all, but changing and changeful human beings). And whatever 'objective' measuring devices are used (questionnaires, interview schedules, check-lists and so on) are no more important than the student's own changing reactions, impressions, perceptions. Second, there is an attempt to relate this study of a specific and confined locality to the overall panorama of 'world affairs'. In what ways is this particular locality a paradigm example for major world trends? In what ways does it affect, and in what ways is it affected by, events and processes in other countries? The study at this stage is relatively passive, in the sense that it involves mastering complex theories about global interdependence — hence mainly reading, listening, consulting. But it involves also the active handling and application of concepts: the student is creating an intricate flow chart, with his own research project at the centre, of world-wide influences and repercussions.

The third stage in this exercise involves a return to active participation in the life of the local community from which the study began. The concern now is to affect that community, in however small a way. Work may be of the social kind, or else perhaps directly political, or else an attempt to reflect back to the community some of the insights which have been gained, for example through street theatre or other forms of entertainment, or through a visual exhibition. Fourth, the students link up with students in other parts of the world who have been involved in a similar series of experiences in *their* locality. They exchange examples of their work and reactions, and perhaps visit each other and actually work together. This exchange and mutual visiting can then be a stimulus to a further project, but asking new and more complicated questions, along similar lines. Amongst the many strong points in such a scheme there is the fact that students are meeting with a far greater variety of values and perspectives than is the case with more passive kinds of learning. Such variety could, certainly, be distressing – the variousness and relativity of all things under the sun can lead primarily to world-weariness. But such dangers can be guarded against, particularly if students have a chance to express themselves personally in a variety of ways, including non-verbal art forms, and if it is the excellence of human achievement, not just its variousness, which is being encountered.

To summarise. The study of world affairs, which is becoming increasingly important in the syllabuses and programmes of higher education, can be said to have three main implications for the moral educator: it offers vivid case-studies for consideration; it offers opportunities for the development of moral skills and attitudes; and it offers opportunities to use a public language for the ordering of private experience. But its success or otherwise is linked to the overall educational context in which it occurs. In this respect it is valuable to recall certain crucial controversies at the present time, which can be said to be between broadly 'liberal' positions on the one hand and broadly 'radical' positions on the other. The controversies relate to philosophical questions about epistemology, and to political questions about the distribution of wealth and power within and between countries. Pending resolution of such controversies there seem to be certain practical educational possibilities – for example, the areas known loosely as 'games and simulations' and 'community education' – which are of particular relevance to moral education.

References

1. E. Boyle & J. Lauwerys, in preface to A. Lyall (ed.), *History Syllabuses and a World Perspective* (Longmans and Parliamentary Group for World Government, London 1962) p. ix
2. A. Lyall (ed.), op. cit., p. xv.
3. L. Elvin, 'Education for International Understanding: the Basic Position', *London Educational Review,* vol. 3, No. 1, Spring 1974, p. 3
4. Important books outlining radical positions with regard to world studies are C. Wulf (ed.), *Handbook on Peace Education* (I.P.R.A., Oslo, 1974), and C. Wulf (ed.), *Kritische Friedenserziehung* (Suhrkamp Verlag, Frankfurt 1973). See also *Bulletin of Peace Proposals* (Oslo 1974), vol. 3. Recent polemical books in the U.K., explicitly antagonistic to 'liberal' curriculum reform (though not specifically concerned with world affairs) include J.F. White, *Toward a Compulsory Curriculum*, (Routledge & Kegan, London 1973), and D. Holly, *Beyond Curriculum,* (Hart-Davis MacGibbon, London 1973).

5. For example the writings of Illich; and, extremely influential in many parts of the world, P. Freire, *Pedagogy of the Oppressed,* (Penguin Harmondsworth, 1972); see also the readings in N. Keddie (ed.), *Tinker Tailor: the myth of cultural deprivation* (Penguin, Harmondsworth 1973).

6. For example, N. Chomsky, *For Reasons of State* (Collins, London 1973), passim. Chomsky cites as a text, and with warm agreement, some words of Bakunin: 'The State is the organised authority, domination, and power of the possessing classes over the masses . . .'

7. The term 'structural violence' is developed at length by Johan Galtung, in various articles over the years in the *Journal of Peace Research* published in Oslo. For brief presentations of Galtung's views in the U.K. see A. Curle, *Making Peace* (Tavistock, London 1971), and A. Curle, 'Education for Peace: the international dimension', *London Educational Review,* vol. 3, no. 1, 1974. Curle's own term is 'peacelessness'.

8. B. Bernstein, 'On the Classification and Framing of Education Knowledge', in M.F.D. Young (ed.), *Knowledge and Control* (Collier-MacMillan, London 1971), p. 57.

9. M. Rokeach, *The Open and Closed Mind* (Basic Books, New York 1960). And see Peter Tomlinson's excellent summary in Chapter 2.

10. This is argued at length in R. Richardson & J. Chapman, *Images of Life* (SCM, 1973), ch. 6 and 7.

11. N. Postman & C. Weingartner, *Teacher as a Subversive Activity* (Penguin Harmondsworth, 1971) p. 114.

12. In the U.K. the most accessible account of simulations is J.L. Taylor & R. Walford, *Simulation in the Classroom* (Penguin, Harmonsworth 1972). With particular reference to world studies see D. Wolsk, 'New Approaches to Education for International Understanding', and J. Colclough, 'An Innovative Curriculum Approach to Education for International Understanding', both in *Ideas* (University of London Goldsmith's College), no. 27, February 1974; also H.R Targ, 'Simulation, Teaching and Peace Studies' in Wulf (ed.), op. cit., and various articles (for example 'Peace Games', and 'World Order Values and Inter-Nation Simulations') by G.L. Thorpe & B. Reardon, available from Institute for World Order, 11 West 42nd Street, New York 10036. For more general and brief discussions see references to games in J. Bruner, *Toward a Theory of Instruction* (Havard University Press, 1967), and D. Holly, op. cit., pp. 123-4.

13 EXPERIMENTS IN THE EXPLORATION OF VALUES

Gerald Collier

An Experimental Course

This chapter is an account of an experimental course conducted in three versions during the period 1968-70. On the first occasion it was used in a summer school in an American University in 1968: the 'contact time' was one hour twenty minutes each day for twenty-seven days. Most members of the class of thirty (Class A) were practising teachers working for a Master's degree, with a sprinkling of undergraduates, doctoral candidates and candidates for professional certification. The second occasion was at Bede College, Durham, a Church of England college of education, where it was used in the autumn term of 1969 with a group of twenty-five first-year students (Class B) on a time allowance of 1½ hours a week for ten weeks. On the third occasion it was used with a third-year group of students (Class C) at Bede College in the ten-week period January – March, 1970. In the latter two cases the work was shared with Mr J.A. Thrower, then lecturer in Religious Knowledge at Bede College, now Lecturer in Religious Studies at the University of Aberdeen, and a number of modifications were made as compared with the course given in America.

The course in each case opened with the showing of a film, *Twelve Angry Men*, a study of a jury at a murder trial. The jury's tentative verdict is 'guilty'; a single member pleads for some discussion of the evidence and begins to sow doubts which eventually lead to a reversal of this verdict. The film is a study of an individual of more than usual integrity who is able to maintain his uneasy doubts in the face of opposition and indifference; this character, Davis, is played by Henry Fonda.

At the close of the film the class was divided into small groups ('syndicates') of five persons. In principle they chose one another on the basis of previous acquaintance but in practice there had been little previous mutual knowledge among the members of classes A and B. The syndicates were then issued with assignments, consisting of several questions on the mode of influence of the Henry Fonda character and a final question asking for a definition of 'integrity' on the basis of this film. Each syndicate was required to hand in a report on the questions posed. The lecturer assembled these reports in a formal lecture of 20-30 minutes, accompanied by a duplicated summary, and a plenary discussion was held.

In assignments (2) and (3) a further study of the concept of integrity was undertaken through an examination of Bernard Shaw's *Saint Joan,* Plato's *Socrates* (in the *Crito*), T.S. Eliot's 'Thomas a Becket' (*in Murder in the Cathedral*) and Tolstoy's 'Ivan Ilytch'. In the earliest version of these assignments the above characters were all included in a single exercise, together with Antigone from the play by Sophocles, it being assumed that the members of the class would be familiar with the majority of the figures. With classes B and C, whose members were known to be younger and less widely read, the characters were divided between two assignments, each given to three syndicates. In each of these assignments, which extended the range of situations in which integrity was being expressed, one question asked for a re-definition of the concept to cover the full range of situations studied. The practice in most cases was for a syndicate to distribute the reading among its members, to debate the questions set, and to arrange for their views — whether agreed or conflicting — to be written up.

The first three assignments present a number of 'heroic' figures, with, in addition, one less admirable character, Ivan Ilytch, who may however be considered to reveal a 'heroic' revulsion against his previous life. The next phase of the work was to show a film, *Saturday Night and Sunday Morning,* in which the leading character, Arthur Seaton, is an anti-hero. One question in assignment (4) read 'It may be said that in some ways Arthur Seaton resembles many unskilled manual workers: he is resistant or irreverent towards authority, unpuritanical towards sex, rather willing to resort to blows. What evidence do you find of other qualities, such as (a) a willingness to stand up for his own freedom of decision; (b) a recognition of the restricted outlook and experience of his parents; (c) an understanding of his own defects; and (d) acceptance of a need for eventual conformity to certain social patterns? (The question was not of course intended to imply that unskilled manual workers have a monopoly of such characteristics, only that sociological studies show some differentiation between social classes in the directions indicated).

Assignment (5) moved to a fresh field. The students were asked to study three chapters of Carl Rogers' *On Becoming a Person*[1] and set out the features of what Rogers calles 'a fully functioning person'. Subsequent questions required them to apply these criteria to the six characters so far studied.

Following assignment (5) a third film was shown, *Harp of Burma,* a Japanese film directed by Ichikawa, about a young Japanese soldier in Burma in 1945, who was drawn to becoming a Buddist monk and burying the remains of dead soldiers, as a kind of atonement for the evils of war.

In assignment (6) the questions focused on the evidence assembled by C.S. Lewis in *The Abolition of Man*[2] for the existence of a corpus of moral principles (the 'Tao') widely spread, both historically and geographically, among mankind, and required the student to make cross-comparisons with Carl Rogers' criteria for a fully functioning person. They also required the student to examine the nature of the authority that sanctioned such codes, and to ask themselves how far these were felt to be imposed by a divine agency, by a tradition transmitted by older people, or by the individual conscience, and how far to be accepted by civilised persons as a natural part of civilised life.

In the American course assignment (6) was replaced by three assignments giving a more extended treatment of the psychological basis of moral development.

Analysis of the Processes Involved in the Course

So much for the exercise. I turn to an analysis of the processes.

The first three assignments had several objects. The first was to study a group of figures of exceptional integrity, attempting to get inside their minds, to observe the pressures at work on them, to follow the interaction between them and their associates, and to understand the nature of their influence on other people. The second object was to provide the opportunity for the students to argue out the validity or otherwise of the judgement in specific and complex situations against that of the figures studied and against that of their fellows in the syndicate and the class. The moral judgements of young people are often based on black-and-white principles, on an over-simple interpretation of complex situations, and the present exercise can develop a richer appreciation of balancing factors and claims. The third was to define the moral quality of 'integrity' — one of the virtues most consistently advocated and held up as an ideal by the great figures of the Western tradition — in order to see more clearly what this quality is and what it is not; thus giving the students some experience of the conceptual clarification needed in any fully developed moral thinking. And fourthly there was the object of clarifying the nature of the arguments involved in reaching the moral judgments studied — the kind of evidence selected and inferences drawn, the assimilation of concrete situations to different value-principles, the deciding on the relevance of particular principles or the priorities among them.

In the first and second of these processes the student is acquainting himself with characters of an order he rarely meets in the flesh, in some degree sharing in their motives, their conflicts, and their decisions, in a concrete, operational sense. This is an element that received inadequate attention in many discussions on moral education. In Wilson's *Introduction to Moral Education*[3], for example, the full significance of his components PHIL, EMP, GIG, etc., may well be lost on students unless given vivid embodiment in convincing figures of above-average stature. Whitehead expressed a profound truth when he said, 'There is no moral education apart from the habitual vision of greatness'.[4]

In the second process in particular the students are developing an insight into the various elements John Wilson lists under the headings EMP and GIG. In effect EMP involves the identification of a number of motives and emotions operating in groups of individuals in complex fictional situations, recognising whether the individuals appear to be conscious of them or not, and in the process of discussion uncovering the emotions and responses evolved in themselves by the fictional events and by their fellow students. GIG involves the recognition of the facts and events the fictional characters take into account in their moral decisions, and have a more developed awareness of where to look for such factors in complex situations and how to articulate them.

In the third and fourth processes the student is attempting to conceptualise qualities in which he has vicariously shared, to draw and re-draw their defining boundaries. (Some of the source material drew on existentialist thinking — Marcel, Sartre — since this has been pre-occupied with the exploration of 'good faith'). These latter tasks are emphasised in Wilson's work.

The four processes involve an analysis both of psychological and of moral questions. Students have to ask themselves questions about motives and interaction on the one hand, and, on the other, about moral quality, the basis of justification, of the actions of the six characters. Each process of study involves both types of analysis. The processes are illustrated in the passages quoted from syndicate reports at the end of the paper.

The film *Saturday Night and Sunday Morning* was introduced for two reasons. In the first place it was felt that a discussion of heroic characters can rather easily become airborne, and that this film would bring students down to earth (if they needed it). Secondly, it is necessary at some stage to define where integrity, associated with self-deception, passes over into disregard for other people, and in Arthur Seaton's character the former is a good deal less conspicuous than the latter. Many students in fact were unable to detect the former; but the following extract from an American syndicate's report illustrates the balance of comment as it emerged after the setting out of Carl Rogers' analysis of the characteristics of a fully functioning person in Assignment (5).

'On the surface Arthur (Seaton) seemed to demonstrate the qualities of a man who is "all too human" or even "animal". He was pleasure-seeking, irresponsible, disrespectful and a blatant liar. He was unconcerned about others and showed a definite lack of morality ... He lacked stable relationships in his association and even used others. He was a devil-may-care ruffian who wanted only to enjoy himself. At the same time he demonstrated some of the characteristics of the fully-integrated personality delineated (above). Arthur Seaton was independent and non-confirming. He was not going to be "ground" into a pattern. He did not try to play a role just to please others. He demonstrated self-awareness and self-acceptance. His attitude was self-confidence. "I'm me and nobody else". He believed in what he was doing and knew what he did not want to become.'

In Assignment (5) the psychological elements of the studies of assignments (1) − (4) are extended in a more generalised form. Here the students are asked to note the personal qualities a psychotherapist observes emerging in patients as they become more balanced, or able to cope, and to examine in which respects the six characters by Rogers can be listed, in the following way, as a series of trends of personal development:

1. Away from living behind a facade or mask.
2. Away from accepting the coercive demands (or expectations in so far as these are felt to be coercive) of other people on one's own behaviour or responses; that is away from merely learning to conform, merely trying to please other people.
3. Towards self-direction or autonomy in which one makes one's own decisions on the basis of one's own convictions as to what is right.
4. Towards openness to experience; this is, towards a greater awareness of the freshness of the ordinary experiences of life; and also a greater awareness of one's own inner responses and motives, a willingness to 'accept' those feelings in oneself which one disapproves of and to trust some deeper 'self' one finds within.
5. Towards acceptance of continual change and evolution.
6. Towards acceptance of other people as they are, without criticism, seeing things from their point of view.

In the sixth assignment the task is to make a comparative study of the personal qualities formulated by Carl Rogers with those to which the moral codes of a number of human civilisations appear to point.

The latter have been listed by C.S. Lewis thus:

(1) The law of general beneficence:
    (a) negative: against killing, cruelty, oppression.
    (b) positive: in favour of kindness, good will.

(2) The law of special beneficence: towards one's own family and relations.

(3) Duties to parents, elders, ancestors.

(4) Duties to children and posterity.

(5) The law of justice:
    (a) sexual justice
    (b) honesty
    (c) justice in court, etc.

(6) The law of good faith and veracity.

(7) The law of magnanimity: willingness to defend a good way of life, if necessary at the cost of life.

The juxtaposition of the two lists of behaviour-elements provides a useful stimulus to thought.

The purpose of introducing the Japanese film at this stage was in part to prevent the exercise being too neatly tied up in rational terms: the obstinate problems of evil and suffering cannot be left out of the debate. In fact the film's approach to these problems served to give the summary statements of Roger's principles and C.S. Lewis's Tao a significance beyond the commonsese, everyday meanings; and indeed to set the problems of moral principle more firmly in a world context.

The feature films were used for several reasons. As with television, a story told by a film has an immediacy of impact not shared by purely literary media, since it is conveyed by an amalgam of verbal and non-verbal modes of communication similar to those of everyday experience. The images of personalities and relationships cohere and come across through a richer and more complex texture of words, gestures, tones of voice and facial expressions than in a novel or printed play. Thus if appropriately chosen a film creates an emotional engagement in the students which can serve as a 'carrier' both for the literary texts which follow and for the subsequent analyses and discriminations. This is particularly important for those students whose verbal sensitiveness is not great and for whom the literary classics tend to be opaque. Thus students who have chosen specialist studies other than literature are put in a position of deep involvement in the human situations and problems that are explored in good literature, and this is shared by the other members of the class.

The Relevance of the 'Syndicate' Pattern of Organisation

Finally a comment on the method of organisation of the students' working situation. The central core of the course was the work done within the syndicates, and the essence of this was the arguing out among the members of each syndicate views they wished to report in answer to the questions posed in the assignments. The material of the discussions held within the syndicates came either from the films seen or from the texts read, the latter being selected passaged indicated in the assignments and distributed among the members of each syndicate. When the tutor summarised the syndicate reports in his lecture he revealed as much of his own views as appeared relevant.

This type of organisation has an important bearing on several aspects of moral development. In the first place the students are in general unable to learn the tutor's views on the questions raised, until after their own views have been formulated. They are therefore less likely to be influenced either towards or against conformity with his views. It is true that in the American course there was a final examination and this introduced an element of absolute judgement on the part of the tutor. But this is not inherent in the use of syndicate methods, as I have noted elsewhere[5]. It is true too that a tutor may at times wish to contribute his personal views to a syndicate's discussion. But even so, his contribution will be fragmentary and likely to be lost to sight when he moves on. In short, this pattern or organisation makes it easier for a genuine dialogue to arise between the tutor and the students.

Secondly, the lack of mutual understanding and confidence between the generations can easily, in normal seminar contexts, be masked by habits of politeness and the pressures of examinations, whereas the syndicates are able to formulate their views before the tutor selects them for his lecture summary. It is true that the tutor may still misread the evidence of the reports: nevertheless the evidence of students' thinking is likely to be available in more decisive form than in a seminar discussion. The structure gives the opportunity for the students to move the debate in fresh directions, to explore new approaches to value questions.

It may be argued that the tutor *ought* to be influencing the students' moral judgement, since he is (or should be) wiser and more sophisticated in his views. I suggest that his most appropriate mode of influence is through the provision of assignments felt by students to be relevant to their interests and experience, the bringing of significant texts to their attention in a setting which enables them to make effective use of them, the pressing of certain questions of the kind already outlined, the creation of a climate of genuine enquiry in ethical questions, and the treatment of their views in a way which demonstrates that he respects and values them. To do all this constitutes a fairly severe test of his own 'performance' in the exercise of — in Wilson's terminology — PHIL, EMP, GIG, etc. in this particular type of teaching situation.

Third, in moral questions especially, the personal factors loom large and students who have decided the membership of their own syndicates are likely to be better able to tolerate the inevitable divergences of response and orientation which have to be worked through. Such divergences arise from differences in social class background and in ideology as well as in temperament and outlook, and an important part of a student's moral education lies in learning to accept and appreciate the unexpected depth or shallowness of his own responses as well as the richness and the diverse contributions of other people's. Each syndicate tends to develop its own culture, in which mutual understanding and insight are important factors, and individuals are caught up in a more intimate and detailed searching into one another's outlook. To use Wilson's terms again, the syndicate organisation is likely to result in a further development of PHIL and EMP in the participants.

Finally, the intense and protracted debates *under the above conditions* appear to help students to clarify their judgment and improve their analytical skill. One can observe them developing their powers of deliberation and exploration in dealing with complex issues and strengthening their capacity for joint thinking and judgment. They learn a good deal about themselves, making explicit their own inner, unverbalised responses and discovering in some degree where their own deeper priorities lie. On the cognitive side they learn above all to inter-relate more effectively the abstractions of academic sources with the particularities of personal experience and response. In these particular courses the least successful part, perhaps, has been the training in the analysis of moral argument and inference; the questions in the assignments have evidently offered insufficient scope in this direction.

APPENDIX

Example A

Question (1)   How does the concept of integrity presented by Henry Fonda compare with that portrayed in Eliot's *Murder in the Cathedral?* How is the idea modified when it is a matter of the individual's wrestling within his own mind as to the right action for him to take?

'Although there is no clear question to be answered here, the play poses some difficult questions about Becket's integrity, that of his followers and the knights. Becket was of central interest naturally but the group felt that the knights had a kind of group integrity . . . the fact that they disclaim any self-interest or quest for favour we found of interest, for if

179

it is to be believed then they must have been acting to enforce their ideals which Becket had opposed. They had murdered through 'duty', for Becket had opposed their King to whom they owed their allegiance and their position.

'The King and barons had a sort of integrity to maintain the social order and power stratification, both of which were endangered by Becket, and so the knights had acted as one to defend their position. They are loyal to the Church and see it as being attacked by Becket . . . This does not excuse the murder at all, but they had tried to defend the integrity of their whole class by the only means possible to them, and in doing so perhaps showed that they held the integrity of their class stronger than the other barons who had agreed with them to uphold this integrity but were not willing to defend it to the uttermost.'

Example B

Question (1)   As above.

'This question particularly interested us as an example of the changing emphasis that we put on integrity. It would seem that integrity predicates must change when society changes . . . We as a group could have little sympathy with Becket . . . Becket was merely standing in the way of history. Becket was true to what he believed but . . . he wanted to die not because of the issue itself but for the sake of martyrdom. "To do the right thing for the wrong reasons" . . . Becket and Sir Thomas More are both caught in the same position. They must die to be true to their convictions yet their deaths will not really alter the situation. They will go into the Church's hagiographies but not stem the flow of history to the appearance of the secular society . . . The main point that emerges is the need to be constantly aware that without a real grasp of the situation the person is not acting for the right reasons. Knowledge must be one of the predicates of integrity.

'We spent two hours discussing this question on which each of us held very different opinions, this being due to the insights of each of the members on the question of integrity. Integrity involves shades of meaning that do not at (once) seem to be present but as we discussed this question it became clear that these semantic subtleties cannot be avoided if we are to do justice to this concept.'

Example C

Question (2)   Has the concept of integrity to be modified in such a case as that of Ivan Ilytch in Tolstoy's short story? How far

do you consider Ivan to have possessed integrity in his
early years? in his professional life? in the later stages
of his illness?

'Early years and professional life: Ivan lived within a system . . .
which was based not on the right man for the right post, but rather on
the man with the right position or with access to the right ear getting
the position. This method was well understood by Illytch who after an
initial flirtation with liberalism, accepted the system and worked
within it. He worked efficiently at the job which demanded decisions,
vis-à-vis cases before the court and in the performance of his professional
role he could be said to have integrity.

'The second opinion on this holds the contrary view. In this early
stage Ivan had no integrity because he merely played a passive role in
the system, causing no-one any harm, not distinguishing himself in any
way and because he created no embarrassment to the social order, he
gained steady preferment. This behaviour is sub-human. Ivan failed to
see that jobs are just not to be done, they involve their being done
responsibly. This raises the whole issue of decision making.

'Later stages of his illness: this is the first occasion when anything
resembling integrity is involved. Ivan is in an 'angst' situation – he is
faced with a factor that he cannot cope with – death. He cannot throw
a party and so avoid the issue. For the first time he has to reconcile and
come to terms with the question of his identity. His shock and the
turning point of the story comes when he realises that he has wasted his
life. His life has not been a great success but a total failure – but he can
still do something about this situation – he can *accept* it. Once this is
done he becomes more integrated.'

Example D

Question (1) and (2)   As above.

'Becket was a man who had been ambitious and a frequenter of
Court circles. He had in all this time conformed to the morality of the
group, living in accordance with its values. On his accession to a place of
. . . power in the Church of England, the need to conform to the group
morality was outgrown. Instead of having to conform to external values,
as represented by the tempters . . . he began to be guided by his own
inner values to the extent that finally he lost his life for these values.
Becket's mystical experience confirmed for him the validity of his own
inner values.

Maslow's view was quoted by the group in this connection: 'Something
real' – i.e. starting from one's own experience – 'is the total collapse of
all sources of values outside the individual'. The group came to the

conclusion that values coming from within the individual are the only ones with any validity. Jung was also quoted in this connection. Living by the dictates of the personality is, he says, ' . . . an act of high courage . . . the absolute affirmation of all that constitutes the individual'. It was apparent that Becket had come to realise that, as Montaigne said, 'the greatest thing in the world is to know how to belong to ourselves'.

The concept of integrity as arrived at in considering Fonda's character, that is living by one's conscience, has to be modified in the face of Ivan Ilytch's life, because, as can be seen in the life of Ivan Illytch, such a conscience may be one that has been given to one. In his early life his feelings of self-recrimination ceased 'when he saw that such conduct was practised by people of high standing and not considered wrong by them'. His affairs, his sycophancy, were done 'with clean hands, in clean linen, with French phrases, and, what was of most importance, in the very highest of society and consequently with the approval of persons of rank.' In his business life 'the thing was to exclude everything with the stamp of life in it . . . and not to admit any sort of relations with people except official relations and then only on official grounds.' His own personality was suppressed to the pojnt that only the 'right' people were cultivated, the 'right' sort of parties were given in the 'right' sort of surroundings. It was only in the face of death, when he had to find some justification for his life, that Ivan Illytch was able to admit 'No, it was all wrong', and with this knowledge and genuine feelings for his wife and son was able to die peacefully.'

Example E

Question (4)   In the cases so far examined, integrity has been seen as a matter for the individual in opposition to his enemies or to something in himself; can one envisage integrity which is shared by a group, such as a small group of men trying to reform a corrupted organisation and working together over a long period of time?

'The immediate reaction to question (4) was to search up actual examples of groups holding a forceful group integrity, for all members of the syndicate felt that this was feasible. For example there is a distinct integrity necessary between people working closely together to fight crime. One cannot envisage the success of the Untouchables against the Chicago Mafia as having been so complete had not all its members had the same views on morality, justice and the need to uphold social freedom at all costs, even their lives. The fact that they did this in return for a meagre pittance, danger to themselves and family, despite the opposition of superiors already corrupted by Capone, shows them to have been men of integrity. Doubtless similar views on life and society had first brought them together, but this worked mainly as a bse, after which with time the group developed its own integrity imposed most willingly on its members, so that they owed allegiance to it and its ideals. Presumably this allegiance to the group integrity would continue until the personal integrity of the person in that group is altered by forces external to the group in such a way as to supersede the group allegiance.'

References

1. Houghton Mifflin, USA, 1961
2. Bles, London 1943
3. J. Wilson, N. Williams, & B. Sugarman, (Penguin, Harmondsworth 1967).
4. *The aims of Education* (Williams and Norgate, 1929).
5. 'Syndicate methods: further evidence and comment', *Universities Quarterly*, vol. 23, Autumn 1969.

14 POLYTECHNICS: MORAL EDUCATION?

Valerie Pitt

Polytechnics, for those naive enough to believe what they read in the educational papers, are Johnny-Come-Latelys to higher education: called into being by the wave of a White Paper. Like most Press images this is an illusion. Most of the White Paper polytechnics are metamorphoses of institutions often older than their local university, indeed than all but the most senior of English universities. Their Prospero was the practical instinct of industrial England which, sensing its own future, conjured, more or less from nothing, the nineteenth-century paraphernalia of our alternative education: 'night school', part-time education, technical colleges; the complex of qualifications − City and Guilds examinations, the syllabuses of the professional Institutes, the ramifications of the London External Degree system − provided what the universities neither would nor could supply − the means of training and education in the skills required by an industrialised economy. The polytechnics belong here: whatever the precise date of their foundation they are culturally Victorian as the universities are culturally medieval.

This is commonplace but very important in our discussion. Moral education, any education, is not an unconditioned activity: unless, and the mere thought is intolerable, its end is some kind of social indoctrination, some kind of 'conversion', it is necessarily dialectical: the personal culture of the student reacts with, and sometimes resists, that of his teachers − and so sets limits to their endeavours. So does the culture, the moral ecology so to speak, of the societies in which we educate our young people − and, in this case, we say it is Victorian. It is, of course, a disintegrating Victorianism − crumbling or shattering under strains which may be a stimulus to future evolution, or simply distructive. Still, this is our 'situation'; the ground of our encounter with our students, moral or intellectual, is defined by the history and present dilemmas of our common society.

Victorian, however, is an ambiguous adjective. The polytechnic situation can be more precisely stated: it is local, secular, and extremely vulnerable to market forces. For the polytechnics, like the rest of our alternative education, are a great monument to *laisser faire:* not planned to meet an educational or even a social need but developing, haphazardly, in response to the needs of an increasingly sophisticated economy. It is significant that most of the designated polytechnics were like other major institutions in technical education founded originally at the old centres of commerce and heavy industry – in Manchester or Sheffield, say, or London rather than in Ipswich or Salisbury. What is more, their work, and their reputations, which were often considerable, were specialised or at least dominated by the studies in particular demand in their geographical area: languages and commercial law in Central London, heavy engineering, 'textile technology' and so on in the Midlands and the North. These institutions are, or were, local in a particular sense: like schools they served a 'neighbourhood community' but more importantly they were symbiotic with local industry. This is a situation which had changed or is changing, principally because industry itself is no longer local: that is, based in and limited by a particular geographical area. But it has left its mark on the shape and culture of the polytechnics. Much of the work of the polytechnics is still 'part-time' or 'sandwich' work. The assumption which still struggles feebly through D.E.S. circulars on the Binary system is that local industry will 'release' its talented young men (and women – if they can be found) to fill up the polytechnic courses as it sent its apprentices there in earlier days. Sometimes it does (it depends on the state of the industry in question), but even when the proportion of part-time to full-time students is comparatively small it makes for a certain amorphousness in the student body. It shifts from day to day – and with sandwich schemes from term to term. Again, the increasing number of full-time students in polytechnics is aware – as university students are not – that the life of learning at the polytechnic is only half what they're about: their professional qualification is often, formally, only completed by professional experience and even when it is not, the *raison d'etre* of the place itself, the preoccupations of their teachers and their fellow students, thrusts the work world on them in ways often incomprehensible in 'academic' institutions.

Their relationship in fact with the body which educates them is peripheral. Many of them are centred elsewhere; in their existing work situation if they are part-time students, or in the job or profession for which they are being trained. It is the most difficult thing in the world for a polytechnic to discover and maintain an identity, a cohesion within itself, for the edges of its community overlap and are perpetually merging with those of the community in the local commercial life or the professional communities to which many of its staff and students belong. This amorphousness is increased by fortuitous factors; most polytechnics have as yet no Student Union buildings and no campuses and some of them are on two or three sites some miles, even cities, apart. There is little or no residential accommodation for students, let along for staff, so that outside teaching time the whole community melts away into commuter belts: it dissolves and remakes itself every day.

There are those who would argue that this is a GOOD THING: that there ought not to be any artificial barrier between student society and the working world. That may or may not be true: the point is that it is so, and since it is we have to discard one standard concept, almost the orthodoxy, about moral education — that it is, to use a phrase of William Temple's, 'Education in and through a community'. It was always very much an Arnoldian notion, part of the character-forming ethos with which the public schools infected the whole of our educational system, and as a notion depended very much on the creation of invisible walls, of a network of convention and loyalties within a closed educational enclave. The polytechnics neither have nor can have such an artificial cloister and in that respect they are more of our own time, more revealing of the problems we face in the education of young adults than almost any other institution. For without that inherited web of conventions and traditions, even without an accepted system of impersonal etiquettes and hierarchies, every question is open, every relationship, even the most trivial encounter, is person to person and something of a strain on both. This of course describes the characteristics of modern society, which is more open, looser, less restrictive, but also less sustaining to its members than the more structured societies of the past. The peculiar amorphousness of the polytechnics may very well make them typical, almost instructive specimens of our moral situation.

There is, however, something very odd in their situation. Polytechnics because they are local, are or have been especially vilnerable to the economic fortunes of industry. New technologies, booms, recessions, mergers, bankruptcies, anything which changes the geography of trade and industry forces them into new ways. Their students must be sought further afield, their courses diversified, and, with the increasing subtlety and centralisation of so much modern management, the character of the education they offer is, and has to be, in a constant state of transmutation. They are also, like other institutions of higher education, subject to that other economic nightmare: the aberrations of 'manpower and planning' and the fluctuation of student demand. This being so one would expect them to be politically minded — moved, that is, by their own problems to a concern about the structures of society. We ought to expect that at least one ground of moral encounter with our students would lie in what are commonly called questions of social conscience — about the ways in which the management of our economic life bear hard or easy on the individual. With some students this, of course, is the case and the polytechnics have, like other institutions, their ration of political activists of all varieties and extremities — but not usually amongst students in the traditional

186

disciplines. The tradition in fact among staff and students, to say nothing of governing bodies, is apolitical in the usual English way: acquiescence in the *status quo* is not politics; criticism, question, agitation about it, is. The tradition, indeed, is deeper than that: any agitation, question or debate in matters of philosophy or religion is liable to disquiet the place. Though everything is open to question, the whole culture of the institution inhibits questioning, or indeed any breach of a certain kind of decorum.

This is, partly, an accident of history. Many of the institutions of technical and commercial education in England at any rate were set up in the wake of the great Victorian rows about denominational schools: their founders were determined to keep them out of ecclesiastical squabbles and made them deliberately secular. It is not, for instance, ten years since the London polytechnics were released from conditions in their original trusts which forbade students to engage with religous denominations or political parties on the premises of the institutions. Whatever the beliefs of its members, which were their own affair, the polytechnic itself remained neutral. There were fascinating local anomalies in the understanding of the trusts: for instance, some polytechnics permitted, or at least ignored, the activities of some very aggressive evangelical societies, but became distinctly unhappy about the discussion of religious and political controveries in an academic context, say in the teaching of social history to engineering or chemistry students. The problems here were not, and are not, those of academic freedom but of a peculiar institutional shyness not merely in matters of social and political conviction but, more interestingly, in moral and spiritual questions. To raise such matters at work is almost indelicate: they are felt to be private, intimate, tabu.

This is consistent with the openness of polytechnic communities. Their members are inside the institution in the matter of their professional studies, outside it in the matter of personal beliefs and convictions. It is difficult to see how, given the history of our alternative education, it could be otherwise — or why, indeed, the founders of the London polytechnics felt obliged to write such an inevitable neutrality into their trusts. After all the whole paraphernalia came into being not for *sophos* (there is very little market for the true, the beautiful, the just) but for *techne,* for the multifarious skills without which our economy cannot, now, operate. And even when the 'skill' is the concomitant of a rigorous theoretical discipline, *techne* is intrinsically neutral, secular, amoral: it does not question its own ends.

It is, incidentally, the importance of the polytechnics, and indeed of other institutions in technical education, within a developing industrial economy which makes nonsense of the sentimental claim that they are the universities of the working class. Beyond the economic need for a skilled work force was the deeper, more personal demand of intelligent individuals for status and vocation within the new industrial order and there is no question but that the 'techs' supplied that. That is, they supplied 'qualifications', the guarantee to society of particular acquirements and to the individual a recognised ladder to place and prosperity. Anyone with a working class background two or three generations back knew perfectly well why young men gruelled their way through the uninspired and often outdated syllabuses of various professional bodies. It was *to better themselves:* to work themselves upwards from the artisan classes into a professional elite. It was by no means an endeavour to be despised: it was often, indeed, powered by profound moral, political or even religious conviction — but that was extra, peculiar to the individual, not the system.

The inherited ethos of the polytechnics is, then, in the strictest sense secular, related with Benthamite precision to the achievement of measurable, this-worldly ends, untroubled with speculation about the ends themselves, the value or the justice of the work in hand. This has its own moral austerity: no one should undervalue what the Victorians rightly believed to be the beneficial effect on character of work well done:

> The student must not be daunted by difficulties, but conquer them by patience and perseverance and . . . above all, he must seek elevation of character without which capacity is worthless and worldly succes is naught.

Samuel Smiles is still read in the polytechnics: not surprisingly — *The Lives of the Engineers* is part of their history. There are still men about there (there were more ten years ago) in whom *techne* has become one way to *sophos:* for doesn't Aristotle say somewhere that the just man deals in justice — that moral character is a function of action, not speculation? The practice of integrity in the conscious attempt to understand physical laws and administrative principles, and to apply them to the achievement of order in particular cases is a kind of justice. Such men would find it an unholy embarrassment to be taxed with any such righteousness and, indeed, the essence of this kind of virtue is that it is totally unself-conscious. It remains, however, true that the culture of the polytechnics is rooted in a stratum of conscientiousness, decency and sobriety which belong, undoubtedly, to the Victorian gospel of work.

That of course is a museum morality — or ought to be: as dead and gone as the steam train and the stovepipe hat. Certainly it is passing, for whatever the righteousness of individuals no polytechnic, or none that I know, presents the pleasing, Carlylean vision of a community united by the work ethic. How could we, since so much of our time is devoted to programming work processes, whether intellectual or physical, from human to electronic agents? That isn't a joke, or if it is it's an irony of the *Zeitgeist,* that great God of *laisser faire.* For the industrial economy which called our alternative education into being is now so massive in scale and so complex that the *techne* it requires from it is different both in kind and scope from traditional commercial and industrial skills. The more sophisticated the society the more its professional elite require a conceptual and theoretical education in principles and problems rather than in the detail of practice. Moreover, the management of advanced economies throws up questions which are really not yet understood, though it is clear that solving them requires and will require the mastery of theoretical disciplines not, hitherto, thought of as vocational. This is not a revelation to the polytechnics any more than it is to the universities: their courses have had to be adapted and diversified over generations not only with the change in demand but with advances in knowledge. The problem here lies in the pace and the kind of change. The polytechnics have had to respond, however awkwardly, to public pressures *against* the merely vocational education. Everyone talks of the need for trained manpower: no one officially loves the intensely specialist career education which they still insist it requires. All students, it is decreed, must therefore acquire an understanding of society and, more ominously still, some insight into value judgments. Superficially, of course, the requisite discipline can still be made to serve the binary mammon: social science becomes management, English becomes communication, and all faces are saved. But it won't do. Just as the natural sciences resist subordination to political and economic ends, so the humane disciplines necessarily call into question the utilitarian certainties of our alternative education. Their power to do so has been greatly strengthened by two developments in the last five years. Some of the polytechnics exist by a species of forced marriage between institutions like colleges of art and education of a very different history and ethos. All of them have had to come to terms with the customers' requirements — which is now for courses in the social sciences and in humanities. The polytechnics have had, in fact, to become new kinds of institution within the matrix of their own history. And that, because of the well known lag between administrative and cultural change, is not so easy. The attitudes and assumptions of the polytechnic communities — especially perhaps of their more senior staff and their governing bodies — are often a generation or more behind the situation they are, actually, creating. This, though inevitable, is extremely dangerous because the new communities, both of students and of staff, drawn into the polytechnics have different values, different assumptions and different life styles from the existing communities.

It is the more dangerous because the older polytechnics' culture does resist the discussion of ends, which are the breath of life to the

189

new communities. Hitherto, our alternative education has been carried, morally speaking, by the unselfconscious ethic of self-reliance and the job done well. That had and has its defects, which are still those noted by the generation which invented it — Dickens, for instance, and Matthew Arnold in *Culture and Anarchy*. Like other kinds of righteousness it is ungracious, unimaginative and insensitive in the nuances of human relationships. It also has one very considerable virtue: it enabled a man to recognise, even in the unpromising environment of urban, industrial England, his own dignity as a human being. It was not for nothing that the Psalmist, looking for some catastrophe of self-loss to mark his grief in exile, says 'Let my right hand forget her *cunning*' for the achievement of knowledge through skill, the responsibility in the exercise of *techne*, is a peculiarly human, a personal act. At least, it has been so in almost all the earlier stages in human history: not in our economy. True the system would collapse without *techne:* so it would without oil. For *techne* is, precisely, manpower: educated, gifted manpower, rather like a high octane fuel, but the fact that it is personal is economically insignificant. This is emphasised for the polytechnics by the binary philosophy: they are in business, they are told, not least by their own directorates, to service 'industry'. It hasn't quite worked out like that: partly because the economy is a more subtle beast than committees on scientific manpower always realise, partly because people are not, in practice, computer circuits. Still, the effect of all this is, or could be, to tighten the seals between the personal world of the student and his teachers, the world in which they *are* concerned with ends, and the work world, the educating society in which, if we are not very careful, we shall find ourselves 'programming' people for definable social roles.

This is the problem, education is difficult enough in situations of rapid and sometimes resented change. It is virtually impossible, especially in the field of morals, when the consensus shifts under us. This, I suggest, is not only a polytechnic problem. It is surely a kind of whistling in the dark to talk of the moral education of young people who are not in our world or at home with our assumptions and don't want to be. The difficulty is however, compounded in the polytechnics because, historically, they are inexperienced in the questioning and criticism of ends, of the roles laid on them by society. The system, unless resisted, would have us treat our students simply as trainees or transients on their way to a place in economic life — not as persons. The old prophylactic against this, the fact that the work itself made the personality, is disappearing from our culture. Now it is no use walking into this situation with a scheme for teaching English literature to accountants, or sociology to engineers — there are other reasons for that. What is far more important is a kind of moral witness, not a dramatic declaration of principle, but a habit of self-consciousness, of encouraging self-consciousness about what it is we are doing. Much of this consists in the wearing business of creating the person-to-person relationships, the justice between persons, which are so vital and so fragile in open societies. Oddly enough, the most important area here is probably in the educational process itself, for it is there that the student has to be treated as a person and to learn to treat himself as a person, not merely the passive recipient of useful, 'relevant' knowledge. Programmed learning — however great its merits — should, for instance, be viewed with suspicion in the polytechnics, where ironically, the old Oxbridge concept of the joint enquiry of the teacher and the taught ought to be restored to its proper place. Our students have to be encouraged, cajoled, and bullied out of their school-conditioned habits to become the masters of their own enquiry and to take it to the questioning of ends, even our ends. What is more, the administration of the polytechnics has got to be made in a variety of ways to create and sustain within the impersonality of its large-scale working the small groupings within which it is possible to create personal links between students and staff, staff and staff, administrators and the people whose work they administer. That means that the process of moral education — which means, amongst other ends, the business of learning to treat people as persons, not things — has to begin not with the students but with the whole polytechnic community — Directorates, Governing Bodies and so on. It means making a fuss on committees; it means persuading one's colleagues to question their own assumptions, to raise those terrifying moral and social questions which they have always thought faintly improper at *work* and even, occasionally, to question the endless stream of clichés showered on us by our political masters and the committees they employ to do their thinking for them.

The fact is that it is not in the long run the slightest use talking about moral education if, at the same time, one acquiesces in conditions which one believes to be immoral. And that isn't only for education in the polytechnics. For historical reasons they happen to be especially vulnerable to forces in our society which, increasingly, operate both against the individual's discovery of himself as a person and the achievement of sustaining relationships within the community. Yet all the evidence is that the universities are at least as uncritical, at least as determined not to be drawn into embarrassing discussions of trends: to play with moral philosophy and religion as if it were a game of conceptual chess or a particular *Times* Crossword, and with the analysis of society as if people were units on a statistical table and nothing more. If we talk about moral education we talk about moral responsibility and that means asking ourselves, surely, how, with all our advantages, we happen to have exercised it — in the polytechnics or elsewhere.

15   INSTITUTIONAL CONTEXTS

Stephen Hatch

Organisational arrangements can readily be altered by human effort. Hence they become the instruments of purposive change, the vehicles through which we seek to fashion a good society. However, in considering the relationship between organisational arrangements and moral development, it needs to be said at the outset that the relationship is not a direct one: it acts through the medium of social life. Cardinal Newman put it in a way that avoids recourse to sociological terminology.

'When a multitude of young men . . . come together . . . they are sure to learn from one another even if there be no one to teach them; the conversation of all is a series of lectures to each, and they gain for themselves new ideas and views, fresh matter of thought, and distinct principles for judging and acting day by day.

'. . . that youthful community will constitute a whole, it will embody a specific idea, it will represent a doctrine, it will administer a code of conduct, and it will furnish principles of thought and action.'[1]

What Newman does not explain, and what is important for understanding the contemporary situation is that the nineteenth-century Oxford collegiate system he had in mind was a carefully structured one, recruiting its students from a limited social milieu and placing them in an environment in which their intellectual and moral development was closely attended to. Today institutions of higher education are much more open and diverse in their membership: it may be difficult to detect in them a youthful community like that described by Newman, and even if one does exist the values it embodies will not necessarily be desirable ones.

There is a large body of empirical evidence about the effect of higher education on students' attitudes and values. Nearly all of it is from the United States, and in a sense much of it is tangential to the main concerns of this book, since it is about attitudes and values rather than the more fundamental components of moral development identified by Wilson. However, it does bear upon the relationship between institutional arrangements and moral orientations, and provides an empirically-tested basis for discussing that relationship.

Fortunately this mass of American evidence has been able summarised by Feldman and Newcomb.[2] Taking into account the very many studies that have assessed changes that occur between entering and leaving higher education, they detect a remarkably uniform pattern. American students tend to become more open-minded, less authoritarian, dogmatic and prejudiced; there tends to be a growing sensitivity to aesthetic experiences and for the most part a declining commitment to religion and an increase in intellectual interests. There have been hardly any comparable studies in this country, but my own examination of student residence[3] suggests, insofar as it goes, that similar changes occur among students in Britain. More remarkable than the actual changes that take place is the consistency of the pattern between institutions. Moreover, such differences as there are between institutions, tend to be of a self-fulfilling and reinforcing kind:

> 'Whatever the characteristics of an individual that selectively propel him toward particular educational settings − going to college, selecting a particular one, choosing a certain academic major, acquiring membership in a particular group of peers − those same characteristics are apt to be reinforced and extended by the experiences incurred in those selected settings.[4]

The implication of all this is that individual institutions have little if any effect, and insofar as they do have an effect it consists simply of amplifying trends already present. Modern universities are large institutions which offer their students a considerable range of choices as to what they study, where they live, what activities they take part in, which friends they make. Given the diversity of people and choices, any individual can choose a social and intellectual environment that suits him and, if he so wishes, insulates him from any influences the institution as a whole may be seeking to bring to bear. Moreover, insofar as there are general influences upon the student, these can more readily be explained as the product of a widespread student culture, which permeates all institutions irrespective of their particular characteristics and provides norms and expectations against which the student takes his bearings. It may be more realistic to think of the university or college as providing a cafeteria service rather than giving any particular shape to the development of its students.

However, even if this is an accurate picture of most institutions of higher education, there are some institutions which seem to have or to have had a more potent influence. In the present context these atypical cases are the ones most fruitful to examine. One is Bennington College. Bennington was studied by Newcomb in the 1930s, during the early years of its life,[5] and a repeat study was carried out by Newcomb and his associates in the 1960s.[6] It is a small, women's liberal arts college in New England. In the 1930s Newcomb discovered that the college was having a marked liberalising and radicalising impact on its students; drawn from affluent, conservative family backgrounds, they emerged as proselytising New Dealers. Summarising Newcomb's interpretation crudely, the change seemed to be due to the following factors: those who came to staff the new college were young, progressive and liberal; the small size, physical isolation and newness of the college led to close personal relationships; the leading personalities among the students took on liberal attitudes from the staff and from the general climate of the times, and the dominant ethos of the student body was derived from them. When Newcomb went back in the 1960s he found that the ethos of the college had not changed a great deal. However, there was a change in the nature of its impact on those who entered the college. By the 1960s its reputation had become known, and its entrants were drawn from liberal instead of conservative families, so the college was confirming instead of changing the outlook with which its entrants arrived.

Another interesting finding concerned the persistence of the attitudes and values acquired by those who had graduated from the college in the 1930s. On the whole the attitudes they acquired in the college had persisted. They remained liberals and had not reverted to the attitudes of their parents.

Another study of considerable interest is by Burton Clark.[7] He examined the factors contributing to the distinctive character of three well known liberal arts colleges; Antioch, Reed, and Swarthmore. Unlike Newcomb, he was not concerned with attitude changes among students, or any measurable impacts on them, but more with ethos, organisational characteristics, programmes and reputation. In each of the three colleges distinctiveness was initiated by a charismatic president with a clearly developed range of educational ideals, arriving at a time when a variety of circumstances created conditions appropriate for radical innovation. Foster at Reed was building up a new college, and Morgan came to Antioch when the college was on the point of collapse. Swarthmore when it appointed Aydelotte was not facing a crisis; consequently Aydelotte's changes were introduced more gradually.

The reasons for this persistence of distinctiveness are as significant as the reasons for its initiation: Clark summarises his conclusions as follows:

'Although emphasis differs and idiosycratic habits catch the eye, we can observe certain elements common to the building and maintenance of an organisational legend. First, believers collect in the faculty and gain the power to protect their cherished ideals and practices. Second, features of the curriculum, determining everyday behaviour, reflect and express the saga. Third, a social base of external believers provides resources, including moral support, and interests a certain kind of student in the college. Fourth, the students develop a strong subculture that significantly incorporates the central idea of the college. Fifth, the saga itself − as ideology, self-image, and public image − has forceful momentum. Personnel defense, program embodiment, supporting social base, allied student subculture, ideological force − these are the essential carrying mechanisms.'

Certain pre-conditions should also be mentioned. Clark's conjunction of elements took place in small colleges that were able to become selective in the staff and the students they recruited.

More generally it is important to realise that distinctiveness is not due to one specific factor, but to the combination of a variety of factors. For example student participation in college government at Antioch was both an expression and a reinforcement of student involvement in college life and of the democratic values of the college. In other contexts organisational arrangements for participation might have a different function. The same can be said of student residence. In some situations outwardly similar residential arrangements are the setting for quite different moral and social milieux. The findings of an enquiry into student residence suggest the following general conclusions.[3] Residence does tend to foster interaction between the students in one residential unit, to increase involvement in student life and to provide opportunities for greater contact between staff and students. However some residential units produce no common ethos, no entity that might be described as a community. Others do have a distinct identity, but not one the quality of which can be predicted from the formal character of the residential arrangements.

Two Cambridge colleges included in the enquiry illustrate the point. These are of similar size in terms of student numbers, possess in common the many formal characteristics of Cambridge colleges, and the students participated equally in the life of the University. However the ethos of the two was very different, the one being a cohesive, conservative community valuing the 'well rounded college man', the other individualistic, permissive and in some senses radical. The difference between the two colleges lay not so much in the range of values represented among the students as in the location of the centre of gravity. Both colleges had distinctive centres of gravity, and in this sense one can speak of a college sub-culture embodying and transmitting norms and values of its own. In both colleges, too, by a variety of measures, the senior members had played a crucial part in deciding the character of that sub-culture.

Thus the informal social system acts as a medium through which values are made real; and the character of the informal system is not determined in a unique way by any particular formal characteristics of the organisation. This point has been developed further by Royston Lambert and his colleagues;[9] although they discuss secondary schools, their general analysis is equally applicable to higher education.

Policy makers and other people pursuing particular goals generally look for specific rules, institutional arrangements or programmes that will have predictable effects of the kind they seek. But the line of argument being pursued here suggests that this is often an unrealistic approach. The achievement of a desired state of affairs is likely to depend on an array of elements interacting together, and is not susceptible to simplistic social engineering. This seems particularly true when the issues at stake are as intangible and personal as moral development. It may be more appropriate to explain the acquisition of values not as the product of rational argument or the exercise of cognitive skills, but as a response to the institutional ethos, personal charisma, the influence of peers, indeed as a form of psycho-social adaptation.

But is this argument as applicable to the components of moral development discussed in this book as to specific values? The components of moral development embody a specific way of looking at the world, which students need motivation to acquire. In bringing in motives one enters the same field as values. Acquiring commitment to a rational as much as to an irrational system of moral thinking requires a psychological leap, the impetus for which lies partially beyond reasoning.

It might be concluded that purposeful action based on a rational relationship between ends and means is futile. But that is not the intended drift of this argument. What is being reiterated is that the effect of organisational arrangements on moral development is complex and governed by psychological and social needs as much as by rational argument. There is no simple causal sequence. Nevertheless the relationships are not incomprehensible. It is possible to trace the mechanisms by which norms and values come to inform the life of students.

If the relationships are comprehensible, then in principle they should be subject to purposive change. Such nineteenth-century institutions as the public schools and the Oxford and Cambridge colleges are indeed monuments to the moral purpose of the educators of the Victorian elite. Here, however, comes the rub. Most institutions of higher education in Britain are now so large, so diffuse in their functions and so diverse in their membership that they can no longer pursue common purposes. Rather, they offer their members a means of pursuing a number of private ends, and are held together by limited agreements on means rather than ends.

The creation of institutions capable of making a distinctive impact on their students depends on the articulation of moral commitments, organisational arrangements and staff and student needs and aspirations.

This demands autonomous leadership at the institutional level. As this country moves towards a system of open, mass, higher education, central planning, bureaucratic administration and a student culture independent of particular institutions become more prominent. In these circumstances there is less and less scope for autonomous leadership, or for the pursuit by the institution as a whole of goals concerned with student socilisation. Unless existing 'enclaves' can be protected or new ones created organisational arrangements are likely to prove something of a *pis aller* for those concerned with moral development. The avenues explored by other contributors will probably offer more hopeful lines of advance.

References

1. Cardinal J.H. Newman, *The Idea of a University* Discourse VI 'Knowledge viewed in Relation to Learning', section 9.
2. K.A. Feldman & T.R. Newcomb, *The Impact of college on Students* (Jossey Bass, 1969).
3. Joan Brothers & Stephen Hatch, *Residence and Student Life* (Tavistock, London 1971).
4. Feldman and Newcomb, *op. cit.,* p. 323.
5. T.M. Newcomb, *Personality and Social Change. Attitude Formation in a Student Community* (Dryden, New York, 1943).
6. T.M. Newcomb, et. al., *Persistence and Change.* (John Wiley, New York, 1967).
7. B.R. Clark, *The Distinctive College* (Aldine, London 1970).
8. B.R. Clark, *op. cit.,* p. 246.
9. R. Lambert, R. Bullock & S. Millham, 'The Informal Social System' in R. Brown (ed.), *Knowledge, Education and Cultural Change* (Tavistock, London 1972).

16   THE INFLUENCE OF COMMUNITY

John Barnett

The influence of community on the moral development of persons
engaged in higher education raises not only questions of how this can
be achieved but the much more fundamental question of whether it
should even be attempted. One can assume that for those who founded
institutions of higher education in earlier centuries this was not a
question to be asked. We have the familiar prayers for universities,
colleges and schools, containing the hope that they should prove to be
places where godliness and good learning would thrive together and in
the phrases — 'in statu pupillari' and 'in loco parentis' — there is the
implication that the staffs of those institutions undertook more than
the instruction of those who attended or were in residence.

In recent years, however, the lowering of the age of majority, the
democratisation of the government of institutions in higher education,
the break in the assumption that moral education equals religious
education, the rise of student power and the radical changes which have
taken place in accepted moral standards have all contributed to the
bringing about of a situation where the link between godliness and
good learning can no longer be maintained in any but the most rigidly
denominational of institutions. The influence of community therefore,
unless it means no more than the unstructured and chance interaction
of person upon person resulting from their being brought together for
the purposes of teaching and learning, is at this time highly suspect if
not totally rejected.

In only one major section of higher education has it persisted to any
recognisable degree through the decade of the 'sixties as a planned
feature of the institutions and that has been in the colleges of education
and particularly in the voluntary colleges provided by the churches.
This survival can be attributed to a variety of causes. Colleges of
education have, on the whole, been comparatively small institutions;
they have had a higher proportion of resident places; their financing
and grant procedures have fostered a greater sense of dependency in
their students. The fact that their staffs have been drawn largely from
the ranks of those who have previously taught children and young
people in schools, has brought into higher education a relationship
between teacher and taught more appropriate to school than post-school

education.

To speak pejoratively, however, of the paternalism of the colleges of education is to place too great an importance on staff attitudes and to lose sight of the one constant characteristic in their make-up which more than any other has continued to make it possible for them to engage indirectly even more than directly not only in the personal and professional education of their students but also, through the influence of the community, in their moral development. This, of course, has been their exclusive concern with preparing their students to enter the teaching profession. An institution which is required by the Government to enter into an undertaking for each of its leaving students that he or she is a fit person to work with children and young persons, cannot be indifferent to moral as well as academic and professional competency.

For the most part however the colleges have relied on some three or four well-tried means for achieving this goal. The first and most obvious has been to bring together a community which has all the obvious signs of being predisposed towards the moral standards the public looks for in teachers — academic success at school, favourable reports from head teachers and other responsible referees, active participation in the acceptable social activities of a school, and a recognisable sense of vocation for teaching. A second and powerful influence has been the spacing throughout the course of periods of practical experience in schools, constantly renewing the sense of responsibility for the well-being of others as well as exposing the student teacher to the strongly conformist attitudes of the teaching profession. Third has been the living together in community with others who identify closely with the individual's own chosen style of life. Drunkenness, promiscuity, drug taking, political activism, idleness and all the more extreme manifestations of a determination to experience in its totality the whole range of personal freedom have been frowned on as antisocial, irresponsible and in some vaguely felt yet powerfully influential way, letting down the children who will ultimately be the student teacher's responsibility; and frowned on not simply by college authorities but by the student body as well.

By the side of these three, the structured steps taken by colleges to provide a system of personal tutors, counsellors, chaplains and the like, and to order the life of the college according to a set of rules of conduct and behaviour have done little more than add the final formal blessing to an almost irresistible grouping of forces.

The beginning of the seventies is seeing the final disappearance in the colleges of education as elsewhere, of what one might term the traditional approach to moral development through the influence of community, as these three or four basic forces give way to change. With a trebling of their numbers, colleges can no longer be highly selective of those whom they will admit for training. Just as academic standards have hardly risen and in many cases have declined, so in all other respects the colleges of education have been compelled to accept as students many whom they would earlier have considered to be unlikely to make acceptable teachers. The members of the college community no longer share an identity of interest; although teaching still has to be the declared goal of those who enter, substantial numbers of those who have been accepted see the college of education as simply providing an opportunity for post-school education and have only vague and often distant expectations of working in schools. Those whose colleges are in close proximity with other institutions in higher education find a greater identity of interest with the freer and less committed student communities in these institutions and are more resistant to the assumptions about their objectives which the colleges still cannot avoid making. Even the periodic sessions of teaching practice exercise a less compelling pressure as authoritarian, subject-centred, teacher-directed patterns of instruction give way in schools to more pupil-centred and participatory ways of learning.

All of this might be a cause for rejoicing if it were not for the fact that those who work in higher education cannot happily shrug off as matters of no concern the ever increasing toll of misery and unhappiness, the drop-outs, abortions, suicides, mental breakdowns, drug addiction, and the waste of potential which are becoming the commonplace experience of the college and university scene. Even less happy are those who, in a post White Paper situation which will remove the last traces of the monotechnic institution, know that it will still rest with them to recommend to the Secretary of State fit and proper persons to work with children, children who will in the future even more than in the past need as teachers persons who are 'successful performers' in John Wilson's sense in the moral field; and we may have cause to regret that for too long we have relied on indirect and external forces for producing the desired goal rather than planning directly for the moral development of those engaged in higher education not simply because they are going to become teachers but because without such development, the education of a whole person is incomplete.

The 'sixties, however, have not been without their experiments and in one college of education, Culham College, Abingdon, the staff attempted to solve a problem which is not unlike the one posed above. The relevance of the solution for teacher education has been set out elsewhere.[1] The importance to the present debate lies in the objectives identified at the beginning of the exercise. These were:

1. To help each student develop an awareness of his own abilities, potentialities and limitations.
2. To enrich the quality of his life.

3. To promote in him a greater sense of responsibility.
4. To encourage a stronger impulse to study in his chosen field.
5. To widen his knowledge and experience both of people and their environment.
6. To increase his awareness of the abilities, potentialities and limitations of others.
7. To develop skills in interacting effectively with others.
8. To enable him to contribute towards the establishing of a community of purpose in any organisation to which he belongs whether as a student in college or later as a member of a staff.

Some of the members of this staff group could be individually described as lecturers in mathematics, science, history, geography or any of the other main courses studied in the college; others as lecturers in the philosophy, sociology or psychology of education or any of the other relevant areas of professional study. Their list of purposes, however, was constructed in terms of interpersonal relations and personal growth in a way which suggests that they saw their role as one in which they were primarily concerned to help students discover for themselves the personal significance of the material they were studying so that their behaviour might be fundamentally affected and changed as a result.

If this was to be achieved, then it required a new focus for the work of both tutor and student. A tutor must feel that the whole pattern of college government, the structure of the academic board and other decision-making bodies in the college are such as will enable him to feel involved in and committed to the totality of the college's work with students; his programme of work and not simply his participation in committees must allow him to experience this involvement and commitment through direct participation in the achieving of the purposes of the college. Similarly the student must feel that he is an active partner in the total exercise, recognising that every part of his course is designed to contribute positively towards his obtaining a richer and more extensive grasp of his chosen areas of study, a more sensitive understanding of people, a deeper knowledge of himself on which he can base more surely his feelings of personal competency and adequacy, a surer awareness of the purposes and processes of education and a greater experience of and skill in the methods of realising his purposes.

Though the phrase was not used at the time, it could be said that the purpose which the staff had identified was the moral development not simply of the students but of the whole membership of the community. Agreement over purposes is one thing: finding ways of achieving those purposes presented a new range of problems. The college had deliberately set aside all of the traditional ancillary means of community influence in favour of a central activity in which all were to be engaged. The identification of that activity was the critical issue and it was found in what came to be termed the supervision group. This was the assembly of about fifteen students of varying ages, sex, background and subject interest, who met together with a group supervisor on two occasions of one and a half hours in every week throughout the course. It was not unlike the syndicate pattern of organisation described by Gerald Collier in his contribution to this symposium but differed in three fundamental characteristics. Every student and almost every member of staff in a college of 600 students belonged to a supervision group; the groups had no more direction from the centre than that they were to explore together their growing understanding of the theory and practice of education; the group life was three years rather than ten weeks.

At the simplest level the supervision group corresponded to any group of human beings brought together to achieve a common task. As a learning group it had similarities to the groups of children and young people which each of its members would later be teaching. As a professional group it corresponded to the staff groups of the schools they would later be joining. Every member, including the staff member, was an individual with his own gifts, skills and experience which could only be used if they were recognised, appreciated and respected by the other members of the group. At the same time every member had his own personal problems and difficulties which could hamper or restrict his contribution unless he was helped to resolve them by the sensitivity, thoughtfulness and consideration of the others. One of the first things, therefore; that the supervision group had to learn to do, with the help of the group supervisor, was to work together in a way which made the most of individual gifts and abilities and minimised the effects of individual problems and difficulties. In the supervision group the growth of Carl Rogers' 'fully functioning person' or John Wilson's 'successful performer in the moral field' went side by side with the preparation of a teacher. The community was a community of people at work.

In most of its other activities, the college followed orthodox methods of teaching and learning. Lecturers in Geography, for example, conducted lectures, seminars and classes for those who wished to specialise in their discipline. There was a central core of lectures, demonstrations and workshops which attempted to give a coherent picture of child growth and development and the part played by education and the school. There was a wide choice of optional courses ranging from 'Guitar in the classroom' to 'Learning Theory' which students arranged into a personal programme with the assistance of their group supervisors. But common to all of these was the element of choice. The tutor chose to teach in those areas where he felt he had a degree of competency and the student chose to study where he felt his need and interest lay.

The confidence generated by these more familiar ways of working and the freedom of choice for both tutor and student were essential supportive elements which made the strain and tension of the unfamiliar experience of the supervision group more acceptable and therefore more fruitful. At the time of this experiment Carl Rogers had not written his book *Freedom to Learn*[2] but there would have been whole hearted agreement with his theoretical assumptions about education listed in Chapter Seven:

1. Human beings have a natural potentiality for learning.
2. Significant learning takes place when the subject matter is perceived by the student as having relevance for his own purposes.
3. Learning which involves a change in self organisation is threatening and tends to be resisted.
4. Those learnings which are threatening to the self are more easily perceived and assimilated when external threats are at a minimum.
5. When threat to self is low, experience can be perceived in differentiated fashion and learning can proceed.
6. Much significant learning is acquired through doing.
7. Learning is facilitated when the student participates responsibly in the learning process.
8. Self initiated learning which involves the whole person of the learner — feelings as well as intellect — is the most lasting and pervasive.
9. Independence, creativity, and self reliance are all facilitated when self criticism and self evaluation are basic and evaluation by others is of secondary importance.
10. The most socially useful learning in the modern world is the learning of the process of learning, a continuing openness to experience and incorporation into oneself of the process of change.

The threat to members of staff of this way of working was considerable. There had been little in their earlier experience which had positively prepared them for a role where the greatest indication of their success lay in the achievement of interdependence between the members of a group in a horizontal relationship, rather than in a vertical dependence upon their teacher. It was an exacting and highly skilled role which all felt hesitant about filling and which some felt quite inadequate to meet. Yet it was the only role which could genuinely be filled by all tutors regardless of their subject specialisations since the group supervision was concerned principally with processes and approaches rather than subject matter. Staff training and staff support were essential but the agencies for this scarcely existed and still are far too few on the ground. The most effective training and support organisation was an hour-long weekly meeting of groups of supervisors, ostensibly to plan and comment on the central programme of lectures but providing an opportunity for sharing and self-discovery in a way analogous to what was going on in the student supervision group.

How successful was the exercise? In advancing the moral development of those involved, it is impossible to tell. No evaluation machinery was built into the scheme to measure this as this was not the main purpose of the experiment. In general terms one can say with confidence that academic performance measured by end of course examinations and other tests was improved; external examiners commented on the maturity and articulateness of close of course students; and the whole period was marked by a feeling of confidence and an absence of unrest in the student body. Notably absent, also, was any feeling of distance between staff and students. If, then, one can take the signs of a mature and purposeful community, drawing its maturity and purpose from its method of operation, as an indication of maturity and purpose in its individual members, and if maturity and purpose are significant indications of progress in moral development, then the scheme was successful.

It was, however, essentially a practical enterprise coming totally within John Wilson's description of those 'which have not been clearly thought out, either with reference to the aims of moral development or with reference to the general findings of psychology and other disciplines'. It could be argued that as teacher education is no longer to take place in monotechnic institutions, it now has no more than historical interest and that further 'hunch' experiments will be needed before an authentic place for the influence of community in moral development can be identified in higher education.

To hold this view is to ignore some significant sentences which occur in the White Paper on *Education in the Seventies*. Here the view is expressed that all young people expect their experience of higher education 'to prepare them to cope more successfully with the problems that will confront them in their personal, social and working lives'; that there is a 'sincere desire on the part of a growing number of students to be given more help in acquiring — and discovering how to apply — knowledge and skills related more directly to the decisions that will face them in their careers and in the world of personal and social action.' To meet this need, the Government has proposed the inauguration of new courses leading to a Diploma in Higher Education. It seems likely that the responsibility for mounting these new courses will rest largely with the Colleges of Education and that they will attract not only would-be teachers but a wide variety of young people who share a common concern for the well-being of others. It should not be difficult to build out of this initial concern, a ground for sharing and developing knowledge, skills and experience in the context of a supervision group such as has been described here. If this can be done, it will be of value to take the Culham experiment as a trial run in the creation of a working community of teachers and learners who set the maturity and purposefulness of the working community at the centre rather than on the periphery of their studies.

References

1. Trends in Education No. 25, January 1972 (H.M.S.O.).
2. Carl R. Rogers, *Freedom to Learn* (Merrill, 1969) pp. 157-63.
3. *Education: A Framework for Expansion* (H.M.S.O., 1972), pp. 107-9.

17 THE ROLE OF STUDENT SERVICES IN STUDENT DEVELOPMENT – A POLYTECHNIC VIEW

Denis Coe

A recent survey of eight polytechnics, *The Attractions of Polytechnics* by H.V. Swann, has shown that most students who go to such institutions do so from deliberate choice. It is claimed from this survey that, whilst universities may have superior social facilities and better accommodation, the polytechnics offer an equally good range of career opportunities and are given high marks for offering 'more practical' courses and greater contact with the world outside.

The significance of these findings, if they are representative, is that the polytechnics are being more successful than is sometimes claimed in attracting students who are motivated to opt for a polytechnic from choice rather than as a second best having been refused admission to a university. In the three to four years which have elapsed since polytechnics were established this is no mean achievement. The attitude of a student coming to a major institution of higher education is bound to have a significant influence on his expectations regarding his academic course and on the community in which he finds himself. In short, if polytechnics can provide the academic stimulus to achieve his intellectual potential and are also seen to be a community with which he can identify, the student is likely to adjust satisfactorily to his new surroundings.

Perhaps the greatest advantage to be claimed for polytechnics is their newness which provides them with many opportunities to experiment. Established traditions and procedures have not yet taken root and whilst staff and students of polytechnics often yearn for the stability and decorum of their colleagues in universities they have also responded to the innovators within their midst.

They are not, of course, the only education institutions which are open to change. The whole field of higher and further education has altered radically over the last ten years. Apart from academic innovations a network of consultative processes has been established which involves students and staff in the management of their institutions. Even if students sometimes doubt the effectiveness of such methods they would seem to be here to stay. And polytechnics, learning from the student unrest which occurred in 1968 before polytechnics were designated, have been quick to establish student representation at virtually all levels of polytechnic activity.

Alongside these developments has been the extension of student support services. Ten years ago college welfare officers were a rarity, doctors even rarer (except in a number of universities) and student counsellors were a group whom our American friends may have found essential for their colleges but were certainly not often found in British institutions. Again, the polytechnics have been able to gain from the experiences of universities and other colleges in building up student services. The pattern which is emerging demonstrates an attempt to create student services which are integrated within a unit or a department and which are seen to be providing both a supporting role for students and an educational role. Given the general development of polytechnics which has already been referred to, this particular chapter attempts to show how far student services can help to provide a suitable environment in which students can develop and achieve a satisfactory life style.

Yet if institutions of higher education are, rightly, to avoid a paternalistic attitude to students, how can they nevertheless establish a caring community within which students have opportunities to develop both academically and personally? This would seem to be a central question in assessing the role of student services within a polytechnic. The examples in this chapter are drawn from the North East London Polytechnic where the author is Dean of Students.

The polytechnic has been created from three former colleges of technology within an area of 20sq. miles. There are over 4,000 full-time/sandwich students and a similar number of part-time students. Following the formation of the polytechnic new student services were established and others were extended. It was then decided in 1972 to create a Department of Student Services under the direction of the Dean of Students. This Department consists of Services concerned with: health, counselling, Welfare and Accommodation, and physical education. A Chaplaincy Service works in association with the Student Services Department and there is also close contact with other central polytechnic agencies such as Careers & Training and Vocational Guidance. In addition, the Department has helped to initiate such additional services as a pre-school playgroup, a voluntary legal advice centre staffed by lecturers from the Law Department, and a comprehensive bookselling service which is provided by a major commercial supplier. Finally, the Dean of Students has the task of monitoring the effectiveness of the personal tutor scheme throughout the polytechnic. He is helped in carrying out this task by close contact with the various student services in his Department and also with the autonomous Students' Union in his capacity as Dean of Students.

Such is the structure of student services which has emerged at this particular polytechnic. How far can it be said to have an effect on the life of the polytechnic community in general and on the lives of individual students? Because these services are relatively new, answers to these questions must necessarily be tentative. But it is already clear that the Student Services have a positive educative role in an institution such as a polytechnic and, therefore, they must have some influence on the development of those who study there.

The experience of the North East London Polytechnic indicates a number of ways in which this may occur.

The provision of student services suggests that the polytechnic is a caring community. Many polytechnic students are away from home for the first time in their lives. Apart from the many adjustments which such a break from home involves there is the added likelihood that, at this stage in their development, many polytechnics, including NELP, can provide only limited accommodation. The students are therefore denied some of the advantages of living on a college campus in reasonable surroundings. Problems of indifferent landlords, poor home study facilities and high rents can hit the new student before he has had a reasonable opportunity to make adjustments to his new life. In short, polytechnic students often have a number of everyday problems to face which are more acute then their university colleagues and the reassurance and help which they receive from Student Services can influence their attitude to the institution. For example, the Senior Welfare Officer at NELP was told that a student had been missing classes for some time. He decided on a home visit and discovered that the student was extremely short of money and not maintaining an adequate diet. The Welfare Officer was able to see that the student's difficulties were resolved and this student, who had been in danger of 'dropping out', successfully completed his course. When the Welfare Officer went to see him at his lodgings the student expressed first surprise, then gratitude and pleasure that the Polytechnic cared sufficiently to want to know what had happened to him.

Clearly, some students would resent what might be considered an intrustion of their privacy. So much depends on how such a situation is tackled. It means striking a balance between recognising a right to privacy whilst ensuring that an offer of help is made. Evidence that student resentment to this type of approach is minimal can be seen in the increasing use which is being made of student services. And students are not only helped themselves. They are able to see the benefit which others derive from the services which are provided.

The implications which have been referred to also react on the organisation and administration of the polytechnic. Administrative procedures can be influenced by welfare considerations which have been highlighted by the Student Services. When a student who is in receipt of a local authority grant is absent from the polytechnic for more than twenty-eight days the Grant Awarding Authority must, by law, be informed. This rule against the misuse of public money could be interpreted quite correctly by a college simply maintaining a rigid attendance record and, at the end of twenty-eight days, informing the Local Authority. At NELP the Welfare Service is informed before the twenty-eight days have elapsed to give the service time to contact the student and to make an offer of help. This is sometimes ignored but, on other occasions, students have been able to resume their studies after assistance by the student services.

Quite apart from the general view that Student Services can demonstrate that the polytechnic is a caring community for all its students, it is worth examining in more detail the possible influence on particular students. Though students are a pretty healthy bunch of people, they are nevertheless prone to a number of stresses which can seriously hamper or even destroy their academic careers. Before Student Services were established, students who, for example, experienced examination or personal stresses, might have been lucky in finding a sympathetic lecturer or friend to see them through the crisis period. Even with comprehensive student services they may still choose to contact a lecturer rather than a doctor or counsellor. The important point is that all these sources of help are now available and skilled counselling can obviously help a troubled student very considerably. Student Services have enabled many students to continue their studies who would otherwise have dropped out or, in extreme cases suffered physically and mentally.

The acute form of examination stress which may manifest itself as a breakdown or blackout in the examination room is only one aspect of the problem. If a student has this type of breakdown it is possible, although certainly not ideal, to award an aegrotat certificate. More common are the large number of students who suffer some form of stress which is not necessarily related to a fear of an examination or assessment, but stems from exceptional circumstances which affect their ability to perform at their true level.

If it is accepted that these exceptional circumstances should be taken into account by Assessment Boards then student services staff can play a vital role. Student Services can offer two forms of support to students. First there is the help which might be available to meet a particular stress situation prior to an examination. Second, if a judgement is made that the student was unable to perform adequately in an examination, evidence can, with the student's permission, be revealed to an assessment board. It has been the author's personal experience that the availability of this type of evidence has not been abused by students who exaggerate their difficulties.

Apart from playing an increasing role in assessment and appeals procedures the Polytechnic Student Services ought to be concerned with student selection. The selection of students for a course should not be haphazard or a matter of chance. Since the demand for a course will govern how far any choice can be exercised, the possession of adequate examination grades ought not to be the sole criterion for selection. It is increasingly accepted by universities and polytechnics that when they select students they must take into account a number of factors in addition to academic standards. At NELP the admissions procedure specifies that in choosing students, tutors will have regard to the principle of 'ability to benefit most' rather than 'ability to succeed'. The practical implications of this policy and the consequent involvement of the student services can be demonstrated by referring to one particular aspect; that of admitting physically disabled students.

It was evident to the Academic Board at NELP that if the selection criteria for physically disabled students were to be more than a pious expression of interest, facilities would have to be provided for this group of students. A Working Party under the Dean of Students was established and, in its subsequent Report, Student Services were given a very important role in this field. A Co-ordinator for Disabled Students was appointed. He is a member of the Student Services team and his task is to monitor the admission of physically disabled students and to give them every assistance. Clearly the actual decision to admit a student must rest with academic departments. But, in the case of physically disabled applicants, staff from the Student Services Department interview the applicants on the same day as the academic department and it is their responsibility to discuss with the applicants the problems which might need special attention if they are accepted. It can be claimed that the existence of Student Services in these cases makes it possible to admit students who previously might have been rejected.

If a polytechnic or other institution demonstrates in these ways that it is a caring community, it can ask applicants to set down frankly any difficulties that they have experienced in the past. This is more likely to happen if it can be shown that student services are available to help and therefore the contribution of such services in the selection process is a very important one.

These questions of student assessment and student selection demonstrate the two-fold contribution of student services within an educational institution such as a polytechnic. The services clearly have an advisory and supportive role but, if they are to realise their full potential, they must also be seen as an integral part of the educative process. Another important way in which this is shown is the co-operation which ought to exist between Student Services staff and the personal tutors in the academic departments. Personal tutor schemes vary from one institution to the next. At NELP personal tutors normally teach their tutees and expect to remain as tutors to the same students throughout the students' courses. They are responsible for monitoring academic progress and, apart from regular meetings with tutees, they are available to help and advise on personal matters.

It is essential that this type of scheme should operate in a large institution like a polytechnic, and conscientious personal tutors are usually the first to notice when the performance of their tutees is not up to standard. If there is genuine trust between the personal tutors and their students, and a readiness by the tutors to use Student Services for advice or referral, students will benefit from such co-operation and will appreciate the complementary roles of the two groups of staff in the Polytechnic. Ideally this co-operation ought to involve academics explaining to the staff of Student Services the requirements and difficulties of their courses and the staff from Student Services passing on aspects of their skill to personal tutors.

Student Services can also make a unique contribution to the educational work of an institution. In the field of research for example, student health units are carrying out projects into the incidence of particular medical conditions amongst students. This work is still in its infancy but it is already clear that it will have an important bearing on student development in the future.

One of the themes of this contribution is that Student Services are not some additional option to the total resources of an educational institution; they ought to be an essential part of the institution and complementary to the academic departments. This is made more obvious to students perhaps when Student Services staff are engaged in various learning commitments with students. At NELP, for example, the Senior Medical Officer lectures to the Youth & Community Course, the Senior Counsellor holds group counselling sessions, the Physical Education Service has a large teaching commitment with the education students and the Assistant Dean of Students lectures to a variety of other academic courses.

It is difficult to assess acurately the influence of Student Services in the development of students. It has been suggested that their presence in an educational institution demonstrates that it is a caring community and that students thereby benefit from being part of that community. It has been further claimed that Student Services play an important part in the educational process and therefore have a role in influencing the development of students.

The third main area of influence which must be considered, even if it is somewhat artificial to separate it from the foregoing, is the extent to which a student is helped to adjust to society outside the polytechnic community. Any help which a student receives during his course will have some influence on his life style. Let us consider some examples of specific help which has been given by student services.

In a large institution like NELP two-thirds of the students live away from home and, as it was pointed out earlier, for most of this group this is their first experience of dealing with landlords. Understandably, there are many conflicts or anxieties created as a result. The help which Student Services can give over accommodation is substantial, although in a large urban area such as East London pressure on accommodation is very great and regrettably a number of students live in accommodation which is far from ideal. In these circumstances it is important that students are aware of their rights and those of their landlords under the various Housing Acts.

Another field in which Student Services can help is in student attitudes to personal relationships. The all too common and mistaken view of students as being amoral and uncaring obscures the fact that many of them look for guidance and help in the same way as their peers who have already taken up employment. Being away from home means that they often look for support from people outside their family circle, and the staff of Student Services, being available for this purpose, can provide this support and advice.

One particular group of students who may need specialised advice are overseas students who have newly arrived in the United Kingdom. Staff in the student services and others in the polytechnic are faced with a real dilemma in attempting to help such students. There is a reluctance to treat overseas students differently from their fellow students. Nevertheless, students who come from overseas and have had a very sheltered upbringing can be severely disorientated by the cultural and environment shock of living in a big city, particularly London. At NELP we have come to the conclusion that a course for newly arrived overseas studants should be organised so that these students may have an early opportunity to discuss the practical problems which may face them in this country. They are also given information about British customs and institutions. In short, an attempt is made to help them to adjust to a different life style.

Many of these developments concerning Student Services would be nullified if the student body in the Polytechnic was either indifferent or antagonistic to them. At NELP the Students' Union is an autonomous body with an income of £20 per head for every full-time student. This amounts to an annual income of approximately £80,000. The Students' Union has a number of sabbatical union officers and supporting administrative staff. At NELP one of the Vice-Presidents of the Union has student welfare as one of his special responsibilities. He is invited to attend meetings of the Student Services Department and he and other

Students' Union officials work in co-operation with Student Services staff on a number of welfare matters. This has not detracted from the work being done separately by the Students' Union in this field, which is very significant.

One interesting co-operative effort between the Students' Union and the Student Services Department concerns the establishment of a Playgroup. A proposal to establish a Playgroup was put forward by the Students' Union and supported by Student Services staff. Together they were able to convince the Governors of the need for a Playgroup and the Students' Union contributed £500 towards the initial cost of establishing it. Their representatives play a prominent role on the Management Group of the Playgroup.

On occasions the students are ahead of the Student Services staff in pressing for extensions to the Services which are available. This in itself is a measure of their concern and their acceptance that Student Services have an important role in the institution.

It is right to conclude this contribution on a note of caution. That student services can have a significant influence on the life style of many students can be shown quite clearly from the case notes of staff. Yet it is easy to overestimate the importance of the Services. Try as one might, large educational institutions like NELP can be very impersonal, and students who may benefit from help and advice either do not know of the services available or are unwilling to use them. Even when they do use the services there are difficult questions of confidentiality to overcome. It is one thing to know that a personal problem is likely to have affected a student's academic performance; but if this information is to be passed on to the appropriate quarters the student's permission must be given. This is usually forthcoming, but the student must have the right to refuse. There is the difficulty of knowing when to refer a student to another person whose expertise is more appropriate to the needs of that student. Care has to be taken that the student does not feel rejected when he has placed his confidence in the person he originally consulted. A large network of welfare services can also cause problems of overlap in the work being done by the different services. It requires a sensitivity amongst the staff of Student Services to resolve any such difficulties as they arise. On occasions the Student Services staff will be identified by students as being part of 'the establishment'.

In one sense of course they are, but if by this identification there is a suspicion that the staff are part of an unfeeling bureaucratic machine then this will obviously hamper the work of Student Services. Finally, there will be accusations that Student Services are guilty of 'pampering' students; that part of developing at a place like a polytechnic is being able to learn to be independent, and that if the support services are extensive this can positively hinder this development.

Maybe this is a reasonable criticism. It is certainly incumbant on the staff working in Student Services to guard against any such tendency.

To sum up the argument, it has been claimed in this contribution that the Department of Student Services helps to demonstrate to students that the Polytechnic has a concern for individual students both in their academic progress and in their personal lives and that this in turn can make a significant contribution to student development. It is clearly too early in the life of both the Department and the Polytechnic to provide conclusive proof of these claims, but the various criteria for personal development which John Wilson sets out in Chapter 1 of this symposium are ones with which the Student Services Department is closely concerned. This fact reinforces the view that such a Department can help students to achieve a satisfactory life-style.

POSTSCRIPT

John Wilson

It would of course be grotesque to attempt anything like a summary of the wide-ranging contributions which are included in this book; but there are nevertheless one or two points which may be of use to the general reader to bear in mind, now that he has steered his way through the various chapters.

First of all, it is important to see that a summary is for logical reasons impossible: not just a very difficult task, but one which could not in principle be successfully undertaken. We have been looking at a murky area, best defined negatively as those aspects of education which are *not* already neatly pigeon-holed under headings like 'mathematics', 'English literature', 'metalwork', and so on: and titles like 'moral development', 'learning to be human', 'personal education', etc. are only attached very loosely to these aspects. In Part I of the book I attempted to set out the aims somewhat more precisely; but as soon as we step into the area of practicalities, it becomes clear that there are no quick answers or simple solutions. Many people will regard education as like some aspects of medicine, in that they think 'researchers' or 'experts' are able to 'tell them what to do' rather as doctors may tell one what medicine to take. But in fact there are no educational experts in that sense: nor can there be. This is not only because education is very complicated, the 'variables' are many, research is insufficient, etc. There are two more important reasons. First, the individual teacher must (within limits) necessarily be free to pursue his own values in his educational work, or at least to determine priorities for himself from among a number of nationally-established values. Hence only he can determine the *relevance* of what 'experts' say: they can, up to a point, tell him *how* to achieve this or that goal, but the choice of goals is largely up to him. Secondly, and just as importantly, educational methods — unlike pills and medicines — are for the most part only effective when used by those who understand their point and rationale.

The kind of understanding required here makes a summary as impossible in this case as in the case of (say) 'summarising' a play by Shakespeare: nearly all of what is important would necessarily be left out. The preceding chapters have not been like cooking recipes, but attempts to show how people placed in very different practical or theoretical situations have thought and acted in relation to their disciplines and their students — with, we hope, perhaps a little more conscious deliberation and reflection than we sometimes use, but certainly not with the intention of producing 'right answers' or 'research findings' in any strict sense. The state of play in this area of education is simply not like that: and, to a great extent, can never become like that.

This is why the editors would be quite unworried by such criticisms as 'The book doesn't hang together', 'No definitive thesis is advanced', or 'The contributors' hypotheses are only dimly outlined'. Terms like 'hypothesis', 'proof', 'findings', 'thesis' and so on are out of place here. What we have done is to approach the extremely vague and general question 'How, both in general and in a particular role (as a teacher of physics or liberal studies, a lecturer in a university or college, etc.) would one *start to think* about this area of education, and what might one do which seems worth looking at?' We have tried to move from the general to the particular: from the abstract aims, via important theoretical generalisations, to practical methods; but even here the reader will often wish to reverse this movement, referring back from an account of a method to the aims, looking once more at the empirical generalisations of psychology, back to the method again, and so forth. And this is entirely appropriate: indeed, it is necessary. It is just this kind of to-and-fro movement which the subject needs.

On the other hand, it would be too easy (and presumptuous) to say merely that the various contributions 'illuminate' or 'stimulate thought' in this area. Or rather, if they do, it is worth considering *how* they do. If the reader is not to be given 'answers', then what exactly is he given? What *use* can he make of it? Here, I think, it may be worth listing a number of points at which those involved in tertiary education (or indeed in other educational contexts) may find some help:

(1) How the individual *tutor* (or the institution) *sees his task:*
(2) How the *students see* the tutor's or the institution's expectations:
(3) The general *background working-conditions* of the institution:
(4) The use of *particular teaching-methods* or approaches.

Sometimes there may be sufficient similarity between the reader's own conditions and those of some one or more contributors to make the latter's account particularly relevant; but in all cases the contributions should shed some light, and make more explicit the connections between 'personal development' (or whatever we want to call it) and the other factors in our working-conditions.

I mention these four points — there are many others — because we are perhaps sometimes apt to suppose that 'answers' or 'recommendations' must always take the form of new techniques or teaching methods.

Sometimes this may be true; but in this area the general background is crucially important. Good and bad decisions will follow, not only from a clear understanding of the philosophical aims and the psychological generalisations, but from a thorough understanding of the particular institution in question: and this is why (1), (2) and (3) above are in practice as important as (4). 'Personal development' is not like learning chess, for instance, where only minimal preconditions are required (a chess set, a competent teacher, and a tolerably high degree of motivation). It is very much influenced, for good or ill, by the institutional background.

This is, of course, something we all know well enough. But we are perhaps too often tempted to dismiss it under over-general headings, such as 'the atmosphere' of the college, or 'the ethos' of the school. Many of the contributions in Part II will, we hope, make certain aspects of 'the atmosphere' more specific and clear to the reader. They should also be of service in highlighting the institutional preconditions without which some teaching methods or approaches could not succeed — however desirable and impressive they might seem on paper. Some of these preconditions obviously relate to the empirical psychology brought out in Part I; and even here the *kind* of force or relevance which such psychological generalisations have in practice can only be properly determined by inspecting particular and practical cases. We are inevitably involved in a constant movement from one aspect of the subject to another.

Somebody who has engaged in this sort of movement would, I am quite sure, be much better equipped to attempt practical moves in this field: even though — or one might say, because — he would not be bewitched by some *particular* 'answer' or 'approach', or thought that 'research had proved' so-and-so or such-and-such. The position here is, I think, very hard to tolerate: one has on the one hand to grant the absence of 'answers' or recipes, but on the other hand to avoid relapsing into fantasy, or prejudice, or over-general talk. It is essential, so to speak, to continue all the time to juggle with the various factors involved: to bear everything in mind at once. A person who does this will still need to engage in a lot of trial and error — there may always be factors which have not even been *thought of* (let alone weighed by any strict research). But he would be in a very much better position to try than somebody who had not been through this arduous process of self-education. The mere mentioning and explication, in the preceding contributions, of many of these factors can itself act as a defence against fantasy: we at least become aware of some of the streams and cross-currents, the rocks and shoals. And so long as we retain our enthusiasm, we have hope at least of making more intelligent and well-informed guesses.

I say 'guesses' and not 'hypotheses': not because there is much in the linguistic point, but because it needs to be made clear that the state of research in this area is, and must for long continue to be, in much the same position as that described above. Researchers must, of course, first of all devise assessment methods relevant to some such detailed breakdown of aims as that given in Part I — it is no use employing 'criteria of evluation' which are not logically linked to what we *mean by* such terms as 'personal development', 'morally educated', etc. They must also familiarise themselves with the generalisations mentioned in Part II, if they are to have a rough general idea of what sort of factors ('variables') could in principle be relevant as causes. But, even then, they will need something much more like a developed imagination, or an informed intuition, if they are to make intelligent guesses about what factors, in particular institutions, are likely to be the relevant ones; and any attempt to erect strict 'hypotheses' relating to over-specified 'variables' is likely to be premature for a long time to come. This is, in part, because the factors are so many and so various; but it is also because many such factors come in constellations — so closely connected with each other (both logically and empirically) that it may be almost impossible to separate them out. In such a situation the researcher can only learn what sort of weight to give to each factor in the constellation by first immersing himself — more in the style of a descriptive anthropologist than a physical scientist — in the understanding of particular institutions and the methods they use: and here the contributions in Part III will be valuable to him.

I have concentrated above chiefly on the empirical or factual aspects of this area; but it should not be thought that these are the only aspects that we need to understand better. At certain stages of our thinking, perhaps, they may not even be the most important. For it will not have escaped the reader's notice that different contributors differ in their *concept* of 'personal development', 'moral education', etc.: that is, they differ (more or less overtly) in regard to what we are *trying* to do here — in regard to our basic aims or objectives. As a philosopher and author of Part I, I tried to construct a list of aims which would be logically complete and logically defensible; and almost all that other contributors have said can be seen to relate, directly or indirectly, to one or other of these detailed objectives. But, first, this list of aims can of course be challenged: essential items may have been omitted, unnecessary items incorporated, or no adequate defence given for them; and secondly, it is inevitable that different contributors — and different readers — bring certain concepts, values or pictures to this area which will, at least, colour or distort the objectives as stated in Part I — whether rightly or wrongly is here irrelevant. Hence, although we have written on a broad basis of agreement, there are naturally differences —

218

none the less real and important for being partly unconscious rather than overtly spelled out.

It is, I think, of particular importance that readers concerned with this area should go further than we have been able to do in reaching and clarifying agreement about aims. This is (if we must use grand words) a philosophical task, and we did not want this book to be primarily a work of philosophy; but it is very obvious that if brief statements of aims — perhaps in very broad or global terms like 'maturity', 'development'. 'an adult attitude', and so on — in fact *mean* different things to different people (as very often they do), then we need to clear this up as soon as possible. Otherwise we shall not be in any real sense engaged in the same task. To take extreme cases: a Nazi or a Chinese Communist might mean something so different by 'maturity' or 'development' from what any of us might mean that our respective aims in higher education could be, not only different, but in direct conflict. A 'developed' Nazi, we might think, is not at all the same as a 'developed' *person*. We usually have some sort of semi-conscious idea of our aims; but such ideas need to be clarified and thoroughly analysed at the *first stage* of our understanding. Otherwise we shall be trying to play different games on the same board.

Even if the aims are agreed, there is still the task of explicating them in more detail. By 'explicating' I do not mean 'trying to realise them in practice'. I mean, for instance, that it is not enough to agree that one aim involves 'the understanding of other people's emotions', or 'empathy', or 'concern'. We need to ask 'Just *what is it* to understand someone's emotions? How, in principle, can one do this? Exactly what *is* an "emotion"? Is "empathy" the same as "sympathy"? What *is it* to be "concerned" for another person as such — what do we *mean* by this?' These questions may at first sight appear 'academic' or 'philosophical'; but it is surely clear that in answering them we acquire a much better idea of the sorts of methods and practical conditions that we need to look at, just because we get a better idea of just what we are talking *about*. It is easy to use the word 'concern': much harder, and much more important, to be able to spell out exactly what this word implies.

I stress this, not simply in order to promote the image of 'philosophy', but because this particular kind of understanding is conspicuous by its absence in most educational theory and research. We have somehow to bridge the gap between high-sounding 'aims' — 'concern', 'maturity' and so on — and what we call 'the facts'. One essential way of bridging it is to concentrate much harder on achieving a more detailed breakdown of the aims. There is nothing particularly new in this. If, for instance, we were called on to produce such a breakdown in the case of some well-established subject — mathematics or physics — we should list the particular concepts, skills, types of knowledge, etc. required *by the subject:* we know, more or less, what it is to be 'a competent mathematician' or 'a knowledgeable physicist'. But we are not so clear when it comes to 'personal development'. My point is simply that, unless and until we become clear, a lot of our empirical work may well be misguided: for we shall not know *what* 'facts', 'working conditions', 'psychological generalisations', 'practical experiences', etc. to look at as being relevant.

Finally, a quite practical point about the conditions under which the further study of this area best flourishes: perhaps of particular importance, since (whatever else this book may or may not do) the contributors have at least shown the need for such further study. The point is strictly one of common sense: it is that we need contexts in which a great deal of prolonged and tough-minded thinking and argument can take place. This sounds truistic; but it is a truism that needs stressing. In higher education — indeed, in education generally — many of us are concerned or compelled to take action: to plan new courses, produce research projects, advise on future action, give our opinion on an ever-increasing number of committees, and so on. In this welter of activity and bureaucracy the social context required for genuine and sophisticated *reflection*, together with the stringent criticism and no-holds-barred argument which is also necessary, is nearly always absent. Such a context needs *time* and *dedication.* The questions are not such as can be settled after two or three conferences: nor can they safely be left to 'researchers'. A solid weekend of well-informed argument may achieve something: the occasional meeting, or 'joint seminar', or 'working party', is usually quite inadequate. We have, I think, to fight hard for time to think, and for conditions in which the right sort of thinking is possible: the battle is constant, because there are many causes which make it easier to do almost anything else than actually thrash out a difficult question at the appropriate length.

This book will, I hope, even if it does nothing else, leave the reader with the sense that further studies are urgently needed: that there are no 'experts' on whom he can, whilst sitting back, rely for 'answers': that it is, in a way, quite shocking and intolerable that we have only just begun to think seriously about this obviously important area: and that a good deal of intense teamwork is required from the reader and his colleagues if we are to make any real progress. And if our contributions offer him a satisfactory stimulus and starting point, we shall be well satisfied.

Notes on Contributors

John Barnett is Principal of St. John's College of Education, York, and was formerly Principal of Culham College, Abingdon. He has been chiefly concerned in devising new academic structures to respond more effectively to the changes in the patterns of teacher education and is currently Chairman of the Council of Principals of Church of England Colleges of Education.

Maurice Broady is a sociologist and holds the Chair in Social Administration in the University College of Swansea. He is particularly interested in social planning and has written a number of papers on the education of planners and architects.

Gabriel Chanan is Senior Editor at the National Foundation for Educational Research, before which he lectured for five years in English and Drama in further and teacher education.

Denis Coe is currently Assistant Director for Student Affairs at the Middlesex Polytechnic. Until June 1974 he was Head of the Student Services Department and Dean of Students at the North East London Polytechnic. From 1966-1970 he was Member of Parliament for Middleton and Prestwich, prior to which he lectured in Political Science at the Manchester College of Commerce.

Gerald Collier has been Principal of Bede College, Durham, since 1959. He has been Visiting Professor at Temple University, Philadelphia in 1965 and 1968 and member of a Council of Europe committee on teacher education during 1964-1972.

David Edge is Director of the Science Studies Unit in the University of Edinburgh, where he teaches courses in the social relations of science. He was formerly a producer in the Science Unit, B.B.C. and holds a doctorate in Radioastronomy. He is active in youth work and has for many years been an adviser to the Scout Movement.

Douglas Hamblin is Lecturer in Education with responsibility for the Diploma in School Counselling in the Department of Education, University College of Swansea. He has been Headmaster of a school for intelligent disturbed children, has worked in an advisory capacity with probationary teachers, and has undertaken Jungian analysis.

Stephen Hatch lectures in the Department of Social Science and Administration at the London School of Economics and is an elected member of the Inner London Education Authority. He is the author (with Joan Brothers) of *Residence and Student Life* (Tavistock, 1971).

James L. Henderson is currently Senior Lecturer in History and International Affairs at the London University Institute of Education. He is Chairman of the World Education Fellowship and Editor-in-Chief of PROBE: his interests include Analytical Psychology and the advent

221

of the psycho-historian.

Roy Knight is Principal of Whitelands College of Education and was formerly Head of the Department of Drama, Film and Television, Bede College, Durham. He was a UNESCO Consultant in drama and media studies in Australia during 1970 and Visiting Professor of Drama at the University of Michigan in 1966 and 1968.

Valerie Pitt is Head of the School of Humanities at Thames Polytechnic, where she teaches English Literature. She was previously a Fellow of Newham College, Cambridge and is currently Chairman of the C.N.A.A. Board of Theology and Religious Studies.

Robin Richardson is Director of the World Studies Project, a curriculum project which began in January, 1973. He was formerly Director of the Bloxham Project Research Unit, Oxford, concerned with aspects of religious and moral education in boarding schools, and is author of *Frontiers of Enquiry* (Hart-Davis, 1971) and co-author of *Images of Life* (SCM, 1973).

James Robertson is at present Secretary of the United Society for the Propagation of the Gospel, London, having been on the staff of the Church of England board of education. He was formerly Head of the Department of Education, Bede College, Durham and his earlier work was in teacher training in Zambia.

Peter Tomlinson lectures in psychology in the Department of Education, University of York, having previously been Research Fellow in Psychology at the Farmington Trust Research Unit on Moral Education, Oxford. His chief interests are in the psychology of cognitive and social development, and the relationships between Philosophy and Psychology.

John Wilson is currently Lecturer and Tutor at the Oxford University Department of Educational Studies, and Director of Research for the Warborough Trust, which is continuing the research in moral education initiated by the Farmington Trust. His interests and many publications are mainly in the philosophy of educational research, and in moral and religious education.